ANATOMY OF A GOLD MINE

MICHAEL D. DUNN

ANATOMY OF A GOLD MINE

Copyright Michael David Dunn 2016.
All rights reserved except for fair use.

Editor: Cathy Collins
Front Cover Image by Michael Dunn
Author's Photograph by Erin M. Dunn

Books and copies of the photographs are available.
Write Michael D. Dunn, 1001 Mica Road, Mineral, Virginia 23117.
Email: michaelsharondunn@msn.com

To my wife Sharon,
who has continually supported me
during the writing of this book; all the while
dodging stacks of files and papers

TABLE OF CONTENTS

ACKNOWLEDGMENTS ix
INTRODUCTION xi

HISTORY 1
PLACER MINING IN THE 1800'S 4
THE END OF AN ERA 13
MINE SPECULATION 17
THE CRASH 20
PROSPECTING 24
THE COMEBACK 28
ANOTHER CHANCE 33
THE HEAD FRAME 50
SHAFT HOUSE 58
AT LAST 87
ONE STEP CLOSER TO MILLIONS 99
MANEUVERING 116
THE CARROT AND THE STICK 135
GOING UP 144
A SQUABBLE 153
ROLLING ALONG 168
GETTING UP STEAM 192
GOING FOR THE GOLD 199
!! BLACK GOLD !! 208
SUSPICION 223
WHERE'S THE GOLD ? 245
ANOTHER IRON IN THE FIRE 258
DISAGREEMENTS 266
THE CAVE-IN 277
KNOCK DOWN DRAG OUT 287
THE WHYS AND WHEREFORES 328
THE RETURN 331

TABLE OF CONTENTS

LIST OF PHOTOS

COLONEL THOMAS R. MARSHALL 7
VIEW OF THE TINDER FLATS MINE 8
GOLD BEARING "WALTON VEIN" 9
MINERS USING A LONG TOM 11
MINERS WITH GOLD PANS 12
SHAFT COLLAR 21
CHARLES B. SQUIER 28
FRONT OF THE DOLAN MINE 37
LEFT SIDE OF THE DOLAN MINE 38
WOODEN TRACK WAY 38
WAGON LOAD OF GOLD ORE 39
REAR VIEW OF THE DOLAN MINE 39
RIGHT FRONT OF THE DOLAN MINE 40
INSIDE OF THE HOIST ROOM 40
FRONT VIEW OF THE DOLAN MINE AND GOLD 41
VIEW OF THE MINE SHAFT 45
HEAD FRAME BEGINNINGS 51
BOLTING TIMBERS IN PLACE 52
HOISTING OPERATION 52
PRE-FITTING BEAMS 55
HEAD FRAME FINAL STAGES 55
BULL WHEEL INSTALLED 56
ARRIVAL OF THE BOILER 56
BOILER UNDER HEAD FRAME 57
SHAFT HOUSE FOUNDATION 58
FRAMING SHAFT HOUSE 60
LEFT FRONT OF SHAFT HOUSE 61
STEAM HOIST FRAME 62
RIGHT SIDE OF SHAFT HOUSE 63
BRICKING THE BOILER 63
HOISTING THE SMOKE STACK 66
THE HOIST ROOM 66
LEFT SIDE OF THE SHAFT HOUSE 68
REAR VIEW OF THE SHAFT HOUSE 71
WOOD PILE AT RIGHT THE SIDE OF SHAFT HOUSE 71
CONCRETE MIXER 99
MAN IN A SUIT SHOVELING 100

TABLE OF CONTENTS

MAN IN A SUIT SUPERVISING 101
DIGGING LAST OF THE FOOTINGS 101
CONCRETE PIERS..102
SCREENING GRAVEL...105
STEAM ENGINE ON RAIL ROAD CAR...108
ENGINE'S FLYWHEEL ON CRIBBING...109
STEAM ENGINE BED ON A TRUCK 109
STEAM ENGINE ON CRIBBING 110
BEGINNING OF HEAVY FRAMING 145
FIRST LEVEL INSTALLED..145
BEGIN SEQUENCE OF 2ND LEVEL, 1 OF 4 150
INSTALLATION OF 2ND LEVEL CROSS PIECE, 2 OF 4 151
SIDE VIEW OF 2ND LEVEL, 3 OF 4..151
ORE BIN SUPPORTS, 4 OF 4 152
UNDERGROUND VIEW OF GOLD BEARING VEIN..154
SNOW ON THE ROOF..158
ROAD CLOSURE..159
THE POINTER 165
THE BOILER FOR THE MILL ARRIVES 169
MACHINERY PARTS...170
ROD MILL AND BOILER...172
MOVING ROD MILL 172
RELOCATION OF THE BOILER 173
BOILER INSTALLED IN FRAME..173
PHOTOGRAPH NO. 62 REAR VIEW OF THE BOILER..176
CLOSE UP OF ENGINE PARTS..179
BLAKE CRUSHER 180
INSTALLING THE CRUSHER 180
SMOKE STACK INSTALLATION SEQUENCE 1 OF 5...182
HOISTING STACK, 2 OF 5...183
CELEBRATION, 3 OF 5...183
ALMOST THERE, 4 OF 5 184
STACK INSTALLED WITH SMOKE EXITING, 5 OF 5..184
A FEW MORE PARTS...188
STUMP REMOVAL 1920'S STYLE..195
NEW YORK INVESTORS ARRIVE..240
COMPLETED HEAD FRAME 241
MINE INSPECTION 241
GOING DOWN IN THE MINE...242

TABLE OF CONTENTS

LIST OF ILLUSTRATIONS

ILLUSTRATION NO. 1: MINE SHAFT STEAM PUMP, ENGINEERING AND MINING, JOURNAL, VOL. LXVI, NO. 20, SEPT 24, 1898, PG 12 27

ILLUSTRATION NO. 2: ALLIS-CHALMERS FACTORY CATALOGUE NO. 107, 1919 ALLIS-CHALMERS MFG. CO. 29

ILLUSTRATION NO. 3: STAMP MILL UNITED STATES PATENT AND TRADEMARK OFFICE 36

ILLUSTRATION NO. 4 AND 5: MILL PLANS ALLIS-CHALMERS MFG. CO. DEC. 12, 1923 87

ILLUSTRATION NO. 6: GRIZZLY CATALOGUE NO. 107, 1919 ALLIS-CHALMERS MFG. CO. 88

ILLUSTRATION NO. 7: BLAKE CRUSHER CATALOGUE NO. 107, 1919 ALLIS-CHALMERS MFG. CO. 88

ILLUSTRATION NO. 8: ORE FEEDER CATALOGUE NO. 107, 1919 ALLIS-CHALMERS MFG. CO. 90

ILLUSTRATION NO. 9: ROD MILL ALLIS-CHALMERS MFG. CO. 90

ILLUSTRATION NO. 10: DORR CLASSIFIER THE DORR CO. JULY 1, 1920 91

ILLUSTRATION NO. 11: PIERCE AMALGAMATOR 92

ILLUSTRATION NO. 12: "TANGYE" BED THROTTLING STEAM ENGINE 110

ILLUSTRATION NO. 13: ERIE CITY IRON WORKS ERIE CITY IRON WORKS, 1909 112

ILLUSTRATION NO. 14: BLEICHERT WIRE ROPE TRAMWAY THE ENGINEERING AND MINING JOURNAL, VOL. LXVI NO. 20, NOV, 12, 1898, PG 35 157

ILLUSTRATION NO. 15: BOILER INSTALLATION ERIE CITY IRON WORKS......... 174

ILLUSTRATION NO. 16: WORTHINGTON 6 X 4 X 6 DUPLEX STEAM PUMP UNITED STATES PATENT AND TRADEMARK OFFICE 181

ILLUSTRATION NO. 17: KOHLER ELECTRIC PLANT 205

ACKNOWLEDGMENTS

My thanks to Mr. Hugh Pagan of Hugh Pagan Ltd.
My thanks to The University of Virginia Law Library

INTRODUCTION

"Anatomy of a Gold Mine" is the story of a 1920's style gold rush involving the expenditure of large sums of money by a New York financier with ensuing lawsuits, fights and squabbles between the Mine Manager and the financier during their quest for millions in gold. A world famous Geologist and a future Governor of Virginia lend their services to the cause. The story is accompanied by previously unpublished photographs detailing the step by step construction of the mine itself-showing how men accomplished difficult tasks without the advantages of modern construction equipment. The Twin Vein Mine buildings and equipment were almost identical to those found in other mining areas around the country. Correspondence detailing many of the mines day to day challenges beginning in 1921 and continuing until late 1925 is included.

When gold was first discovered in Virginia, the property owners mined placer deposits when they were not engaging in agricultural endeavors. Placer deposits contain gold bearing gravel and sand. These deposits are the result of the weathering of rocks which contain gold and the concentration thereof in rivers, creeks and waterways.

The gold found in Central Virginia is located in what is called the Virginia Gold-Pyrite Belt which extends from Fairfax to Buckingham County, Virginia. Gold has been mined in Central Virginia since 1830 employing both placer and hard rock mining methods. There were several very rich gold discoveries near the present day town of Mineral, Virginia and miners still search nearby Contrary Creek for gold they hope their predecessors missed. There is nothing more exciting than the presence of gold in white quartz rock or a pay streak in a gold pan.

HISTORY

The earliest reference to the existence of gold in Virginia, was by Thomas Jefferson, in 1782. Jefferson described a sample of ore weighing about 4 pounds that was found on the north side of the Rappahannock River, about 4 miles below the falls. The gold ore yielded 17 pennyweights of pure gold. This sample was the only gold found in the area."[1]

Gold and other precious metals are weighed using the Troy Weight System. In this system 20 pennyweights or 480 grains equal one Troy ounce and one Troy ounce weighs 31.1035 grams compared to one standard ounce which weighs 28.3495 grams.

The next discovery of gold after Jefferson's 1782 description was in 1806 at the Whitehall Mine in Spotsylvania County, but mining did not begin until 1848.[2] The Tinder Flats Mine on Contrary Creek near present day Mineral was first operated in 1830.[3] The Virginia Mining Company of New York operated a gold mine on the Grasty tract of land in Orange County, Virginia from 1831 to 1834.[4] By 1836 there was considerable gold mining activity in the State, and production was reasonably steady from the rediscovery to 1850. The annual value produced was between $50,000 and $100,000. Gold mining activity had increased in the State during the early 1850's, but The Civil War almost completely stopped gold mining in Virginia and the South.[5]

---

1 Transactions of The American Institute of Mining Engineers. Vol. XXV. 1895. New York. The Institute. Pg. 679
2 Sweet, Palmer C. and Trimble, David, 1983, Virginia Gold-Resources Data: Va. Division of Mineral Resources Publication 45, 196 pgs, pg 185
3 Sweet, Palmer C. and Trimble, David. 1983, Virginia Gold-Resource Data: Va. Division of Mineral Resources Publication 45, 196 pgs. pg 131
4 Sweet, Palmer C. and Trimble, David. 1983, Virginia Gold-Resource Data: Va. Division of Mineral Resources Publication 45, 196 pgs. Pg 141
5 Watson, Thomas, L. Mineral Resources of Virginia. Lynchburg, Virginia. J. P. Bell. 1907 pg. 549

ANATOMY OF A GOLD MINE

The Walton Gold Mine located on Contrary Creek near Mineral, Virginia was one of the richest gold deposits in Central Virginia. It was first worked by Native Americans and was described by Forrest Shepherd of New Haven, Connecticut in 1836. "Near the southern boundary of the gold mine tract, directly upon and at the sides of the main vein, we discovered what evidently appears to have been ancient excavations and embankments. . . .They are therefore necessarily referred to the operations of a people long since sunk in oblivion."[6]

In 1836 the Walton Mine was also described by Benjamin Silliman in his report; "The workings consisted of two mine shafts, one shaft was seventy feet deep and the second was forty feet deep. The two shafts were one hundred and five feet apart."[7] Samples taken in one area averaged $5.92 per bushel or 100 pounds of ore, which would yield $118.40 per ton. Another test was conducted on a sample with no visible gold, however, it yielded a value of $20.41 per 100 pounds or $408.20 per ton. One other test was conducted on quartz showing gold the size of the head of a pin, and this yielded a value of $133.69 per 100 pounds of ore, or a staggering $2,673.80 per ton.[8]

This is an astonishing amount and equaled that of some better mines in the American west.

Benjamin Silliman was one of our country's first professors of science and a leading chemist at Yale University. He had a great deal to do with the development of the sciences of Mineralogy and Geology in the United States.[9]

An additional account of a gold discovery along Contrary Creek in 1836 by Professor William B. Rogers referred to a tract of land that belonged to Benjamin Jenkins which was located near the Tinder and Allah Cooper Mines. The Jenkins property at that point was producing $2,000.00 to $3,000.00 in gold per year. A vein of quartz was discovered on the property which, according to a Master Miner had pieces of gold approximately five eights of an inch in diameter projecting from it.[10]

---

6 Forrest Shepherd, Walton Mine Report. New Haven, Connecticut 1878, Library of Virginia
7 Silliman, B, Fredericksburg, Virginia, September 21, 1836, Library of Virginia
8 Silliman, B, Fredericksburg, Virginia, September 21, 1836, Library of Virginia
9 Jones Bob, Giants of Early Mineralogy, Rock and Gem Magazine, Aug. 2015, Beckett Media LLC, Dallas Texas
10 1836 Report, Rodgers, William B. Charlottesville Virginia, University of Virginia

HISTORY

This is an example of just how rich the gold deposits of Louisa County were in 1836 when gold was worth $19.598 per ounce. Professor Rodgers was the Director of The Geological Survey of Virginia from 1835 until 1841 and was also President of The National Academy of Sciences.

PLACER MINING IN THE 1800'S

Placer mining employs water to separate gold and other material according to their specific gravity, with gold having the greatest specific gravity. The Placer-gold deposits found in creeks and waterways originated in quartz veins and other types of rock which have been eroded over a long period of time. The action of the water caused the gold to collect in areas where the velocity of the stream flow slowed, allowing the gold to settle to the bottom of the stream and eventually onto bed rock. These deposits were mined using gold pans, log rockers, sluice boxes and miners cradles and later steam powered machinery. Gold miners also would follow the trail of gold upstream until it stopped. It was then traced to its origin above the stream and a prospect pit was excavated to find the vein. After the vein had been located a shaft was sunk and the vein was mined, sometimes the vein would be cut by the creek and it would be mined in each direction by digging a trench until it was necessary to sink a shaft to reach the vein.[1]

"The Tinder or Tinder Flats placer deposits which are located along and on both sides of Contrary Creek, near Mineral, Virginia, were perhaps the best known and most productive source of placer gold in the early days of Virginia gold mining." These deposits were also mined using gold pans, log rockers, miner's cradles, sluice boxes and later steam powered mining equipment from 1830 until 1867. In 1895 the placer deposits were tested again to determine if the gold remaining justified the purchase of modern machinery for working them on a large scale, but no mining was done.[2]

---

[1] Watson, Thomas, L. Mineral Resources of Virginia, Lynchburg, Virginia. J. P. Bell 1907 Pg. 558
[2] Sweet, Palmer C, and Trimble, David, 1983, Virginia Gold Resources, Data. 1983, Virginia Division of Mineral Resources, Publication 45, 196 p, pg. 131

PLACER MINING IN THE 1800'S

Gold pans are used for prospecting and by miners who are operating on a small scale. When one uses a gold pan, approximately 20 pounds of creek gravel are shoveled into the pan which is then submerged under water and shaken a few times to settle the material it contains. The pan is then rotated in an elliptical pattern by the miner as he tilts it slightly to the side allowing the organic matter and lighter material to be ejected from it. This shaking and rotation cause the gold to collect on the bottom of the pan. The pan is again submerged, filled with water and the process is repeated until only gold, a small quantity of black sand and other heavy minerals remain. Black sand is an indicator of the presence of gold, but not a guarantee. The remaining minerals are heavy, but not as heavy as the gold and the majority of them can be panned out leaving the gold visible.

Panning is not an exact science, but an art and every miner has a different technique. Frying pans and even pie plates have been used to pan for gold and some miners coated their pans with Mercury. A tool called a miner's spoon is sometimes used to take small samples believed to contain gold.

Very early gold miners employed a homemade piece of mining equipment known as the log rocker. It was made by cutting a log longitudinally in half, hollowing it out and cutting a series of slots into the bottom. The rocker was installed on a slight slope and the lower end was left open which allowed water and worthless material to be discharged. As the log was rocked from side to side, water and gold bearing material were introduced into the upper end. The gold would settle into the slots which contained mercury that bonded instantly with it, forming an amalgam and the tailings exited the lower end.

Another type of mining equipment used in placer mining is the Rocker Box or Miner's Cradle. This piece of equipment can be made any size one desires, but usually they are about four feet in length and are also installed on a slight incline. It is operated by shoveling gold rich gravel into a hopper on top which has a screen in the bottom. The hopper fits loosely in a frame, and as the cradle is rocked, the hopper slides from side to side bumping into the edges of the frame as water is poured onto the contents. This bumping helps to settle the gold to the bottom of the screen. The water then washes the gold and finer material through the screen where it falls onto what is called an apron. The apron is constructed of a piece of canvas with a small depression made into it which is nailed to a square frame that is installed on a slope in the rocker box. The apron catches the larger pieces of gold and allows the fine gold and worthless material to be washed over its edge.

The remaining material containing fine gold is washed onto the bottom of the rocker where the gold is trapped behind riffles made of strips of wood, which are nailed at regular intervals over a piece of burlap or miner's moss to the bottom of the rocker. The worthless material or tailings are washed out of the lower end. The cradle is especially useful when larger pieces of gold and stones containing visible gold are present because they are easily picked out as the process continues. The burlap in the bottom of the rocker will trap the fine gold which can be separated by washing the gold out of the burlap or by burning the burlap and panning the remains. The Rocker Box is very effective in catching coarse gold, but flour and flake gold (thin, flat pieces of gold) is frequently lost to the tailings.

Sluice boxes were also used to recover gold and are about four feet in length. They are constructed by building a wood trough with what is called a head box at one end where gold bearing gravel is introduced. The sluice also has a layer of burlap or miner's moss on the bottom over which riffles are nailed at regular intervals. The sluice is placed in the creek with a slope of about 1 inch for every foot in length. As water flows through it, gold-bearing material is shoveled into the head box located at the upper end of the sluice. The water washes the lighter material out and the gold is trapped behind the riffles. Sluice boxes have the same drawback as the rocker; they lose flour and flake gold to the tailings pile. To remedy this problem a small amount of mercury was placed behind the riffles, but today mercury is not used in such an uncontrolled way. An extended version of the sluice box is called a long tom which can be twelve or more feet in length, and is used in the same manner as its shorter counterpart. The extra length minimizes the loss of flake and flour gold.

Interest in the Tinder Flats Mine was renewed in 1909 and a mine report was written by Colonel Thomas R. Marshall in May of that year for Mr. Charles Heath of New York City.

Colonel Thomas R. Marshall, was a graduate of The Virginia Military Institute and Commandant of Cadets in 1892.[3] Early in 1909, Colonel Marshall came from New York to Louisa County as an Engineer of Mines and was employed at a pyrite mine in Spotsylvania County, Virginia later to be known as the Valzinco mine. **Photograph 1**

PHOTOGRAPH NO. 1
COLONEL THOMAS R. MARSHALL

Most of the successful mining operations employed a Mine Superintendent. The Mine Superintendent usually was a Mining Engineer from one of the recognized Schools of Mines or a Military Institute. His job was to insure that the

---

3   Letter to inspector General U. S. Army, Washington D.C. May 30, 1893

mine was constructed and run employing the most up to date mining practices of the day.

This report sheds more light on the progression of mining on the Tinder Flats property. The mine encompassed a large area and some of it is shown in **Photograph No. 2** taken in 1909 by Colonel Marshall.

PHOTOGRAPH NO. 2
VIEW OF THE TINDER FLATS MINE

The Tinder Fats Mine is located approximately five miles north of the town of Mineral, Virginia on Route 522. The mine property is adjoined by the famous Sulfur Mine property on its western boundary, and on the north and east by the Allah Cooper Gold Company. The Colonel stressed the value of a three quarters of a mile long, standard gage railroad spur which had been completed to the center of the mine property and the fact that it was owned by the Tinder Flats Mine.

The mine property consisted of slightly more than three hundred acres with Contrary Creek running through a valley in the center of the property. Contrary Creek is believed to have broken through and eroded the quartz dikes located in the western part of the property which created the quartz gravel and gold deposits

PLACER MINING IN THE 1800'S

in the flats down stream. The actual valley was comprised of approximately one hundred and ten acres out of the three hundred.

The gold deposits on the property were described by the Colonel as containing, bright, angular, free gold which was at the time worth $20.67 per troy ounce. The Colonel said that the celebrated "Carrubus Nugget" and the gold ore which won the prize at the Centennial held in Philadelphia, Pennsylvania in 1876 came from the placers of Louisa County.[4] Actually, the "Carrubus Nugget" came from the Reed Mine in, Cabarrus County, North Carolina for which it was named. The Reed Mine was known for producing large gold nuggets, some in excess of twenty pounds.[5] The gold ore samples the Colonel referred to did come from the Walton Mine on Contrary Creek in Louisa County, Virginia.

**PHOTOGRAPH NO. 3
GOLD BEARING "WALTON VEIN"**

Free gold was found in four quartz veins running Northeast to Southeast across the Tinder Flats property, the most prominent one being known as the "Walton Vein," its name was taken from the Walton Mine which was successfully worked before the Civil War. The last reliable assay from the Walton property reported a value of $27.00 per ton. The value of the gold at the Walton Mine at this point is a mere trace compared to what was found in the 1830's and is a testimony to the effectiveness of

---

4   Tinder Flats Mine Report, Col. Thomas R. Marshall, 1909
5   Engineering and Mining Journal, Vol. XXI, June 24, 1876, Scientific Publishing Co. No. 27 Park Place, New York. E-Book, Google Books, 6-15-15 2:45 P.M. pg. 611

the early miners. The Walton vein was explored by miners hired by the Colonel in 1909 and the actual exposed gold-bearing vein is shown in **Photograph No. 3**.

According to the Colonel, the first development of the Tinder Flats Mine began in 1832 by Fred Rawlings but the mining was not well organized. When the crops did not require attention, the slaves were moved to the flats and the gold bearing gravel was washed using the old log rocker or sluice box, their primary interest was to save the coarse gold. The mine changed hands several times and was worked by the Miller Bros.-Fisher & Dobney in 1856 and later by Miller & Watkins in 1867.

No accurate records could be found detailing the production and associated costs, but from memorandum and notes found by Colonel Marshall, it appears that in all approximately 60,000 cubic yards of gravel were washed and $120,000 in gold was recovered. There were many rich gold pockets found, one pocket was discovered while a hole for a gate post was being dug. This pocket was so rich that it took two weeks to work it entirely and $7,500.00 in gold was recovered.

In 1890, the property was bought by a Mr. Shields, who contracted to supply the C. & O. Railroad with quartz gravel to be used as ballast for thirty five cents per cubic yard. He planned to process the gravel for gold and then sell the tailings as ballast. Shields built a three story mill house, installed second hand machinery and constructed the 3/4 mile long railroad spur, which was paid for by the ballast he sold. The Colonel said Shields had every opportunity to make the venture a success, but his outside speculations bankrupted him and all of his properties were tied up in litigation which stopped mining until the Court ordered a sale in 1908, when it was bought by Mr. Heath.

The Colonel's examination of the property consisted of panning the gravel taken from pits which were sunk to bed-rock. More than a hundred pits were sunk at regular intervals on both sides of the creek and extended through the entire length of the property. No pits were sunk on the hill portions of the property, but he followed Silver Creek, a small creek which flows from the south into Contrary Creek. Approximately two hundred yards up the creek there was evidence that the creek had cut through the gravel to bed-rock. There the Colonel measured the depth of the gravel and was able to find gold. He also found a small sluice box six feet long that was being worked by a very old, local miner, who told the Colonel he

PLACER MINING IN THE 1800'S

was making good money by working a few hours a day. The Colonel's examination convinced him that the gravel would yield $1.25 of gold per cubic yard and he believed it was a safe estimate considering that even the most expert panner will lose from 25% to 30% of the fine gold.

The Colonel had the gravel assayed by Ledoux & Co. of 99 John St., New York. Three cubic feet of gravel was taken from each of the 28 pits that were sunk on the flats. The Colonel found the average depth of the gravel deposit to be four feet. The average of all samples was $1.20 in gold per cubic yard. On the north side of Contrary Creek, the depth of the overburden was approximately one foot and on the south side of the Creek the average depth was two feet. Overburden is a term that refers to the depth of non gold bearing material which rests on top of the gold deposit.

Miners sometimes used a long tom to separate gold from the worthless gravel and it was one of the methods employed by the Colonel to determine the value of gold on the property in **Photograph No. 4**

PHOTOGRAPH NO. 4

MINERS USING A LONG TOM

The Colonel believed they could make money by selling the tailings (valueless rock left after the gold is extracted) to the C. & O. Railroad. The Railroad offered Heath a long term contract to buy 300 cubic yards per day of washed gravel for ballast, at $ 0.50 per cubic yard, f.o.b., which would, hopefully, cover the operating expenses. This led the Colonel to believe if Heath could process 300 cubic yards of gravel per day, for 300 working days per year the property would produce 90,000 cubic yards annually. Colonel Marshall added that if one cubic yard of the gravel yielded $1.25 in gold the mine would produce $112,500.00 per year and selling the gravel at the rate of 90,000 cubic yards per year would exhaust the entire deposit in ten years.[6]

The Colonel also evaluated some of the samples by panning them and a miner holding a gold pan stands by a small creek which has been dammed up using boards in **photograph No. 5.** The pool of water created would supply the water necessary for panning gold. Two other miners use wheel barrows to transport the gold bearing gravel so it can be tested.

PHOTOGRAPH NO. 5

MINERS WITH GOLD PANS

---

6   Tinder Flats Mine Report, Col. Thomas R. Marshall, 1909

THE END OF AN ERA

In addition to gold, iron was mined from deposits of weathered pyrite known as gossen, which is what remains after the sulfur has been leached from the pyrite. Pyrite is a combination of one atom of iron and two of sulfur. It is said that some of the iron ore refined by the Victoria blast furnace, which is near the Tinder Flats Mine, was sold to The Tredegar Iron Works in Richmond, Virginia. Tredegar produced a wide array of metal products such as railroad rails, iron plates and different types of Confederate Ordnance.

Iron and pyrite mining began in the Mineral area as early as 1834, and at the turn of the 20th. Century, Louisa and Prince William Counties provided nearly 50 percent of the total pyrite production in the United States.[1] Pyrite was mined as a source of sulfur and was processed in furnaces to produce sulfuric acid. The acid was used in the production of explosives, fertilizer and many other products.

The larger mines were completely self-sufficient and even had a commissary where the miners used mine script to buy the necessities of life. In those days, town was more than just a short ride away for the majority of them because the modes of transportation consisted of horseback, wagon, train or walking. There were very few cars. The mines had small areas nearby where some of the miners and their families lived; not the best places to live, but close to where they worked. Skillet Hill and Scrap Town were two such villages that were located near the Sulfur and Arminius Mines. There was also a blacksmith shop on the property where repairs were made to the machinery and a carpentry shop complete with a wood lathe capable of producing any round wood parts needed.

---

[1] Young, Robert, S. Sulfides in Virginia, Virginia Minerals, Vol. 2 January 1956, Division of Geology, Charlottesville.

Mining companies employed steam engines which were at that time the only source of mechanical power available. Electricity was later generated by the same steam engines which supplied mechanical power throughout the mine and processing plant. The electricity generated by the engines provided light in the mine and at the processing plant. The use of electric lights allowed the mines to operate 24 hours a day, 7 days a week if necessary. Steam engines were manufactured in many different sizes and designs ranging from small shop engines to engines capable of producing over 3,000 horse power. Some of the small mines had steam engines and electric lights if they were profitable, many were not. At the Arminius Mine, steam was transported inside of pipes, some as large as 8 inches in diameter, to different areas of the mine where it powered processing equipment, steam drills and other types of equipment. Early miners employed candles, lanterns and lamps underground before electric lights were available. Electric power was a rarity in those days and the Town of Mineral did not have electricity until years later.

"The Boyd Smith, Arminius, and Sulfur Mines which are located along a narrow ridge immediately northeast of Mineral are perhaps the most famous mines in the State of Virginia. Beginning in 1834, these mines were successfully and intermittently worked for iron, copper, and sulfur. During the period of most intensive development, 1882-1905, the mines were operated for pyrite, although some lead and zinc was recovered.. The Arminius Mine was first opened for pyrite in 1865."[2]

"In 1882, pyrite was being mined on a scale large enough to be reported to the United States Geological Survey and 12,000 tons were produced in the United States that year."[3]

"Prior to 1915 Virginia produced about 45% of the domestic output of pyrites. During the years 1915, 1916, and 1917 the quantity of pyrite supplied by Virginia represented about 35% of the total production.

"In 1918 only 30% of the total output of pyrites was credited to Virginia. This reduction in Virginia's share of the total production of pyrite was not due to less production in Virginia but more production in other parts of the nation. In 1919

---

2   Young, Robert, S
3   Industrial Readjustment of Certain Mineral Industries affected by The War, Washington, Government Printing office 1920 pg 216

THE END OF AN ERA

a number of other locations in the United States including Georgia, Alabama, Tennessee and New York, began producing pyrite which further depressed the price."[4]

An additional factor which affected Virginia pyrite production occurred in 1916 when the Arminius Mine suffered a catastrophic cave-in which is said to have been heard in Mineral. "The old workings caved in during the latter part of January which impacted both the No.3 or operating shaft which was 1,200 feet deep and the new development shaft which was 1,014 ft. deep. Production originally was expected to be stopped for three or four months. During the recovery process the miners were being employed on the surface and in development work."[5] The Arminius Mine recovery from the cave- in was a long process and by August 16th., 1919 they had only cleared the 200 and 400 foot levels of debris and had sunk a new 750 foot inclined shaft which connected with the original workings on the 700 foot level. The miners were hoisting ore from the mine and de-watering the shaft as they progressed downward.[6]

"The Sulfur Mine first opened for pyrite in 1882 and in 1906 the property was developed by 8 shafts the deepest had reached 720 feet."[7] In 1917 The Sulfur Mine was owned and operated by the Virginia Carolina Chemical Co. which processed all of its product for sulfuric acid. The deepest shaft was still down 720 feet and they were pumping 100 gallons of water per minute out of the mine to prevent it from flooding. "The mine was producing 7,000 tons of ore per month and they were in the process of enlarging the mill to bring production up to 20,000 tons per month."[8]

The Sulfur Mine changed hands, and in August of 1919 The Sulfur Mining & Railroad Company mill was producing only 100 tons of pyrite daily, a great deal less than its full capacity of 500 tons per day. Little to no development was done in

---

4   Phalen, W. C .Sulfur, Pyrite and Sulfuric Acid in 1914 Washington, D.C. Government Printing Office 1915 pg 141
5   The Engineering and Mining Journal. Vol. 101, No. 7 February 12, 1916 New York, Hill Publishing Company pg 334
6   Engineering and Mining Journal, August 16, 1919 Vol. 108 No. 7, pg. 285, McGraw Hill Company, Inc. New York
7   Watson T. Leonard, Mineral Resources of Virginia. Lynchburg, Virginia. J. P. Bell Company 1907 pg 201
8   Thomas E. Fisher, Mine Report 1917

1919 and all of the ore was coming from the old pillars left to support the roof of the mine because the deposit was nearly exhausted.[9] The Sulfur Mine was worked out before the closure of the other pyrite mines in 1921.

In 1921 competition for the sulfur market was stiffening. The Union, Freeport and Texas Gulf Sulfur Companies were producing 7,000 tons of pure sulfur per day.[10] This was an important contributing factor leading to the end of pyrite mining in Mineral. The use of sulfur in the production of sulfuric acid provided several advantages; the process was less involved and produced a purer product. The second factor leading to the demise of the pyrite mines, according to Arthur E. Wells of the Engineering and Mining Journal was, "The termination of hostilities of WWI in November of 1918, and the almost immediate abrogation of all war munitions contracts left the large consumers of pyrites and sulfur with considerable reserves of raw material and finished product on hand. A considerable amount of sulfuric acid was also left in the plants of the large explosive manufacturers. The demand for acid during the first quarter of 1919 was only about 50% of that prior to the signing of the armistice. There was little activity in the pyrites and sulfur situation during that period until the reserve stocks were mostly absorbed and it appeared that the price for sulfur-bearing raw material and acid had dropped to what was considered a fair post-war price."[11]

---

9   Weed, Walter, Harvey. The Mines Handbook Tuckahoe, New York. Mines Handbook Co. 1922, E-Book, Internet Archives Nov, 29,12:24 P.M. pg 1624
10   Wells, Arthur E. Sulfur, Pyrites and Sulfuric Acid in 1919. Engineering and Mining Journal, Vol.109 No. 3 New, York, McGraw Hill pg 222
11   Wells, Arthur, E. Sulfur, Pyrites and Sulfuric Acid in 1919, Engineering and Mining Journal Vol. 109 No. 3, New York, McGraw Hill. Pg 222

MINE SPECULATION

In 1910 Colonel Thomas R. Marshall, now the local mining property speculator, was busy buying and selling the smaller mining properties. Every mining town has at least one speculator and they all say the mine they have for sale will produce a fortune. The Colonel would purchase an option to buy a piece of property for a small amount of money, make some improvements, write a mine report and market the property to parties interested in investing in the development of the mine. Some of Colonel Marshall's clients were businessmen in New York, New Jersey, Richmond, Virginia and, in one case, a mining company in Canada.

In May of 1910 Colonel Marshall was marketing the Julia Pyrite Mine property located just outside of the town of Mineral. The Colonel had shipped a sample consisting of 1,070 pounds of pyrite to the Ricketts and Banks laboratory in New Jersey for analysis. According to the mine report written by the Colonel, the mine was in the very early stages of development. There were two shafts. The number one shaft was down to the 100 foot level, with a horizontal tunnel or drift at the 50 foot level driven a distance of 55 feet. This shaft was vertical as opposed to some which were inclined and it measured 6' x 7' inside and was timbered for the first 15 feet. A second or number 2 shaft was located 1,100 feet from the number one shaft and had been sunk to a depth of 100 feet with a drift having been driven toward the number one shaft at the 70 foot level.[1]

After Colonel Marshall had secured an option on the Julia Mine, he made some improvements which were to accompany the sale of the property. They consisted of, one building covering shaft number one, a building to house the boiler and hoist for shaft number one. There was also a tool house and blacksmith shop. Shaft number two also had a building covering the shaft and a building for the boiler and

---

[1] Thomas R. Marshall, Mine Report, Mineral, Virginia 1910

hoist. The equipment included two steam powered pumps, one steam powered drill with tools, one steel ore car with rails, picks, shovels and other mining tools.[2]

The Colonel was unable to sell the Julia Mine right away but later was contacted by several interested parties. He issued another report containing data nearly identical to the 1910 report in March of 1916. On May 2, 1917 Dr. Pierre de Ricketts, a New York Mining and Metallurgical Engineer told the Colonel that he knew of a party interested in purchasing a pyrite mine. The Colonel said, "If you have friends who are interested in pyrite ore I can make the terms so attractive that the proposition will appeal to them. If you can get them to put up $15,000.00 cash, which is needed to install the equipment necessary to mine and ship 50 tons per day, I will deliver to them all of the output of the mine for the next six months."[3] (50 tons per day for 150 days would produce 7,500 tons of ore.)

On the 21st of May he presented more details of his proposition to Mr. William Seton Gordon of 141 Broadway, New York, who was associated with Dr Ricketts. The Colonel told Gordon, "At the present market price the 7,500 tons of pyrite ore would be worth $75,000.00. It is a good business and one that will grow larger and continue for a long time. I can begin to mine immediately and produce 50 tons of ore per day, and after six months of operation the output could be rapidly increased to an output of 250 to 300 tons per day after the first twelve months."[4]

Questions were raised by New York Mining Engineer H. P. Henderson to Thomas E. Fisher a local Mining Engineer, as to whether the Colonel's claims were possible relative to the quantity of ore he could produce. This question was based on the small size of the ore bucket at the mine. Henderson later wrote to Fisher asking him to please advise as to whether or not he believed the Colonel's estimate, that he could ship 100 tons of pyrite ore and 40 tons of lead and zinc ore weekly at the substantial profit stated.[5]

---

2   Marshall, Thomas R, Mine Report 1916
3   May 2, 1917 Letter from Thomas R. Marshall to Dr. Pierre de Ricketts
4   May 21, 1917 Letter from Col. Thomas R. Marshall to Mr. Gordon, New York, City
5   December 14, 1916 letter from H. P. Henderson to Thomas E Fisher

MINE SPECULATION

According to the Colonel's records, the property was sold during the middle of July in 1917 and a 100 ton per day mill was later erected on the property. The mine was operated on a limited basis. After producing approximately 15,000 tons of low grade ore it closed in 1919 and the equipment was removed.

THE CRASH

In the early part of 1921 Colonel Marshall purchased an option to buy the Dolan Gold Mine property from Mrs. Gertrude L. Dolan, the wife of. R. E. Dolan. R. E. Dolan had worked as a salesman in a clothing store prior to marrying Gertrude. Mrs. Dolan agreed to sell the mine property for $35,000 and she promised the Colonel $5,000 as a sales commission provided the bond was paid on or before the maturity date. The gold mine he hoped to sell had been re-timbered, a shaft collar had been installed and all he needed was a buyer. At some point prior to August 2, 1921, the pyrite mines near Mineral closed. The Colonel found himself in an instant financial vise because he had money tied up in the development of the Dolan Gold Mine and he could not collect any of the money owed him from previous deals. The Colonel, however, was not going to give up yet because he had another iron in the fire, and the pay off could be really big. The pending deal on the Dolan Mine necessitated that he go to New York for an important meeting with the potential purchasers, but Colonel Marshall found himself short of cash with money tight.

The development work on the Dolan Mine done by Colonel Marshall can be seen in **Photograph No. 6,** the shaft collar has been installed and a ladder protrudes from the left side. This is the same collar that will eventually have a head frame constructed over it. Quartz vein material, possibly gold-bearing, has been stock piled to the left of the two posts in the photograph. Ore is frequently piled up in advance of being processed for the gold it contains, and this pile is referred to as an ore dump.

On August the 2, 1921, the Colonel was desperate to raise the $100 needed to pay for the trip to New York City for his meeting with the group of investors to whom he hoped to sell the Dolan Mine. He sent out five letters during the month of August seeking financial assistance. The people he reached out to responded quickly.

THE CRASH

PHOTOGRAPH NO. 6

SHAFT COLLAR

Moorehead Wright, President of The Union Mercantile Trust Company of Little Rock Arkansas responded on August 9, 1921.

> "I am sorry that it does not seem proper for me to meet your request. I do not know enough about your business credit to lend you $500 and I could not afford to give you that amount. I regret your hard luck and hope you will find some emergency solution. With personal greetings running back to memories of a long time ago."[1]

Colonel Marshall scrambled, desperately trying to raise the $100 needed for his business trip to New York. The prospects were J. H. Coghill and Eugene Perry, members of a New York business syndicate, who may be interested in investing in the development of the Dolan Gold Mine property. If the Colonel succeeds, Mrs. Dolan will put $5,000 in his pocket which was a considerable amount of money in 1921.

---

[1] August 9, 1921 Letter to Col. Thomas R. Marshall from Mr. Moorehead Wright, President Union Mercantile and Trust Co. Little Rock Arkansas

The Colonel contacted Graham C. Lacy, Vice-President of the Tootle Lacy National Bank of Saint Joseph, Missouri. On August 17, 1921, he responded, "I am sorry I cannot meet your wishes with regard to a loan."[2]

More bad news arrived on August 31, 1921 from Mr. B. H. Rulluh of Fletcher, North Carolina.

> "I shall not be able to do what you require. Just at present I am strapped up beyond description and I suspect I find myself in pretty much the same position as you are, plenty of money due me, but not a cent of cash, and from the present outlook, I do not see any chance of getting any. We are simply all of us up against it excepting that it is very unfortunate to have fellows holding the whip handle over you."[3]

The Colonel continued to search for the badly needed funds and more letters were sent.

On December 20, 1921 J. C. Miller, owner of Miller Supply company of Huntington, West Virginia wrote,

> "I wish it were so that I could be able to assist you in the matter you mention. I am very cramped myself. Owing to the fact that business is more depressed now than it has been at any time in the 25 years I have been in business. I wish I were in a position to assist you."[4]

The Colonel sent additional letters to friends and business acquaintances asking for monetary assistance but the reply always ended with the same answer, I am sorry, but wish I could help.

---

2   August 17, 1924, letter from Mr. G. G. Lacy, Vice President, The Tootle-Lacy National Bank Saint Joseph, Mo.
3   August 31, 1921 Letter to Col. Thomas R. Marshall from Mr. Rulluh
4   December 20, 1923 letter from J. C. Miller to Colonel Thomas R. Marshall

THE CRASH

The Colonel pleaded for help on April 12, 1922 from J. L. Sperry of Norfolk, Virginia,

> "You will be astounded to read my letter, but I am putting my pride in my pocket and am writing to you to ask you to be my friend in a critical moment. Briefly all the five big mines here have closed down. I opened three of them, not a wheel is turning and I can't collect the money due me. There is no one here in this little place that can help me and I am caught so that I can't get away. It is imperative that I go to New York at once to complete the sale of a property I have developed up to the point where the equipment must be put in. I must go to see the New York people who are taking over the property. I will make on the deal some $18,000, but if I let the bunch know how stifled I am for cash they will commence to trade my eyes out so that precludes my applying to them at this juncture. I can get some money soon after I get to New York but I need $100.00 so Sperry I am writing to ask you to send it to me so that I can be in New York on Monday. I will be able to return it soon and to show my appreciation of your helping me, I will send you some of the preferred shares of the company's stock as a reminder. I know that I lost $72,000.00 on the Valzinco lead and zinc mine, and now that Huddleston has defaulted I am badly crippled for ready cash, but this sale will give me relief. I hate to ask anyone to help me but I must do it as it is so urgent to act quickly to complete the sale. I will recognize the obligation in any way you wish it done. Please write me by return mail and help me over this critical moment."[5]

The plea was answered by more bad news.

---

[5] April 12, 1923 letter from J. L. Sperry to Colonel Thomas R. Marshall

PROSPECTING

Colonel Marshall hoped his potential investors would be capable of investing $50,000 in the Dolan property which would allow him to make a quick profit. Perry and Coghill were interested, but money was hard to find. The time frame for the sale was governed by the terms of the option the Colonel held and he clearly needed more time to close the deal. Things began to move along as interest in the mine built, Perry and Coghill took the first step by ordering samples to be taken from the mine.

One of the first things done prior to committing to a contractual agreement to lease a property for mining is to have ore samples taken from the mine and sent to a reliable laboratory to be assayed. (An assay is a process devised to test ores and minerals by chemical or blowpipe examination; said to be in the dry way when done by means of heat (as in a crucible), and in the wet or humid way when by means of liquid tests. An assay is different from a complete analysis because only certain ingredients such as gold, silver or other specified components are tested for.)[1] There were a number of very reliable laboratories located in New York City. Perry and Coghill contacted the Ricketts and Company, Mining and Metallurgical Engineers to perform the assay tests on the ore samples which were to be collected from the Dolan mine.

Colonel F. S. Tainter, a Mining Engineer and Geologist, was sent to Mineral to collect samples from the Dolan mine property, especially from the old Louisa Mine shaft. Twenty samples were taken from various locations in the mine including what are called grab samples (samples picked up at random locations) from the Luce mine dump, the Slate Hill Mine dump and additional grab samples from the Dolan Mine property.

---

[1] Raymond, R. W. A Glossary of Mining and Metallurgical Terms, New York, American Institute of Mining Engineers. 1881 pg 5

PROSPECTING

All of the samples taken were placed in cloth bags and each was labeled stating the location where it was collected. Sample 19 was listed as being collected from the north end of the open cut, and was mailed in by R.E. Dolan.[2] This sample should have been suspected as a high grade sample from another location and possibly excluded. At this point the old Louisa Mine was 220 feet deep with several drifts or tunnels, the longest stretching 62 feet from the shaft.

A Certificate of Analysis from the Ricketts and Company Incorporated dated July 7, 1922 showed 14 of the 20 samples contained only a trace of gold. One sample collected on the 40 foot level of the shaft, 25 feet from the North face and 20 inches from the bottom of the wall, showed 1.59 ounces of gold per ton which was worth $32.52 per ton. The sample from the 40 foot level, 30 feet from the North face at the bottom 20 inches up showed .32 ounces of gold per ton worth $6.61 per ton. Sample number 19 listed as special, from the North end open cut assayed at a stunning 4.85 ounces gold per ton, yielding $100.10 per ton of ore.[3] (Ore is, "a natural mineral compound, of the elements, of which at least one is a metal.")[4]

On July 29, 1922, another assay was performed on an ore sample from the mine which showed zero ounces of gold per ton. This assay could have destroyed the Colonel's chances of selling the mine to the New York investors. On August 15, 1922, samples 9,10, 11 and 14 were re-assayed and the results ranged from $2.20 to $8.00 gold per ton. This assay was conducted by Ledoux and Company, Engineers, Chemists and Assayers located on 99 John St., New York. This assay was commissioned by Mr. A. Alexander of Flynn, Marburg and Curran Incorporated (Mining Engineers) also of New York City. After receiving the report, Mr. Alexander was of the opinion that, "these results while better than Ricketts and Companies assays of the same samples, were not sufficiently encouraging to warrant our advising that the Dolan property negotiations be continued."[5] Not good news for the Colonel.

As of May 1920, Dr. Alfred Ledoux's laboratory, "had been existence in New York City for 40 years. Doctor Ledoux was past president of the American Institute

---

2   Tainter F. S, 84 Pine Street, New York, Mine Report Feb. 15, 1923
3   Tainter. F. S, Report
4   Raymond R. W. A Glossary of Mining and Metallurgical Terms, New York, American Institute of Mining Engineers. 1881pg 63
5   April 3, 1923 Assay Report by Ledoux & Company, 99 John Street, New York

of Mining and Metallurgical Engineers. He was born in Kentucky in 1852 and entered the Columbia School of Mines in 1870 and in the third year went to Berlin to study chemistry, mineralogy and geology. In 1877, the State of North Carolina created an agricultural experiment station, and Doctor Ledoux became its first director. In April of 1880, he opened a laboratory and office in New York, in partnership with Professor P. de Ricketts, under the name of A. R Ledoux & Co. Later the name was changed to Ledoux and Rickets, and after five years of association the partnership was dissolved. Doctor Ledoux continued the business under the firm name of Ledoux and Company. He was frequently called upon for mine examinations in Canada, the United States and Mexico and was respected worldwide as a Mining engineer."[6]

The money crunch continued to plague the Colonel, and he had asked his old friend, R. E. Dolan for help, and on August 9 Dolan had sent him $10, saying, " I am sorry I cannot send more but you understand the situation, this will enable you to hang on a few days longer." The Colonel thanked Dolan for his assistance and mentioned that he was still short of his goal.

In another letter three days later Dolan told the Colonel, "Yours of yesterday read. Enclosed $10.00, I just could not send more for the reason I did not have it on hand and your letter coming this afternoon too late to get out anywhere to try to get it. This is lowering me now down to bedrock. Hope this will see you thru as it is the best and all I can do."[7]

Dolan Mine samples 9, 10, and 14 were again re-assayed on August 25, 1922 by Ricketts and Company, the results showed an average of .28 ounces of gold worth $5.97 per ton of processed ore. All of the assayed samples contained small amounts of silver.[8] At a recovery rate of $5.97 of gold per ton and processing 50 tons per day, the mine would produce $298.50 worth of gold per day. This figure does not represent actual profit; the cost of mining and processing must be subtracted from this figure.

---

6   Mining Engineers of Note, The Engineering and Mining Journal, Vol. 109, No. 3. May 22, 1920, New York, McGraw Hill Co. Pg. 1167
7   August 9, 1922 from R.E. Dolan to Col. Thomas R. Marshall
8   August 15, 1922 Assay Report Ricketts & Company. New York

The conflicting results of the assays were answered by Dolan who was very confident that the assays would prove satisfactory and he suggested that if the consulting engineers, Marburg and Lynn were not impressed with the results of assays and were still interested, he would dewater the mine so samples could be taken at a greater depth. Dewatering is necessary in mines because of the constant inflow of water from the surrounding water table which can range from a few gallons per hour to hundreds of gallons per hour. This inflow had to be pumped out using steam pumps. Dolan also agreed to allow them 30 additional days to conduct further investigations, at their own expense, in an effort to satisfy them. He was positive that his property would stand investigating and added "It is not necessary for anyone to buy pig in a poke."[9] The Colonel moved quickly to find the needed pump.

With the closure of the pyrite mines around Mineral there was plenty of surplus mining equipment to be bought at very good prices and a pump to dewater the mine was easy to find. Colonel Marshall wrote to The Sulfur Mining and Railroad Company in Richmond asking if they had a steam pump for sale or rent. He was able to rent a Worthington steam pump with 100 feet of one inch pipe and 150 feet of one and a half inch pipe to dewater the mine so that further samples could be collected.[10] **Illustration 1**

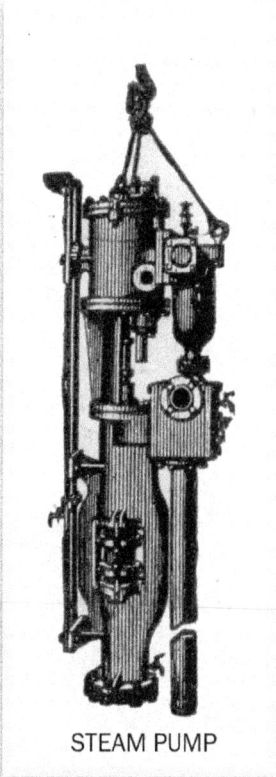

STEAM PUMP

ILLUSTRATION NO. 1: MINE SHAFT STEAM PUMP, ENGINEERING AND MINING, JOURNAL, VOL. LXVI, NO. 20, SEPT 24, 1898, PG 12

---

9   August 12, 1922 Letter from R. E. Dolan to Thomas R. Marshall
10 August 12, 1922, Letter from Col Thomas R. Marshall to The Sulfur Mining and Railroad Co.

THE COMEBACK

Perry and Coghill were in no financial shape to advance the $50,000 which was going to be needed for the development and operation of a gold mine. They told the Colonel they would see if a "man of means" might be interested in the proposition. This man was none other than Financier, Charles B. Squier Jr., whose grandfather William C. Squier, co-founded Manning and Squier which later became part of the New Jersey Zinc Company. His father, Charles B. Squier Sr., served as the Secretary and Treasurer of the new company beginning in 1897 until his death in 1904.[1] In 1923 Charles B. Squier, Jr,.a very wealthy man, resided in an apartment at 521 Park Avenue, New York. The spacious apartment was comprised of fourteen rooms, four bathrooms and a staff of four servants and a governess.[2] In the photograph of their camp near Mineral, Charles Squier is standing with his hands on his hips in the right side of **Photograph No.7.**

**PHOTOGRAPH NO. 7
CHARLES B. SQUIER**

The Colonel, in spite of being short of funds, continued to move the deal forward by letter and on November 1, 1922 asked for and received a seven month extension on the

---

1   Hardenberg, Henry, The First Hundred Years of The New Jersey Zinc Co. New York. The New Jersey Zinc Co. 1948 pg 21
2   H. Ray Paige vs. Charles Burnham Squier, 957 New York Supreme Court, February 25, 1927, Appellate Division, First Department.

contract to buy the Dolan property. With this extension the Colonel had more time to broker a deal with the new syndicate formed by Charles Squier.

Colonel Marshall wrote to Dolan in Cripple Creek, Colorado asking him to look around for a used 25 ton per day amalgamation plant which was smaller than the one the Colonel really wanted. The used equipment, would allow them to set up the processing plant much more cheaply than if they bought new equipment, but would process substantially less ore per day than the 50 ton per day plant recommended by the Colonel. Mining operations usually start small and work up if the ore is not proven. Squier had written to the Allis-Chalmers Manufacturing Company located in Milwaukee, Wisconsin requesting specifications and a price quotation for a 50 ton per day amalgamation plant. In 1920 things moved a great deal more slowly than in the modern world with the internet. Squier's advance research concerning the cost of the plant before committing to financing was just good business. **Illustration 2**

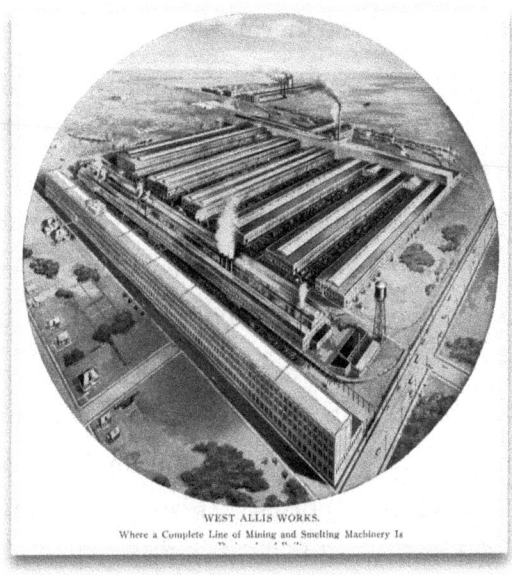

ILLUSTRATION NO. 2: ALLIS-CHALMERS FACTORY CATALOGUE NO. 107, 1919 ALLIS-CHALMERS MFG. CO

An amalgamation plant employs several types of crushing machines which reduce the ore to the fineness of powder, after which it is passed over copper plates coated with mercury which bonds on contact with gold thereby trapping it and allowing the tailings to pass out of the plant.

Squier decided to move forward with the development of the mine itself without the official formation of a corporation. This development entailed making improvements to the shaft and constructing a head frame and shaft house. Construction began with the pouring of concrete which would support the headframe timbers. He hoped the small amalgamation plant at the old Dolan mine would provide income as development of the mine proceeded.

On December 15th., 1922, the Colonel told Squier in a short note,

> "I have used the two bottles of whiskey you gave me to accomplish more than a hundred dollars would have done."[3]

The whiskey was probably shared with the miners as an inducement to work harder. This was just a little tiny violation of the 18th Amendment to The Constitution called Prohibition.

On January 7, 1923, the weather had been terrible, it had been sleeting and snowing for the past three days and the thermometer had been as low as 6°. The weather for the moment had prevented the Colonel from pouring concrete but he had everything ready to resume as soon as the weather would allow it.[4]

Dolan had conferred with Mr. Willard of the Mine and Smelter Supply Company in Colorado who showed him their new Marcy Rod Mill, (a type of rock crushing machine). Dolan told the Colonel, "it's a dandy", the best he had seen yet and it had several advantages over the Allis-Chalmers Mill. He asked Willard to write the Colonel and explain the advantages of the Mill.[5]

James H Coghill hired Colonel F. S. Tainter to again examine the mine and write a report on it. On February 15, 1923 Tainter submitted his report on the mine he had visited during the first week of February. He made a careful examination of the mine as his rather limited time would allow and described the mine property as consisting of approximately 800 acres, well watered and heavily timbered, with probably 30% of the timber being marketable.

---

3 December 15, 1922, Note from Col. Thomas R. Marshall to Charles B. Squier
4 January 7, 1923 Letter from Col. Thomas R. Marshall to Charles B. Squier
5 January 12??1923 Letter from R. E. Dolan to Col. Thomas R. Marshall

THE COMEBACK

"The remaining timber would provide all of the material necessary for mining operations for many years to come. Water is plentiful and of extremely good quality. The land is well suited for the impoundment of water for general development work, and is entirely sufficient in volume for all purposes in reason. The main workings lie within two miles of the town of Mineral and the railroad station. A new concrete road passes the property and the railroad station is within one-half mile of the mine at Pendleton, Virginia.

"There are two distinct fissure veins running across the entire property in a north easterly to southwesterly direction. He found that only one of the veins had been worked, or prospected, they were about forty feet apart, and continued across the property for approximately 5,000 ft. The vein is pitched at about 70° and is in a white crumbly quartz shot with brownish yellow streaks. It carries a varying overburden of clay which will probably average six feet in depth, although it frequently outcrops. Over its entire length it has been uncovered at intervals by cross cuts, and at its highest point nearly midway of its length a shaft has been sunk 220 ft. and drifts or galleries run out on the 40, 80, and 120 foot levels. In working it is necessary to care for a small inflow of water, but this should not be bothersome. At the bottom of the shaft, sulfides (pyrite etc.) are encountered which are said to carry about $30 to the ton at and near the point of contact. At all points uncovered by the shaft, and drifts a width of vein is revealed averaging a good four feet. In a nut shell we have a vein 5,000 ft. x 4 ft. or a tonnage of approximately 300,000 without taking into account the parallel vein which as yet is unprospected."[6]

Tainter took samples at various points across the property, at various points in the shaft, and drifts, the samples were panned with rather astonishing results. Not

---

[6] February 15, 1923 Mine Report By Col. F. S. Tainter

one pan failed to yield gold, and in sufficient quantity to be rated better than color. A 20 pound gold pan was panned with slightly less than half its capacity, and the average value ran in excess of $40 per ton which was about the minimum value found and some ran much higher. Tainter believed if they accepted only one-half of the $40 value, and assumed the cost of running and handling to be $6 per ton, a total net value for the working of one ore vein would seem to be in excess of $4,000,000 Tainter said there was a steady market for tailings at $2 per ton and this could increase the profit. He believed that with the proper equipment, and honest administration the figures would prove up fairly well. This is incredible news to the potential investors who had another sample assayed on April 3, by 1923 Ledoux and Company which reported 1.37 ounces Gold per ton that was valued at $28.32.

Tainter also advised them to be sure of the title, water rights, mineral rights and taxes before making any definite commitment, and all final conclusions should be based on a satisfactory outcome of the investigations of those issues. He counseled them to have the vein blocked off and sampled at regular and short intervals so that positive values could be established for future guidance.

This looks like very rich ore and at the rate of $28.32 per ton the mine would produce $1,416 for each 50 ton day or approximately $500,000 per year if they can run full time without any major breakdowns. Quite a change from the earlier assays.

ANOTHER CHANCE

On April 30, 1923 Colonel Marshall wrote to John S. Battle, an attorney from Charlottesville, Virginia, to begin the process of chartering and incorporating the Twin Vein Mining Company.[1]

> "John S. Battle was born in New Bern, North Carolina in 1890. He earned an associates's degree from Mars Hill College in North Carolina, a bachelor's degree from Wake Forest University, and a law degree from the University of Virginia. Battle was elected to the Virginia House of Delegates in 1929 and to the Virginia State Senate in 1934, where he served until his election as governor in 1949. In 1956 he was a candidate for the Democratic Presidential Nomination, eventually losing to former Illinois Governor Adlai Stevenson. He died in 1972 at the age of 81."[2]

On May 1, 1923 Squier wrote the Colonel,

> "I am pleased that you have communicated with Mr. Battle as I advised. I trust your trip home was in all ways as pleasant as possible, and that your train was not late as it so often is.
>
> "We have decided at this end that I shall be the president, Mr. Perry and Mr. Coghill respectively vice-presidents. Mr. Van Tassel Sutphen (who has admirably preformed such services before and is one of the syndicate members) secretary and treasurer of the

---

[1] April 30, 1923 Letter from Col. Thomas R. Marshall to John S. Battle
[2] John Stewart Battle Papers, 1954-1967; Accession No. 8599, Albert and Shirley Small Special Collections, University of Virginia School of Law Library, The University of Virginia Charlottesville, Va

proposed company; all of the above gentlemen to be directors, together with yourself, who will also be designated as General Manager of the mine, Mr. Wm. Chappell (of the syndicate) and Mr. Battle, of Charlottesville.

"I think we shall be able to sell between one and two thousand shares of the reserved stock at $5 per share in a week or two. This would bring in between $5,000 to $10,000 in fresh capital for development, which can be applied as the directors see fit. Mr. Coghill Mr. Perry, myself plan planned to come down to the property for several days, perhaps the end of next week or very soon thereafter and can then go into the various details on the spot, which is always much more satisfactory!

"In the meantime, I think you should, first of all get in touch with the Allis-Chalmers Co. agent and have him go down (gratis, on the strength of the probable order of a mill) and inspect the premises, with a view of letting us know exactly what type and size mill we need, and then we can set to work at this end to order same at the best terms we can make.

"After that, the following seems to be of the UTMOST IMPORTANCE, before actually contracting to spend any sums of money, which does not prevent you from taking options (without any outlay) on any new or secondhand equipment in the vicinity you think we need, please submit to us here as soon as possible, a careful, written estimate for the various equipment and other expenses (which you stated would not exceed the sum of $5,000, and might well be much less!) Which you deem all that is in any way required to commence operations, exclusive of the mill, particularly whatever is needed to take out the 1500 to 2000 tons of ore you propose to place on the dump, during the probable three months time it will take to secure the mill and have same fully installed on the property ready to operate at the rate of 50 tons per diem. While we would authorize an expenditure not exceeding $5,000 for the work and equipment above- outlined, I would caution you to be very careful in your estimate, as we would be very dubious about authorizing any further outlay, and might even allow the property to lie idle pending investigations from other sources."[3]

According to deed books at the Louisa County Court House, the mine is located on part of the old R. E. Dolan property previously known as the Louisa Gold Company land tract, which consisted of 766 acres including the Waddy track and the 104 acre Waldorf track.[4] Apparently, Colonel Marshall dewatered, re-timbered and installed the shaft collar in one of three Louisa Mine shafts prior to selling it to the New York investors.

The actual R. E. Dolan mine is located across the road from the old Louisa mine shafts and was a fairly small operation. There are three mine shafts in the area with two in fairly close proximity to each other and one near an elongated rock dump. This dump is the final resting place of waste rock which contains very little or no gold. The ore dump which was parallel to the waste dump no longer exists because this dump contained gold ore which was processed..

There were several photographs of the Dolan mine found in an envelope with "Mrs. Dolan" written on the outside. Additional photographs show a mining operation that existed before the syndicate purchased the property. The mine had a small head frame constructed of poles and equipment consisting of a small steam powered mine hoist, an ore bucket, a wooden mine car, a hand powered two stamp mill for crushing the gold ore and several amalgamation plates.

A stamp mill is a machine that crushes gold-bearing rock to a very fine powder employing what are called stamps which weigh several hundred pounds each. The stamps move up and down and are located inside of an iron assembly called a mortar, the rock is fed in and crushed between the stamp shoe and the die in the bottom of the mortar. Stamp mills were built to run with or without the presence of water. They were manufactured in many different sizes beginning with small

---

3   May 1, 1923 Letter from Charles B. Squier to Col. Thomas R. Marshall
4   Sweet, Palmer C. and Trimble, David, 1983, Virginia Gold resource guide: Virginia Division of Mineral Resources Publication 45, 196 p, pg 132

hand cranked mills used in assay offices to models that crushed many tons of ore per day. The larger mills were powered by water, steam, and later by oil and gasoline engines. They could be disassembled into smaller pieces allowing them to be transported to remote locations. **Illustration 3**

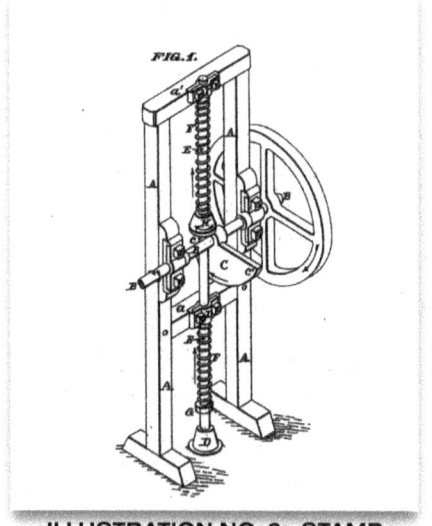

ILLUSTRATION NO. 3: STAMP MILL UNITED STATES PATENT AND TRADEMARK OFFICE

A front approach to the mine is shown in **Photograph No. 8**. The head frame is on the left side of the building which houses the boiler and single drum mine hoist. The wooden track way is pictured slightly to the left of the building and under the head frame. Moving counterclockwise in **Photograph No. 9** the left side of the building is shown with a miner in the process of dumping a bucket of ore into the homemade mine car. The car will be pushed on the wooden track way and dumped out. The two sets of wooden tracks in **Photograph 10** are a substitute for the more expensive iron rails typically used for transporting ore and waste rock. Gold ore from the large pile on the left side of the track way will be transported to the stamp mill by wagon for processing in **Photograph 11**. Also in **Photograph No. 10** The right track way is used to dispose of rock with little or no gold content. The gold ore on the left side of the track way is nonexistent today having been processed for the gold it contained. The two trees at the end of the right track way are still standing today. **Photograph No. 12** shows a rear view of the mine, the dump and track way. Continuing counterclockwise, **Photograph No. 13** shows the mine from the right front with the building on the left. The interior of the building, the steam hoist and operator are shown in **Photograph No. 14**. The man standing in front of the mine wearing a bow tie in **Photograph No. 15** is believed to be R. E. Dolan. The large piece of white quartz rock in the right foreground is probably gold-bearing and may have been placed there for that reason. The dump piles shown in the preceding photographs are very similar to dumps seen at old mines in Colorado and other western states. The photographs of the Dolan mine were labeled personally by the Colonel.

PHOTOGRAPH NO. 8

FRONT OF THE DOLAN MINE

ANATOMY OF A GOLD MINE

PHOTOGRAPH NO. 9

LEFT SIDE OF THE DOLAN MINE

PHOTOGRAPH NO. 10

WOODEN TRACK WAY

ANOTHER CHANCE

PHOTOGRAPH NO. 11

WAGON LOAD OF GOLD ORE

PHOTOGRAPH NO. 12

REAR VIEW OF THE DOLAN MINE

PHOTOGRAPH NO. 13

RIGHT FRONT OF THE DOLAN MINE

PHOTOGRAPH NO. 14

INSIDE OF THE HOIST ROOM

PHOTOGRAPH NO. 15

FRONT VIEW OF THE DOLAN MINE AND GOLD

Acting on Tainter's advice, John Battle began examining the titles to the property and on May 5th, 1923 Squier told the Colonel, "John S. Battle of Charlottesville states he has ascertained that the title to the 48 acres is defective, imperfect and the surveyor believes it lies directly on the veins of gold ore!" They need a deed from Mrs. Flora D. Caring, a former resident whose location is presently unknown. This is a serious matter and Charles Squier hopes the Colonel can straighten it out with Dolan in some way. The Colonel had told Squier in New York that all former owners of the property were living nearby or could be reached. In the event that Mrs. Caring cannot be found, they might be able to eventually get a deed from the court, but it will take valuable time. Squier does not want to delay the final payment and closing of the title any longer than necessary, and asks the Colonel to work with Mr. Dolan and do everything he can to get a clear title to the property as soon as possible.

Squier again asked for the Colonel's detailed estimate of materials and equipment for the head frame and shaft house which he has capped at $5,000. The head frame and shaft house will have to be complete before the mill can be set up. The Colonel informed Squier that the manager of the Allis-Chalmers Co. will go to Mineral as soon as possible, inspect the site for the mill and provide a quotation for the machinery necessary to process the gold ore.

The Colonel had sent Charles Squier some dogwood and azalea blooms which Squier told the Colonel on the 5 of May had

> "Arrived in good shape this morning. I hope the spring flowers will still be fine when we come down on the 14 or 15. I am well aquatinted with the flora of Virginia, having spent many Springs at Hot Springs at the Homestead."[5]

On the evening of May 9 Squier, advised the Colonel that his note and one from John Battle with a copy of the proposed Certificate of Incorporation of the Twin Vein Mining Company had arrived. In the note the Colonel indicated his disagreement with the surveyor as to the location of the 48 acre tract of land.

> "In as much as there is a difference of opinion between you on one hand and the County Surveyor and Mr. Battle on the other, as to whether the 48 acre tract crosses the vein or not, and if it even did not, we certainly do not want to have the title questioned some time in the future-with this I am sure, for our mutual security, you will agree-it will be quite necessary for Mrs. Dolan to get her aunt, Mrs. Caring, of Cleveland, Ohio, to give her the necessary paper signed and witnessed in due legal order to make the title unquestioned. Mr. Battle had these papers prepared recently and forwarded them to you. When this is in due order, the money can be paid down and the deal all closed up.
>
> "We all plan to leave here on the evening of the 15th. or 16th. and come down by the Pullman to Mineral, which leaves here at 8:45 P.M. I hope before that time to have from you to submit to the others your written estimate of all the preliminary expenditures of not over $5,000, which will take care of everything except the mill

---

5   May 5, 1923 Letter from Charles B. Squier to Col. Thomas R. Marshall

itself. We will spend at least two full days in Mineral, that is two days and one night, and I suggest you try to reserve for us at the hotel the three or four best rooms!"

Battle told Squier of the recent sale of the Sulfur Mine, which has a lot of secondhand machinery, which could be bought from the new owner for a "mere song"! Squier suggested the Colonel investigate because the machinery includes a complete mining mill! He is interested to hear what the manager of the Allis-Chalmers Co. has to say about the used mill, "Maybe we can buy the mill in return for some stock"! At this point they have sold about $10,000 worth of stock and are having a prospectus printed which will make it easier to sell stock, Squier sent the Colonel a copy several days later.[6]

The pyrite processing equipment at the Sulfur Mine will not do the job because it was specifically designed to process pyrite. The type of equipment required to separate worthless rock from gold at the Twin Vein mine is specifically designed to recover only gold; they are not interchangeable processes, an amalgamation plant will be necessary to process the type of ore found at the Twin Vein Mine.

The brakes are still on; the title to the 48 acre strip of land which cuts the mine property in half is in limbo. The Dolans have traveled to Cleveland, Ohio in an effort to get a previous owner's (Mrs. Caring) signature on the necessary papers. Without a clear title to the property the Twin Vein Mine will not be one contiguous property under the Company's control. In the event of a major gold strike they would have no choice but pay an exorbitant price for it, or engage in a legal battle that could last for years and bankrupt the company. These types of problems are very common in the mining industry.

On May 12 Squier tells the Colonel,

> "In regard the matter of the title to the 48 acre tract as being highly important, but trust it can be cleared up in view of the fact that the Dolans feel so sure they can secure Mrs. Caring's signature to a full

---

6   May 9, 1923 Letter from Charles B. Squier to Col. Thomas R. Marshall

quit-claim deed to the property, although it does seem strange that Dolan allowed the title to remain in this imperfect condition so long!

"I have written Mr. Battle very fully concerning the two ways in which it will be possible to handle the matter, neither of which will necessitate the Dolans return to Mineral, and should not cause them in any way to object, if they really can, as they say, to secure Mrs. Caring's signature on the necessary papers. There is no other way the difficulty can be overcome, as we cannot accept beforehand their statement without definitely knowing Mrs. Caring's attitude in the matter.

"It is our understanding that you will not expend actually any money until this matter is cleared up, also that you will not expend any money until we have your detailed report as to same, as set forth in your letter. We will not come to Mineral until the above matter of the title is duly straightened out, as we cannot come down twice. If we hear from Mr. Battle in the meantime that the Dolans have accepted one of the propositions, we can then proceed with incorporation, We can come down next Friday or the following Monday morning, clean up all of the details and at the same time go over your estimate for the expenditures for the development of the mine itself. So please do not make reservations for us at the hotel, until we know definitely just what day we are coming."[7]

Everything seems to start rolling at one time, on May 22, 1923 Squier advised the Colonel that, "He was in receipt of his note of the 19th. and was pleased that the quit-claim deed has been executed by Mrs. Caring, and the title, with full rights, to the entire 776 acres is in good shape. Perry, Coghill and I have our reservations on the 8:45 evening sleeper, which leaves here next Thursday, the 24th and arrives in Mineral, around 10:00 on Friday morning. Will you please reserve for us three rooms, if possible, in the hotel in Mineral for Friday night? We will spend Friday going over all the legal details as Mr. Battle will meet us at Mineral

---

7   May 12, 1923 Letter from Charles B. Squier to Col. Thomas R. Marshall

Friday morning. Then we can go over your written figures of the entire expenses up to and not exceeding $5,000.00, exclusive of mill, which I trust you will have prepared. We will spend Saturday in carefully inspecting the property itself physically and mineralogically. Will you kindly reserve for us on the best train out of Doswell or Gordonsville Saturday evening, a drawing room for New York."[8] (A drawing room is similar to a rolling living room, very plush for the day.)

Squier, Perry, Coghill and Battle arrive in Mineral on May 24, 1923 for the inspection of the mine property they hope will make them all very rich. They are shown the improvements to the shaft made by the Colonel and the layout at the Dolan mine.

When the Colonel first had an option on the Dolan property, he had pumped the shaft out, installed new timbering and a shaft collar which is in the right hand side of **Photograph No. 16**. A mine shaft is a very dangerous place due to the danger of someone falling in and losing their life at the bottom. Boards are placed on top of the shaft collar to prevent this event. The top of a ladder can be seen at the rear the shaft collar.

PHOTOGRAPH NO. 16
VIEW OF THE MINE SHAFT

---

8   May 22, 1923 Letter from Charles B. Squier to Col. Thomas R. Marshall

On May 27, 1923 Squier wrote the Colonel,

> "Perry and I arrived, weary, but optimistic, at 11:10 railroad time, at the Penn Station last night, and are glad the deal is closed, and the pretty, and we hope lucrative property is finally ours! We are much indebted to you for your hospitality and for your valuable explanation to us of the potentialities of the property!" (The new owners are getting a taste of gold fever.)
>
> "I will recommend to the other directors that your salary, as general manager of the property, commence at once at the rate of $5,000.00 per annum, and I will POSITIVELY see that you receive not later than Friday of this week at least $3,000.00 in cash that you can use for the payment of the machinery you mentioned to me as having acquired so cheaply in Virginia!
>
> "I trust you will soon inform me that Dolan has finally attended to the satisfaction of the $5,565.00 lien against the property which we spoke to the local banker about yesterday morning, as this is important in the EXTREME! Please send me up some good samples of ore, when you find some, and keep me informed of all important progress-I really feel we have secured a fine property very reasonably!
>
> "It is also very IMPORTANT that you send me at once the specifications for exactly what we must order from the Allis-Chalmers Company in the way of a mill before Thursday morning! I think we have sold some $18,500.00 worth of stock at $5 per share, all to be paid up at once in cash, and we shall probably not sell more than $25,000.00 worth in all!"[9]

---

9   May 27, 1923 Letter from Charles B. Squier to Col. Thomas R. Marshall

ANOTHER CHANCE

On May 31 Squier informed the Colonel,

> "Your special delivery letter of the 30th. came this morning, and I shall be particularly interested in the results of running the little crude mill on the property! I am rejoiced that Dolan has arranged for the payment of the $5,565.00, which was a bit irregular-send me the satisfaction of the loan by registered mail for filing here. I shall also be glad to have the flow sheet and other specifications from the Allis-Chalmers Co. at the earliest possible moment, so we can order all mill machinery as soon as possible-I am anxious to proceed at once as quickly, as well as economically, as practicable! The amount of your salary has not yet been formally agreed upon, but I will vote for $5,000.00 per annum, commencing as of June1st., and presume it will be soon that you will show it is quite justified. I enclose herewith my check from "special account" for $3,500.00 to order of Thomas R. Marshall-General Manager-to cover the machinery you have ordered in Richmond for immediate delivery, and also some balance for labor, etc. You may advance yourself of this amount one twelfth of $5,000.00 for June, if you so need-I am taking some risk personally in so handling the advancement of funds, as the company is not yet in legal being. Please be very careful to take receipts for all expenditures and send me the original receipts (including the $100.00 advanced to you in New York upon the occasion of your last visit for personal expenses), as same must be duly filed and agreed upon. I have not yet heard from Battle that the incorporation has gone through.
>
> "I am quite enthusiastic about our "smug" little property, and know you agree with me-we certainly bought it for a veritable "song"! I am leaving for my country estate tomorrow morning, so please address me henceforth: Merely, Bennington, VERMONT."[10]

---

10 May 31, 1923 Letter from Charles B. Squier to Col. Thomas R. Marshall

On June 6, 1923 Squier advised the Colonel,

> "I am glad the check for $3,500.00-arrived in time as it was sent out last Thursday, May the 30th. Before I left New York I got your letter of the 2nd. containing a letter from Mr. Dennison of the Allis-Chalmers Co. Just as soon as you receive the specifications of just exactly what we will need from the Allis-Chalmers Co., send them to me and I will make a special trip to New York to collaborate with Mr. Perry in ordering it at the lowest cost possible-I had hoped to have ordered it by June1st..
>
> "Also I had hoped the company would be incorporated, so we could have our directors meeting. I have heard nothing from Battle about this and cannot understand the delay.
>
> "I trust you have been <u>very careful</u> not to give out any of the Company circulars we gave you that day at Gordonsville, without noting therein "Stock subject change in price or withdrawal from sale without further notice"! This is most important! What did you think of the little circular?"[11]

Squier scolded the Colonel in his letter of June 7,

> "Since writing to you yesterday I received a letter from Mr. Battle explaining why the incorporation of the company has been held up! It seems that you would not sign the incorporation certificate unless you were mentioned therein as general manager. This is never done in any state as general manager is not regarded as an official such as president, vice president or treasurer. You are one of the directors hence only the incorporating officer. You will readily appreciate that the Board of Directors in any event controls

---

11   June 6, 1923 Letter from Charles B. Squier to Col. Thomas R. Marshall

the appointment of officers. Said offices can be changed from the president down.

Their office duration etc .and the stock of course controls all stockholders meetings and said control rests entirely in me for the next five years. Therefore, please sign the papers which all the others have signed at once and forward same to Battle as it will be most inconvenient to delay incorporation further. I regret I neglected to explain to you when I was in Mineral. It is our intention to make you General Manager as long as you are shown to be capable thereof, even for many years to come, if satisfactory."[12]

On June 10 Mrs. Dolan wrote the Colonel concerning the details of his commission which includes the clause, upon payment of the $15,000 with interest on or before the maturity. If the buyers can make the payment on time she will pay him $5,000. There is also a provision in the sales agreement that states

"In the event of foreclosure of the deed of trust, the $5,000.00 is not to be paid." The mortgage comes due in February of 1924![13]

---

12 June 7, 1923 Letter from Charles B. Squier to Col. Thomas R. Marshall
13 June 10, 1923 Letter from Mrs. R. E. Dolan to Col. Thomas R. Marshall

THE HEAD FRAME

A head frame is a tower-like structure constructed of very heavy timbers with a very large pulley or bull wheel at the top which is secured in place with bearings allowing it to turn without a great deal of friction. A steel cable runs in the grove of the wheel and is connected to a mine hoist at one end and the skip at the other. This structure is used by the miners to raise gold ore and non gold-bearing material to the surface where it will be either piled up for processing or discarded.

Construction of the head frame began with first order of heavy timbers on June 16, 1923 from W. J. Walton at Pendleton, Virginia, totaling 2,449 board feet. The timbers were all white oak and ranged in dimension from 8 by 10 inches, 12 feet long; 8 by 8 inches, 10 and 12 feet in length; to 6 by 9 inch beams, 12 to 16 feet in length.[1] White oak is specified due to its toughness. Construction of the head frame was delayed because the W. J. Walton Lumber Company could not deliver the materials to the mine site for three weeks due to adverse weather conditions.

The lower section of the head frame was constructed of white oak timbers with a dimension of 8" x 10" x 12' long. Timbers 8" x 8" x 12' long were used in the upper areas with smaller timbers being used for cross bracing. The use of very heavy timbers for the head frame was necessary due to the stress placed upon it when the ore bucket was raised with a full load of heavy ore or waste rock by the mine hoist.

Photograph No. 17 demonstrates how the timbers were hoisted into place. Six men employ what is called a gin pole which is located in the left side of the photograph. The gin pole has guy ropes and a block and tackle attached to the very top. The ends of guy ropes are attached to trees, stumps or anything solid enough to provide stability. The item to be hoisted is tied to the end of the rope at the bottom

---

[1] June 16, 1923 Bill of Materials to W. J. Walton

THE HEAD FRAME

and the other is used to pull the item to the top. In the photograph the gin pole is bending under the weight of the beam.

All of the timbers had to be hoisted into place using the gin pole and the men provided all of the power because there were no modern hydraulic cranes to make the work easier. The shorter beams can weigh 300 or 400 pounds each depending on how well cured they are. **Photograph 18** depicts how this was accomplished as the second level of the head frame is now under construction. Lap joints are cut into the ends of the beams so they can be bolted together forming a very strong joint. The mine skip which will be used to raise the ore from the mine can be seen at the left side of the head frame with the shaft collar being located in the center of the new head frame. **Photograph 19**

PHOTOGRAPH NO. 17
HEAD FRAME BEGINNINGS

PHOTOGRAPH NO. 18

BOLTING TIMBERS IN PLACE

PHOTOGRAPH NO. 19

HOISTING OPERATION

THE HEAD FRAME

On June 17, Charles Squier told the Colonel he was glad to hear Dolan had paid the $5,5650 mortgage on the property, and that it was "duly satisfied and recorded by the clerk. Will you please obtain for me the cancelled mortgage, which is very important we have for our files!"[2]

Squier was very confident in John Battle's professional abilities when it came to the drawing up of legal papers and he regretted the unnecessary delay in their plans caused by the Colonel's reluctance to signing the incorporation papers. The Colonel would not sign the agreement because he believed he was losing some of his share of the mine in this deal.

On June 14, Squier while at the Ritz-Carlton Hotel in New York had received a letter, a separate package containing the proposals of the Allis-Chalmers Co., a number of photographs of the work at the mine, and a sample of gold dust from the Colonel. Squier wanted a better sample of the gold from the mine and told the Colonel to "Please send me any very fine rock specimens showing actually small nuggets you may run across!

Squier continued, "I was in New York from Monday to Thursday last and had several important conferences with Perry, Coghill, and Sutphen regarding the mine. We are now waiting to hear from Mr. Battle that the incorporation papers have gone through, and the company actually exists. Then Perry, Coghill, Sutphen, and Chappell, which make up the necessary quorum, will hold a directors' meeting, and elect the officers. Perry and Coghill are spending next week-end here with us. As we cannot very well order any machinery from the Allis-Chalmers Co. until the company has been duly incorporated, I hope you will not delay your signature any longer, if it has not already been affixed!"[3]

Earlier the Colonel was able to purchase a used steam powered double drum mine hoist and the New York investors are very glad to get it. The hoist will raise and lower the mine skip from the bottom of the mine shaft to the surface. A skip is used in mine shafts which are inclined rather than vertical and can transport gold

---

2   June 17, 1923 Letter from Charles B. Squier to Col. Thomas R. Marshall
3   June 17, 1923, Squier

ore, waste rock, miners and materials in and out of the mine shaft. Some skips have a valve in the bottom which allows them to bail out a water filled shaft.

The top elements of the head frame are pre-fitted on the ground prior to being hoisted into place. A close examination of **Photograph 20** reveals the lap joints cut into the timbers which will allow others to be joined at these points. The carpenters are pre-fitting the upper members on the ground to be sure of a good fit prior to hoisting them into place, nothing was left to chance. In **Photograph 21** the head frame is nearly complete with both sides in place. The bracing is the next phase of construction. **Photograph 22** shows that the bull wheel has been installed on the top of the head frame. The hoist cable (steel rope) which runs over the bull wheel is approximately one and one quarter inches in diameter and has a safe working load of about 17,000 pounds. When the mine hoist revolves in one direction the skip is lowered into the mine and when it revolves in the opposite direction the skip will be raised from the mine.

A pile of fire bricks which will be used to brick the boiler can be seen on the very left of the photograph, the lower section of the smoke stack is lying on the ground to the right of the head frame. A second mine shaft with a windlass mounted on the top can be seen in the foreground. The windlass is a very basic means of raising and lowering the ore bucket in a mine shaft, and is usually seen at very small mines. The next best arrangement is the head frame which is nearing completion. This shaft was used by the miners prior to the main shaft being in operation.

Photograph 23 documents the progress being made at the Twin Vein Mine, the boiler has arrived aboard an early version of a tractor and trailer it weighs around 17,000 pounds and will be unloaded by hand. It is very carefully moved off of the truck because any unexpected changes in its speed or direction can result in very serious injury or death to the men.

Photograph 24 The boiler has been successfully unloaded and rests near where it will be installed. The steam hoist frame is sitting directly under the head frame but will not stay there for long as it will eventually be installed in the hoist room.

THE HEAD FRAME

PHOTOGRAPH NO. 20

PRE-FITTING BEAMS

PHOTOGRAPH NO. 21

HEAD FRAME FINAL STAGES

PHOTOGRAPH NO. 22

BULL WHEEL INSTALLED

PHOTOGRAPH NO. 23

ARRIVAL OF THE BOILER

THE HEAD FRAME

PHOTOGRAPH NO. 24

BOILER UNDER HEAD FRAME

SHAFT HOUSE

PHOTOGRAPH NO. 25

SHAFT HOUSE FOUNDATION

Photograph No. 25 Construction had progressed well, and the Colonel had been very busy securing materials and overseeing the work on the head frame and now the shaft house. The shaft house will contain the boiler, mine hoist and other equipment associated with the operation of the mine itself. The foundation for the shaft house had been built and the sills are in place as shown from the rear. The floor of the shaft house will be made of dirt and the boiler's concrete footing will be dug into it. The stones comprising the right rear side of the foundation are

SHAFT HOUSE

still in place today. The mine hoist that rests under the head frame will have to be moved to the small room that can be seen at the right rear of the shaft house. One method for moving very heavy items is to construct a wood track-way of heavy timbers and then use pipe or steel shafts for rollers. The item can then be moved by men, by pulling it with horses or a tractor. As the item moves forward on the rollers, those previously passed over are repositioned in front of the item as it traverses the track-way. Skids are also used to move such items. Part of the used sections of smoke stack for the boiler can be seen in the foreground with the remainder to the rear near the head frame.

On June 19 Squier advises the Colonel he has still not heard from John Battle that the company's incorporation has gone through and hoped it would be soon. This delay is costing valuable time and they need to hold the directors meeting and select the corporation's officers.

Squier informed the Colonel,

> "Perry, Coghill, Sutphen and I decided at our meeting in New York last week that we will formally commence your salary of $5,000.00 per year, payable monthly in advance, on the actual date of the company's incorporation." Squier was careful to say that they cannot personally or individually order the $10,000 mill from the Allis-Chalmers Co. because it must be ordered legally in the company's name. Squier, at this point hoped to hear that the incorporation had finally gone through, because if not, they are suffering unnecessary delays.[1]

The delay in the incorporation caused Charles Squier to hesitate in ordering the mill in his name because he would not have the protection the incorporation would provide in the event of a lawsuit.

The Colonel pushes construction of the shaft house along and orders additional materials on the 20 of June 1923. The order consisted of 6 pieces of 7 inch by 10

---

1   June 19, 1923, Letter from Charles B. Squier to Col Thomas R. Marshall

inch oak, 10 feet long; 20 pieces of pine 4 inches by 6 inches,12 feet long; 52 pieces of pine 2 inches by 6 inches, 16 feet long which were used as rafters; 60 pieces of pine 2 inches by 4 inches, 10 feet long and 12 pieces of pine 2 inches by 6 inches, 14 feet long.[2] The framing for the shaft house is nearly complete in **Photograph 26**.

Charles Squier told the Colonel that Perry and Coghill were spending the week-end of the 22nd. at his country estate in Bennington, Vermont so they could go over everything very carefully. He anxiously awaited news from the Colonel and John Battle that the incorporation papers had gone through so they could hold the meeting. Squier said, "They could have the directors meeting early next week, order the stock certificates to be engraved, and put through the order for the mill with instructions to rush it. Perry is a friend of the most important man in the Allis-Chalmers Co., which will facilitate matters greatly!"[3]

PHOTOGRAPH NO. 26

FRAMING SHAFT HOUSE

---

2   June 18, 1923, Bill of Materials From W. J. Walton
3   June 19, 1923, Squier

SHAFT HOUSE

The Colonel had sent Squier a large rough button of gold with the "flow" sheets for the mill. Squier was impressed with the gold sample and had many questions about it. He was of the opinion,

> "The gold should be worth about $5-do you know exactly how much ore in weight produced it; did the ore come from the dump around the shaft and was it obtained by running ore through the small 3-ton mill or by mere pan washing or panning; and was it smelted or fused into the hard, solid mass it is now in from gold dust?"[4]

The flow sheets show in order, what pieces of equipment are used in the gold recovery process beginning with the introduction of the ore into the mill and ending with the separation of the gold from the worthless tailings.

PHOTOGRAPH NO. 27
LEFT FRONT OF SHAFT HOUSE

---

4   June 19, 1923, Squier

Photograph 27 construction on the shaft house is progressing quicky and the Colonel sent more photographs to Charles Squier. The photograph reveals the left view of the shaft house under construction. The boiler has been repositioned and rafters are being nailed in place over it.

Photograph 28 The massive steam powered mine hoist frame is resting on several heavy timbers. One of the two steam engines which will power the hoist can be seen on the left side of the hoist frame. These small steam engines will rotate the two small gears which are connected to a large shaft on the right side of the hoist, the other gear is located on the right side of the hoist. The other gear is located on the right side of the hoist and to rear of the first. These gears will in turn rotate two 4 ft diameter gears which are attached to the drums of the hoist thereby winding and unwinding the cable wound around them

Photograph No. 29 The shaft house has been framed, sided in and the roof has been installed leaving an opening to accommodate the smoke stack installation. The shaft house is nearly complete except for the installation of the windows.

PHOTOGRAPH NO. 28

STEAM HOIST FRAME

SHAFT HOUSE

PHOTOGRAPH NO. 29

RIGHT SIDE OF SHAFT HOUSE

PHOTOGRAPH NO. 30

BRICKING THE BOILER

Photograph No. 30 The boiler has been set in place and a firebox is being constructed to contain the fuel which will supply the heat necessary for the generation of steam. Steam will power the mine hoist and other equipment such as pumps and drills. The boiler front at the far right will support the fire doors at the bottom and the boiler doors above. On the front of the boiler the fire tubes can be seen through which hot gases from the fire below circulate thereby heating the water contained in the boiler. The smoke stack will be attached to the top of the iron boiler front casting at the top. The upright device attached to the boiler near the front left is the water column which allows the operator (fireman) to observe the water level in the boiler. The water level must be maintained at the proper level or the boiler can over heat and explode.

On June 26 Squier told the Colonel he was glad to receive the photographs he had sent up, which showed the construction work on the shaft house. Squier was impressed and encouraged the Colonel to continue sending photographs as the work progressed. Squier again pressed the Colonel to send,

> "Any especially fine natural unrefined specimens of very rich ore, showing small nuggets, you may happen upon! These things all assist us greatly in the further sale of stock!"[5]

The proceeds from the sale of stock are used to purchase equipment, pay for labor or purchase options on adjacent and, hopefully gold rich property, Squier continued

> "Perry and Coghill were here with me from Friday to yesterday (Monday) and we spent a lot of time in going over everything very carefully. I instructed Mr. Perry to telephone Battle yesterday morning as to the delay in the incorporation papers. A letter from Perry arrived this morning saying he got Battle on the wire, and that Battle had already filed the papers, some ten days ago, without your signature as you did not then desire to sign merely as director, so the incorporation will soon be in order. We can proceed at once to have

---

5   June 26, 1923 Letter from Charles B. Squier to Col. Thomas R. Marshall

SHAFT HOUSE

Perry and Coghill transfer the property now standing in their names as agents to the new company, as incorporated, have the stock certificates engraved, hold the directors meeting (four only need be present) etc. The fact you have not signed the incorporation papers will make no difference, as I have duly instructed the others that you are to be a director in full standing with the others, and you can sign later. It was vital to have no further delay on account of ordering the machinery! It is also understood you are to be General Manager of the property @5,000.00 per annum, this, is however never regarded as an officer, as director, president, etc., or mentioned in incorporation papers!"[6]

At this point the mining company was still operating as an unincorporated business, and the Colonel was told by Charles Squier not to spend more than $5,000 on the head frame and shaft house. The first orders on June 16 and the 20 for materials were under Colonel Marshall's name; a subsequent order of July 3, 1923 was under the name of the Twin Vein Mining Company Incorporated.

After the boiler has been set the smoke stack will be installed on top of the it. **Photograph No. 31** A gin pole is being used to hoist the smoke stack into place. The stack will be hoisted so that the bottom will clear the hole in the roof, and then it will be gently lowered onto the top of the boiler where it will be bolted in place. The opening in the roof will be closed and the miners are one step closer to firing it all up.

Photograph No. 32 The mine hoist has been installed inside of the shaft house and the piping to the boiler is complete. The hoist cable can be seen in the left side of the photograph exiting the hoist drum and continuing to the bull wheel at the top of the head frame. The left side of the mine hoist is visible, and one of the steam engines which provides power for the hoist is located in the lower rear of the photograph. This hoist is much larger than the one in use at the Dolan Mine.

---

6   June 26, Squier

PHOTOGRAPH NO. 31

HOISTING THE SMOKE STACK

PHOTOGRAPH NO. 32

THE HOIST ROOM

SHAFT HOUSE

On June 27 Squier told the Colonel that his special delivery letter had arrived last night, and he could see from the photographs enclosed that he was making good progress. Squier expressed his sympathy concerning the difficulty the miners experienced with unloading and moving the heavy mine machinery, but surmised that they finally prevailed. The Colonel had mentioned a need for more funds, and Squier sent a check made out to the Colonel for $1,500, which Squier said was, "the balance of the original $5,000.00, which is all you said would be needed, exclusive of the actual mill from the Allis-Chalmers Co. I have not yet received word of the incorporation of the company, so I am again taking some personal responsibility in sending you this additional check to avoid any delay in the work! This now leaves us with only $1,500.00 cash of the company's funds on hand and none of the subscriptions sold to out-of-town people by Perry or Coghill have yet been paid, although they should come within a few days.

> "Please send me at once, for my files, all your receipts (original) and letters, or other data, for keeping an audit of the expenditures for machinery, equipment, etc.! I am very interested in the progress made, and I shall come down again probably with Coghill before I sail for Europe on August 11th. If this turns out to be a very profitable mine, we will certainly surprise N.Y. City."[7]

---

7   June 27, 1923, Letter from Charles B. Squier to Col. Thomas R. Marshall

PHOTOGRAPH NO. 33

LEFT SIDE OF THE SHAFT HOUSE

Photograph No. 33 The shaft house is waiting for its windows, and water being pumped from the shaft is exiting the pipe at the rear of the building. The steam whistle has been installed next to the stack and will be used to signal the end of a shift or in the event of an accident, it can summon help. The water tower is located to the left of the smoke stack and holds water for the boiler. The hoist cable can be seen as it exits the cupola and continues over the bull wheel and then down into the inclined mine shaft. The ore chute is located at the right side of the head frame, and directs the ore to the side of the head frame when it is dumped out of the skip at the front. The American flag flies proudly at the top of the head frame.

On July 13 Charles Squier told the Colonel he had received his letters of June the 30 and July 9, and was pleased with the progress he was making. Squier wished Coghill and Perry were making better, "progress in selling stocks and getting in more funds in a dull season and the stock market has been very poor of late! The photographs in your last letter of July 9th. were especially interesting!"

> "Please let me know when all your machinery and equipment excluding the Allis-Chalmers mill is in place and how much ore per

day you will be raising for the big ore dump! Also, send me all the original vouchers for all expenditures for our files. The company is now duly incorporated and stock certificates will be issued within one month so look into all legal peculiarities! Either I, Coghill or both of us will come down for a day or so next month (August) to review the work accomplished!"[8]

The Colonel had again written to Charles Squier detailing the progress being made at the mine and included additional photographs of the construction along with a request for more operating money. On July 27 Squier told the Colonel,

"I received your letter this morning and I would like to take this occasion to complement you upon all you have done so far and the splendid progress you seem to have made from the interesting photographs you have sent! I am sending all of the photos to New York, as I receive them, as this sometimes facilitates the sale of stock! The sale of stock has been very slow lately, as business has turned bad in the stock market and for some time. This has a depressing effect upon all sales of securities, as you can well imagine! If we do not sell more stock soon, I will probably have to personally loan the company $5,000.00 with which to carry on!"

"I was in New York last Monday and Tuesday morning when we had the first official meeting, at which the officers were duly elected, and other routine business was conducted, such as taking steps to have the transfer agent appointed, the great seal, and the stock certificate book ordered. It is quite important that you send me at the earliest possible moment all official vouchers including your own receipts for your salary for the months of June and July. I can then exchange checks with the company, and thus eliminate any further personal liability, which I have assumed for some time, in order to

---

8   July 13, 1923, Letter from Charles B. Squier to Col. Thomas R. Marshall

avoid further delays and all of the various outlays can be duly audited in the books! So please send me these accounts at once!

"Mr. Sutphen now handles the company funds as Secretary and Treasurer, his address is, Van Tassel Sutphen, 22 Franklin Place, Morristown, New Jersey. All checks must be countersigned by me, or for convenience during my absence, by either of the Vice- Presidents, Perry or Coghill. Mr. Coghill is the first vice president and thus next in command to me! I am writing to Mr. Sutphen today to send you a check for $1,250.00, which is all we can spare at the moment-this may take several days, on account of the required countersignatures. I can well appreciate that you want to keep going any good men you have on the payroll.

"I will unfortunately not be able to come to Mineral, as I have a lot to do here, and am leaving for Europe, partly on business, on August the 25th. and will be back around November1st. We will come down shortly before Thanksgiving when we hope all of the equipment will be running. Mr. Coghill, however, has assured me that he will come down sometime within the next month, and he is really a better man to examine everything than I, who know so very little about anything mechanical! I feel optimistic, that, if we only have plenty of ore, all will turn out well!"[9]

Photograph No 34. All of the windows have been installed in the shaft house, water is flowing indicating that they have steam up and are pumping water from the shaft. The photograph of the rear of the shaft house provides more details of the completed head frame, shaft house and water tower. There appears to be a sluice box with water flowing through it in the foreground

Photograph No. 35 The side view of the shaft house reveals what appears to be a large wood supply but it is not large enough to run the boiler for very long in the event of bad weather. These boilers can burn several cords of wood per shift.

---

[9] July 27, 1923, Letter from Charles B. Squier to Col. Thomas R. Marshall

SHAFT HOUSE

PHOTOGRAPH NO. 34

REAR VIEW OF THE SHAFT HOUSE

PHOTOGRAPH NO. 35

WOOD PILE AT RIGHT THE SIDE OF SHAFT HOUSE

Squier sent the Colonel a hand written note at 3 PM on July 27,

> "(1) have you duly taken out in the name of the company employers liability insurance covering the employees under Virginia law. (2) have you taken out fire insurance to cover the boiler, shaft house and equipment? If not, these should both be at once covered in the company's name! Also, how much gold have you recovered from the operation of the small 3 ton mill which was already on the property when we took over? I understood you intended paying for some labor out of this? What is the approximate recovery rate of gold per ton so far? Please let me know at once about these important matters!"[10]

Colonel Marshall had written to Dolan on July 15 in Cripple Creek Colorado seeking information regarding the availability of used amalgamation equipment. Dolan's reply was,

> "Got back from Cripple Creek on Saturday and found your letter, certainly glad to hear from you and enjoyed looking over the photos and from indications you are making good progress with the work.
>
> "I certainly will be glad to hear from you any time, whenever you find time to write, and I will keep you advised of anything new springing up in the working of mines, mining or milling of ore I may hear of. I made a careful canvas of the mills in Cripple Creek last week but found nothing new in any of the processes now in use there, but several of the technical mill men are however talking about installing the Merrill filtering machine and a new vacuum outfit just coming on the market in connection with the cyanide process.

---

10 July 27, 1923, 2nd Letter from Charles B. Squier to Col. Thomas R. Marshall

"Cripple Creek is taking on a new lease of life and now only beginning to recover from the war depression. It is producing monthly upwards of one half $1 million.

"Have a couple of nibbles for our (Cripple Creek) property but nothing yet certain, I am hereinafter negotiating with some parties who want a lease and bond but you know we would rather sell. The Cripple Creek parties wanting the mine could not agree on terms so that is off for the present at least.

"This town has changed greatly since we were here a few years ago. The city is now to be compared in every way to many of our Eastern cities, the place has grown to be twice the size it was when we lived here."[11]

Squier wrote the Colonel on August 9

"I received your letter upon my return from the week end I spent at East Hampton, Long Island and also the package of receipts and vouchers which I examined, and have sent on to Mr. Sutphen, to be audited and filed away for safekeeping.

"I am glad you took out the insurance, and I am relieved to know it is in force! I am happy to hear you received the check from Sutphen for $1,250.00. There was an unavoidable delay because the company's accounts were just recently started! I shall be interested to here what results you get from operation of the crude little mill!

"In regard the matter of the Allis-Chalmers Company, I regret to say we are having great trouble raising additional funds, because this is the dull season, when many people are away on their vacations and chiefly because the stock market and business in general (for several months) has turned very poor, and scared

---

11   July 31, 1923, Letter from R. E. Dolan to Col. Thomas R. Marshall

people with capital!! We have thus not felt "financially able to order the Allis-Chalmers mill, but hope to do so, before I go to Europe, on the 25th. Jim Coghill has finished his work with the Porter Cord Tube Company and will have extra time for a more intensive stock selling campaign! He was here for a night recently, and is spending the week end with Perry in Magnolia, Massachusetts. I am meeting Coghill in Boston early next week, and we now have a lead for some more capital for stock. I have not considered it right for me to advance more funds personally in view of the fact that I put in the original $10,000 and secure the only stock sales of Manning for $6,500 in all, while Perry and Coghill have raised nothing! It is now up to them!

"Do not be discouraged because if nothing in the way of new capital is raised before I go to Europe on the 25th., I will be in New York for several days and I will advance the company $5000.00, thus assuring the ordering of the mill.

"I think you had best not proceed with the mill house, in view of all the above, until the mill is actually ordered and thus conserve our funds-I regret the delay quite as much as you do. This due entirely to the failure of Coghill and Perry to raise the additional funds by the sale of stock, which they had promised to do long ago. We will have to stop expenditures for perhaps a few weeks, unless you can proceed on a three months credit basis, which might be fairly safe! However, from what you say in your letters, you cannot very well start to erect the mill-house until you have your specifications of the ordered mill."[12]

The Colonel received a reply on August 18, 1923, to his letter of August 11 requesting information as to why the mill had still not been ordered. Squier explained the painful details.

---

12   August 9, 1923 Letter from Charles. B. Squier to Col. Thomas R. Marshall

SHAFT HOUSE

"Your letter of the 11th. was awaiting me upon my return from Boston, where I have been for some days on business, and I am replying at my earliest opportunity! I appreciate very much the fact that you have worked very hard, and saved us considerable expenses in the purchase of equipment (all for the general good!), and erected, I doubt not, a very good shaft head enclosure and boiler house! You are naturally very disappointed at the fact the mill is not yet ordered form the Allis-Chalmers Company, but we could not do so without additional funds in hand! For the present, we must close down, and cease further construction operations. As I understand it you can not proceed with the mill house until the plans are furnished by Allis-Chalmers after the mill is definitely ordered. We will have to wait until more funds are in hand-I think I intimated this in my last letter of over ten days ago!

"Perry and Coghill have fallen down on producing the capital they promised, and as we are now a duly incorporated company, I cannot feel personally justified in advancing more funds myself, as this might have the tendency to make them feel they could let things slide some more. I think you will appreciate this point of view as just to me, although I regret just as much as you the delay involved! If we had a small amount left in the treasury ($1,000.00), I would suggest you proceed with cutting wood for engine and boiler fuel, but this we cannot do!

"However, I have to report the following which is hopeful: Mr. Coghill, in whom I have a good deal of confidence, has just completed some work for another company, in which he has a large interest (the inner tube), and he has agreed in writing very definitely to me not to go to Europe this year (as I shall look out for whatever comes up over there), and from now on to give his entire time and attention to the gold mine and to the procurement of additional capital, which he has not been able so far to do!

"He and I made a special four day trip in my auto to Boston and vicinity, and I think we have sold considerable stock (from $10,000.00 to 30,000.00 worth) to responsible parties, who will pay in full! We have relied too much on Mr. Perry, who has not lived up to the $5,000.00 in subscriptions, which he definitely promised. Had we had it in hand by now we could have ordered the mill, and given you $1,500.00, which you could have used for general cleaning up, cutting wood and generally "carrying on"! I hope the above will clear up the situation for you, give you renewed hope and explain an unfortunate situation, which, at worst, is only temporary! I feel quite CONFIDENT that Mr. Coghill will <u>with untiring efforts</u> now raise all of the additional capital we will ever need, which ought not be over $35,000.00 more, including partial payment of the nine months loan of $15,000.00 on the property.

"Please find out from your local bank, if they will extend the present nine months mortgage, as a new loan made by the company, for $10,000.00 or even $7,500.00, as a first lien on the entire property, if we arranged to pay off the balance?

"It is quite impossible for me to come down to Mineral before I sail for Europe on the "Homeric" of the White Star Line next Saturday, the 25th. I have too much to clean up here! I am leaving here on <u>Thursday next</u>, and will be at : 521 Park Avenue, New York City, in the interim.

"Mr. Coghill will be in complete charge during my absence, and will come down to Mineral within ten days. The main thing to do at once is to sell stock! If absolutely "up against it", wire me here, and I will send $1,000.00, but otherwise try to tide matters over! If there are any important things to talk over, please write them to me at once."[13]

---

13 August 18, 1923 Letter from Charles B. Squier to Col. Thomas R. Marshall

SHAFT HOUSE

The lack of money continues to be a problem, the Colonel sends an urgent telegram to Squier requesting money as soon as possible. Squier replies on August 20, "This will probably be my last letter, before departing for Europe next Saturday for two months, as I shall be fearfully busy cleaning up various important matters before leaving!

"You, I hope, understand your last letter did not reach me until last Friday evening, when I returned from our stock selling campaign in Boston and vicinity, and I did not gather from its content that you were so urgently in need of funds, until your telegram arrived Saturday around One O'clock, too late for me to communicate with the bank until Monday, as I wired you at once in reply.

"I have instructed The Farmers Loan & Trust Co. this morning to at once wire you by "Western Union $500.00 which I have to advance out of my private funds (very much against My attorneys' advice!), the first time being $500.00 sent to Battle to defray various legal expenses, etc., when the company had no money in hand. This I am not willing to do again under any circumstances! Please let me know of your receipt of the $500.00 wired today by sending me a formal receipt as General Manager of the company.

"I do not like to discontinue the labor organization you have built up, but I fear it will have to be done temporarily! Besides, there is little to be done now (cutting wood can wait for a week or so without much loss of time until the Allis-Chalmers mill is definitely ordered, and you have their plan for the necessary enclosing structure.

"Also, please hereafter address all communications to our First Vice-President (Jas. H. Coghill, Normandie Park, Morristown, New Jersey, who will now assume full control, pending my absence abroad! Until he lets you know we have more funds in hand, in the best interests of the company, all expenses of any kind will have to be shut down. With the $500.00 sent you today, you can pay your pay-roll of last week, the two insurance policies, and then we must pause until some of the capital promised by Perry arrives!

> "P.S. My address abroad until Oct. 15 will be, National City Bank of New York, 41 Boulevard Haussmann, Paris, FRANCE (if anything <u>very important</u> comes up in the interim before Nov. 1)- I am having a final conference with Perry and Coghill "at the Yale Club, New York, Friday."[14]

On August 30 the Colonel received a post card from Charles Squier now aboard the R.M.S. Homerei en route to Cherbourg, France, "I have thought much about our gold mine since sailing last Saturday. I only hope your very optimistic statements in regard to the value of our property as made by you at various times will be proven by future events to have been ever more than justified! It does seem rather remarkable- so much so that I often doubt it being feasible even!- that we should buy a property for a mere $25,000.00, right in the vicinity of Washington D.C. which would really produce millions in gold over a period of years! However, such things have happened before!-if rarely!

> "I hope that Perry secured for you the promised $1,500.00 cash or check that morning, so you went back to Mineral with the situation at least temporarily relieved. Also, I hope he secured the additional $2,000.00 in subscriptions he seemed sure of getting at once from his relative in Magnolia, Mass. Best of all I hope you, Perry and Coghill will work along in unison with perfect feeling and understanding during my absence-as team work is what counts most!
>
> "Since you have more time for the present, please write me at your earliest opportunity just what you have found out about the other gold vein: how much the mill house will cost (exclusive of the $10,775 machinery to be ordered from the Allis-Chalmers Co.) and if you found out, while in New York how much cash had to be deposited with the Allis-Chalmers Co. to order and start making the machinery. Please let me know at once about these matters.

---

14 August 20, 1923, Letter from Charles B. Squier to Col. Thomas R. Marshall

> "The only thing you can do if Perry and Coghill do not raise sufficient additional funds, is to hoist out the pump, etc. (which you said would cost $125.00) and entirely suspend operations until I return from Europe around Nov.1st. Let us hope, however, that enough will be gradually coming in to keep cutting fuel lumber, keep the pump running and continue increasing amount of ore on the dump, even though the mill cannot be ordered!

The company seems to be teetering on the edge of serious financial difficulty. There is no gold in the ore they are running through the small 3 ton per day stamp mill. Stock sales are flat and there is no money in the treasury, and now the Colonel is concerned about the status of his stock holdings in the company. Squier offers a solution to the Colonel's dilemma:

> "You had better ask them to assign to you at once your 15,000 shares in such way that you have a separate certificate for 3,750 shares and send me your power of attorney made over to me on the 3,750 for 5 years as per your former written agreement covering them. Mention the number of the stock certificate for the 3750 shares aforementioned, this power of attorney should be duly witnessed before a notary."[15]

This maneuver will allow the Colonel's shares to rank with those of Charles Squier in the event of financial disaster, and the Colonel would be entitled to his money before the other stockholders.

The options the Colonel were supposed to secure were still not quite in order, especially the mining option on the Walnut Grove property. Colonel Marshall asked R. E. Dolan for help and Dolan wrote to his friend John Strootman in Buffalo, New York, to see if an agreement on the Walnut Grove property could be worked out. In the meantime, Strootman had written the Colonel and told him he would take a "motor

---

15   August 30, 1923, post card from Charles B. Squier to Col. Thomas R. Marshall

trip" thru Virginia in the near future and he might come to Mineral.[16] John Strootman was a manufacturer of "Foot-Easing Felt Cushions', the inventor of the Strootman Shoe Fitting System, and also held interests in gold mines located in Canada.

The Colonel was hoping Dolan could secure an option on the Walnut Grove property which was adjacent to the Twin Vein Mining Company before the price went up. Dolan had rented a room at the Hotel Alexandria, located at the southwest corner of Rush and Ohio Streets in Chicago, Illinois. Earlier, Strootman the owner of the Walnut Grove property, had refused to give Dolan a one year option on the property when they met in June and Dolan had not heard from him since.[17]

On August 28 Dolan replied to the Colonel"s letter of the 23rd. "if you feel that there is a good chance to do the deal and you can handle it on a shorter time option I will go to Buffalo from here and do the best I can to get it.

I think it best not to contact them in writing and more could be accomplished face to face. I know they will not grant a years option without a payment. I have faith in the Walnut Grove, and further, I think it ought to go to your people, it's the most logical thing to do. Let me know the shortest time you can handle it and be assured I will do all I can, but no use to ask for 12 months open option.

> "If I can find anything new here on amalgamation will send it to you if not and am able to complete my mill arraignments here, will get back to Colorado and find what I can for you together with data on the new process for separating sulfide ores as I have not got it with me. The mill I am arranging for here is a cyanide process for the Cripple Creek low grade ore. Let me hear promptly about the Walnut Grove and I will get busy."[18]

The Colonel is trying to get an option to mine the Walnut Grove Property for gold without paying any more than $10 for a year's option.

---

16 September 1, 1923 Letter from R. E. Dolan to Strootman
17 September 28, 1923 Letter from R. E. Dolan to Col. Thomas R. Marshall
18 October 4, 1923 Letter from R. E. Dolan to Col. Thomas R. Marshall

SHAFT HOUSE

Dolan wrote the Colonel on October 4.

"I have your letter of Oct. 2nd and am quite surprised to hear that my friend Strootman was motoring thru Virginia, altho he told me when I saw him in June he expected to take a motor trip down that way late in the fall but I had no idea he would go this early and that explains why I did not hear from him in answer to my letter. Did he tell you when he expects to be back in Buffalo? If so and you let me know I will do all I can to get you the option, but as I said when I tried to get it in June they would not listen to a years option, maybe they might change their minds. At any rate as soon as I know he is home will go after them again and see if we can get it.

"What you tell me about the lower workings etc. will be held in the strictly confidential and it does not tally with all the different ones told us about the vein at the 75 ft. or 80 ft. level in the shaft and on the bottom where McSween left off work."[19]

Apparently, the Colonel had informed Dolan about the ore running out on the two levels but withheld this critical information from Squier. Information of this type could cause Charles Squier to close the mine in light of the absence of any gold recovery with the small mill already on the property. He would not see any reason to build a mill and spend further money in a mine that may be worked out.

The Colonel received a post card from Charles Squier dated October 8. "Your letter just received this morning-I am glad you are still hopeful, but the situation has been difficult indeed. Did Coghill not go down to Mineral shortly after I left? He certainly promised to do so! I so far have heard nothing from him or Perry since I left on the 25th., Sutphen is quite reliable and honest. He said the trust deed of Perry and Coghill to the company was completed and in order and I saw it myself! I will return by R.M.S. Olympic due Nov. 6th., drop me a line to Berkeley Hotel, Piccadilly London."[20]

---

19 October 4, 1923 Letter from R. E. Dolan to Col. Thomas R. Marshall
20 October 8, 1923 Post card from Charles B. Squier to Col. Thomas R. Marshall

October 10 Charles Squier is staying at The Hotel Lotti, Paris France and replies to the Colonel's letter.

"I note with pleasure you are still optimistic in the face of considerable difficulty. Coghill's inability to raise funds and the general financial gloom which is spreading over America will become much darker and last a long time unless I miss my guess! This readily makes the raising of funds more difficult! It is for the above reason that I must <u>personally</u> be entirely satisfied from some outside scientific engineers findings that the <u>gold is there</u> in good paying quantities of fine quality and easily accessible! Forgive me, if I say I think it feasible that you are too optimistic perhaps in your reiterated statements of the properties gold content and value.

"I will leave here on October 31st., and am due to arrive in New York on November 6th. There is no feasible way at this distance of my doing anything before reaching New York. Just as soon thereafter as feasible I will go to Mineral with some expert which I will employ at my expense. His judgment will determine whether or not I involve myself any further financially in the whole proposition-I think this will strike you as fair. And, as I had already suggested an expert to you. Please drop me a line to Berekely Hotel, Piccadilly London at your earliest convenience and let me know the latest news.

"Of course your salary must remain in abeyance until several months have elapsed perhaps as we have no available funds at all. I only hope with the $1,400.00 I understand Perry finally raised you have been able to preserve from rot or deterioration what we have already expended on the property. Let me know about this in detail when you write next.

"A long letter has just come from Coghill and I think he has been trying to do what he could- but he and Perry have both delayed too long and missed the market in selling stock, when things were booming! I suspect Perry has left Thomson & M..S. Hinnon the brokers, as a means of cutting their expenses in bad business! Perhaps he will devote more time to us! I believe he and Coghill have been down to the mine some weeks ago and will each write me. I am writing Perry and Coghill to sell the balance of the treasury stock-some 7,700 shares @ $5.00 allowing a brokerage firm $1.50 of this per share if they could then raise over $20,000.00-it would be the best way!"[21]

James Coghill told the Colonel on October 16 that the funds he had requested should reach him before he received the letter of the 16th. Perry had sold 200 shares and expected to collect $1,000 very quickly, which he was going to wire to the Colonel.

Coghill was still on the hook for a $500 loan he got from a personal friend and he had little hope of them being able to raise anything further for the next several weeks. Coghill hoped that Perry would be able to generate a little more money using his business contacts. Coghill had wired the Colonel and advised him to impress upon Perry the urgency of their dilemma, because Perry's friends were the only possibility they had for raising any more money.

The Colonel was instructed by Coghill to, send a complete inventory of the equipment and raw materials such as lumber, with the retail price of the individual items. This action was to convince prospective investors that they were fully equipped to operate the shaft. He asked the Colonel to make a check out to his order for $1.60, and then to stop payment on the check. Coghill planned to use it only as evidence that the company was operating on the up and up.

Coghill was also anxiously waiting for the pictures they took during the last visit to Mineral and suggested the Colonel send duplicate prints to Charles Squier.

The Colonel was advised by Coghill that he had spoken to some investors in Richmond who were considering becoming financially involved in the company, and it was quite possible some of them would motor to Mineral and want to look over the property. Coghill asked the Colonel to please show them every courtesy and use the best selling arguments he had.

---

21   October 10, 1923 Letter from Charles B. Squier to Col. Thomas R. Marshall

James Coghill was in constant touch with Eugene Perry and told the Colonel that he could contact Perry in his new office at, the H. L. Horton & Company., 547 Fifth Avenue, New York City.[22] This would allow Perry to relay messages in the event that he was unavailable.

Dolan wrote the Colonel on Oct. 23 from the Hotel Alexandria in Chicago, Illinois with an update on his progress in securing the Walnut Grove property option.

> "Have received your letter of the12th. and wrote to John Strootman telling him of your desire to have an option on Walnut Grove for 12 months and now would be a good time to handle it as your people were hopeful but might not be later on. He wrote me that he had sent you Canadian papers and was interested in your progress and success on the Louisa (Mine property).
>
> "But as for the option on Walnut Grove, he preferred to let that rest for the present. I may go on to Buffalo and if I do you may rest assured I will do my best.
>
> "Was very much disappointed to learn of the ore giving out on the 75 foot level (North). Am wondering if that can be the end of that ore shoot at that point. Did it extend further than the 40 foot where the vein took an irregular course and broke up? Hope the south end will show much better."[23] (This is a serious development, the abrupt disappearance of the vein could mean the mine is worked out and will be closed if the New York investors get wind of it.)

Dolan continues,

> "While in Cripple Creek saw a property that reminded me of yours, they drove for 75 feet or 80 feet on the 100 foot level with a vein varying from 3 feet down to a few inches in width and finally disap-

---
22 October 16, 1923, Letter from James H. Coghill to Col. Thomas R. Marshall
23 October 23, 1923 Letter from R. E. Dolan to Col. Thomas R. Marshall

peared all together, then they drove a cross drift and found the vein about 4 or 5 feet from where they lost it and were working it when I left.

The fact of the vein being in place farther north and carrying values leads one to believe that a fault or horse might occur and some cross cutting would prove that theory."[24]

(A horse is an area of non gold bearing country-rock that interrupts the ore vein.)

"Am trying to bring my affairs to a close here, but nothing definite yet. Certainly takes time and patience. No doubt you will be glad when Squier returns from Europe. How are Messrs Coghill and Perry?"[25]

On November 3 Charles Squier told the Colonel,

"I shall arrive in New York early Wednesday morning the 7th. and will endeavor to come to Mineral the following Sunday morning, leaving New York Saturday evening and returning to New York Monday or Tuesday, do not count on this arrangement unless I write you before hand. I will try to bring with me some new practical mining man merely to give me another outside expert opinion of the property, and he will probably remain for several days to make a full inspection.

"It looks as though I would have to personally finance the company-as I understand since my absence Perry and Coghill have only raised $1,900.00 in all by the sale of stock. Unless something has come through very recently it is for this reason I am unwilling to risk any more of my own personal funds without further expert advice as to the property's certain value. The last of your three letters was received by me in London at the Berkeley Hotel just before leaving. I understand what difficulties you have encountered and

---

24 October 23, 1923, Dolan
25 October 23, 1923, Dolan

compliment you upon having "carried on" as well as you have-you may rest assured something will be done shortly after my return. Although-due to the companie's financial situation your salary may have to remain in arrears for sometime, which should not worry you if you believe in the property ultimately making good.

Squier complains,

"Perry is utterly unreliable in making good on promises, unless continually <u>prodded</u> which I warned Coghill continually to do . Perry means well, but he is too easy-going and fond of "parties!" Jim Coghill did raise over $40,000.00 for The Porter Cork and Inner Tube Co., he has a good mind for business and is smart but appears to have no financial backing! They both made the serious error of not prosecuting more seriously the sale of stock when the stock market was booming in May and June. Times are bad, the public is cagey, and there you have the whole story in a nut-shell! Did Perry and Coghill never go to Mineral until <u>Oct.6th</u>?

"However you need worry about nothing, if the property is <u>really</u> valuable- I can find the money at once, <u>I am quite sure of that</u>. Please let me <u>know at once</u> how much gold you have recovered from operation of the small mill, how much money you have borrowed on notes or otherwise for the company's account, with a full and <u>detailed statement of same</u>. Has the incorporation tax making the issuance of the company's stock legal been paid? I must have these matters in hand<u> at once."</u>[26]

---

26 November 3, 1923 Post card from Charles B. Squier to Col. Thomas R. Marshall

AT LAST

The order for the mill machinery goes out to The Allis-Chalmers Company on November 12, 1923. The gold ore will be processed by the machines as it moves through the plant from one machine to the next beginning with its introduction at the top of the mill building. The means of raising the ore to the top of the mill is not described in the specifications and was left to the ingenuity of the Colonel.

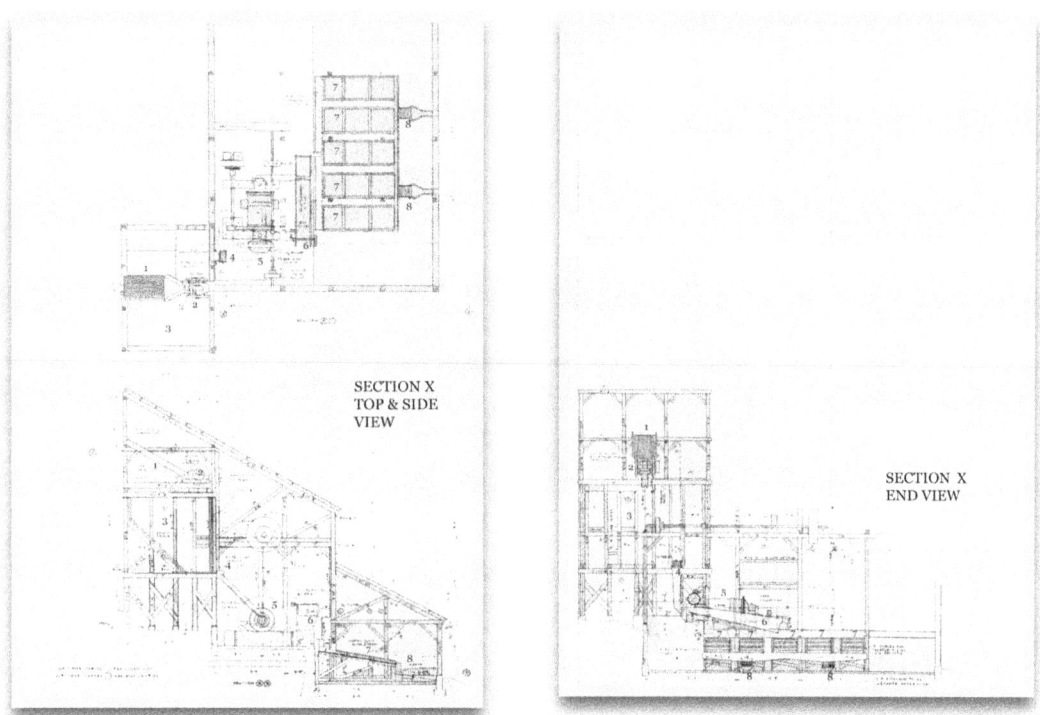

ILLUSTRATION NO. 4 AND 5: MILL PLANS ALLIS-CHALMERS MFG. CO. DEC. 12, 1923

The ore is first dumped on to the sloping grizzly in **illustration 4 location 1** in section x and the grizzly is shown in **illustration 6**. The 4 by 8 foot grizzly was a grate made of steel bars 3/4 of an inch thick and three inches deep and that allowed any material, less than 1 ½ inches to fall through into the ore bin before it reached the crusher. The large pieces of ore slid down into the receiving opening of the crusher.[1]

**ILLUSTRATION NO. 6:
GRIZZLY CATALOGUE NO. 107,
1919 ALLIS-CHALMERS MFG. CO.**

**ILLUSTRATION NO. 7:
BLAKE CRUSHER CATALOGUE NO. 107, 1919 ALLIS-CHALMERS MFG. CO.**

The crusher in **illustration 7 and location 2 in section x.** was a 7 inch by 10 inch Standard Style, "B" Blake Crusher that weighed 6,500 pounds and could be disassembled into individual pieces. All of the parts weighed 150 pounds or less except for one 360 pound piece. The individual pieces could be transported over

---

[1] Specifications by The Allis-Chalmers-Manufacturing Co.1909, Milwaukee Wi.

very rough country and reassembled at remote locations if necessary, or installed in the top of a three story building. The 7 inch by 10 inch measurement referred to the receiving opening of the crusher, the largest Blake Crusher was 30 by 18 inches. The crusher reduced the large chunks of gold ore to 1 ½ inches which were discharged into the ore bin. Power was delivered to the crusher by a single 24 inch diameter flat belt pulley with a 8 ½ inch wide face that revolved at 250 to 275 revolutions per minute.[2] The belt which delivered power to the crusher was connected to a pulley on the jack shaft which ran the length of the mill building. The shaft had additional pulleys that transmitted power to other machines in the mill and was connected to the steam engine by a similar belt arrangement.

The 2,000 cubic foot ore bin, **location 3 in section x,** was constructed by the miners of 6 inch by 6 inch side beams with 6 inch by 8 inch sloping supports for the bottom. The bin was sided with 3 inch planks and it was all was supported by 10 inch by 10 inch vertical posts on top of concrete footings. The sloped bottom allowed the ore to slide down as it was removed from the bottom by the ore feeder.

The feeder, **illustration 8, location 4 in section x** was a 16 inch "Style H, which was connected to the bottom of the ore bin and to the input side of the rod mill. This device insured that ore was fed from the ore bin into the rod mill at a uniform rate.[3]

The Rod Mill in **Illustration Number 9, Location 5 in section x** was a 4 foot diameter by 6 foot long crushing machine which employed as a grinding medium 12,000 pounds of round bar stock ranging in size 2 ½ inches to 4 inches in diameter. The rods were 1 inch shorter than the interior measurement of the rod mill.[4] While the drum rotated ore and water were fed into the mill and the ore was crushed by the action of the rods. The mixture of water and powdered ore form what is called a pulp which was then discharged to the classifier.

---

2   Description, Blake Crusher, The Allis-Chalmers-Manufacturing Co. 1909, Milwaukee, Wi.
3   Description of Feeder, The Allis-Chalmers-Manufacturing Co.1909, Milwaukee, Wi.
4   Description of Mill, The Allis-Chalmers-Manufacturing Co. 1909, Milwaukee, Wi.

**ILLUSTRATION NO. 8:
ORE FEEDER CATALOGUE NO. 107,
1919 ALLIS-CHALMERS MFG. CO.**

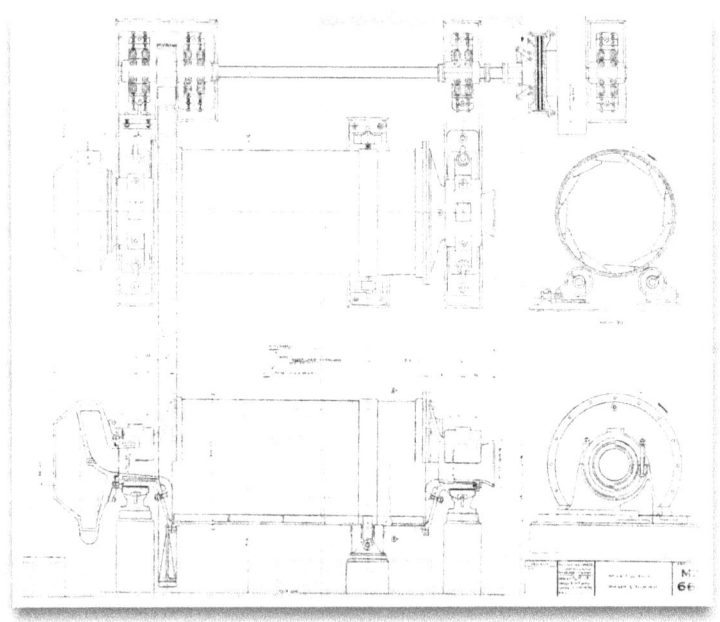

**ILLUSTRATION NO. 9:
ROD MILL ALLIS-CHALMERS MFG. CO.**

The Classifier in **Illustration Number 10, location 6 in section** x was a Model "C" Simplex Dorr Classifier that separated the pulverized ore from the oversized ore which was returned to the rod mill to be re-ground.[5] The ore was reduced to the same size as the particles of gold it contained. This mixture of powdered rock and gold was then conveyed to the amalgamation plates.

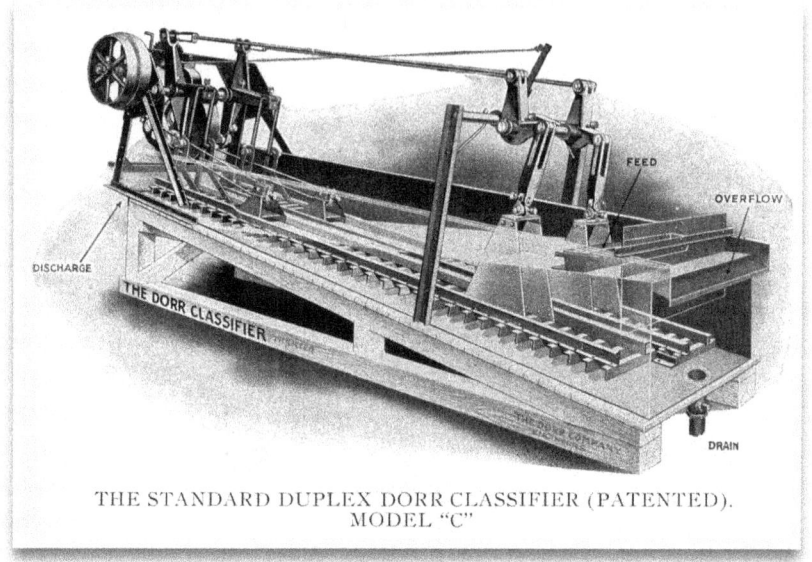

THE STANDARD DUPLEX DORR CLASSIFIER (PATENTED).
MODEL "C"

**ILLUSTRATION NO. 10:
DORR CLASSIFIER THE DORR CO. JULY 1, 1920**

The amalgamation equipment **Location Number 7 in section** x consisted of fifteen 1/8 inch thick, 4 foot by 4' 6" pure copper plates, each one was electroplated on one side with silver at the rate of one ounce per square foot. The plates were mounted on 5 specially designed copper plate tables which were constructed of wood by the miners. Each table held 3 of the plates which were installed in a step down arraignment with a specified slope of 3/4 of an inch per foot or 4 degrees.[6] The plates were coated with Mercury by the miners. The slope of the plates was critical, because it allowed an even distribution of the pulp over the plates, maxi-

---

5   Description of Dorr Classifier, The Allis-Chalmers-Manufacturing Co.1909, Milwaukee, Wi.
6   Description of Amalgamation Plates, The Allis-Chalmers-Manufacturing Co.1909, Milwaukee, Wi.

mizing the collection of gold and the rejection of everything else. If the pulp flowed too rapidly over the plates the gold would be washed over and lost

The 2 Pierce Amalgamators In **Illustration No. 11, Location Number 8 in section x** were the final collection devices. The two 20 to 25 ton per 24 hour day amalgamators were installed at the lower ends of the collection tables to catch any fine or float gold that was not trapped by the plates. They were 22 inches wide, 24 inches long, 5 inches deep and contained mercury.[7]

ILLUSTRATION NO. 11: PIERCE AMALGAMATOR

The Clean-up accessories were also included in the package and consisted of one standard cast iron gold retort complete with the clamp, cover and a condenser to separate the vaporized mercury from the gold remaining in the retort. Additional items used in refining gold were three black lead crucibles with the covers, two sets of crucible tongs for handling the searing hot crucibles and one gold bullion mold.[8]

The total shipping weight for all of the equipment from the Allis-Chalmers Company was 71,700 pounds. The total cost for the complete plant less the used boiler and steam engine was $9,798.00, plus freight, which was payable at either

---

7 Description of Pierce Amalgamators, The Allis-Chalmers-Manufacturing Co. 1909, Milwaukee, Wi.
8 Description of Clean-up Accessories, The Allis-Chalmers-Manufacturing Co. 1909, Milwaukee, Wi.

the New York, Chicago, or Milwaukee Exchanges. The terms required 25% cash on acceptance of the proposal, with the balance due in cash, in exchange for the railroad shipping documents or collect on delivery. Charles Squier was able to secure more favorable terms, allowing payment to be stretched out over several months.[9]

The miners continued stockpiling ore on the dump pile which they hoped would give them a good head start on supplying enough ore to the mill once it was up and operating. They needed to accumulate 1,500 to 2,000 tons of ore prior to the plant becoming operational, which would allow them to run for 40 days at full capacity, while at the same time replenishing the stock pile from the mine..

Charles Squier wrote the Colonel on November 18.

> "I think it no more than just that I, as president, and the Board of Directors, vote you our sincerest thanks for your fine results, in the face of financial and other extreme difficulties this past summer! You need have no more fear as to finances, as our difficulties are now past; this does not, however, mean that the strictest economy be in any way relaxed, but that the mill and other necessary equipment are assured.
>
> "We must have your vouchers for all expenditures during the past summer, and, in the future, all important expenditures must be paid directly by Mr. Sutphen, Secretary and Treasurer in Morristown, N.J., after they have been marked "O.K." by you, except possibly payrolls.
>
> "Mr Battle will IMMEDIATELY rectify the question of the incorporation tax at the Louisa County Court House and have same changed or paid. Kindly let me have your written estimate in detail of your proposed expenditures, with cost, of various items (including labor during the period) for setting up and completing (with machinery to obtained second hand and building housing the plant) for the

---

9   Terms of sale, The Allis-Chalmers-Manufacturing Co. 1909, Milwaukee, Wi.

mill as ordered from The Allis-Chalmers Co. on Monday the 12th. of November.

"We will be down again in three or four weeks with one or possibly two very IMPORTANT men who would like to see the property. Do not sell any stock in Virginia on account of the drastic Blue-Sky Laws, which might cause us trouble. I would like to come down some time and spend a week with you and look over other surrounding "prospective" properties, and generally "comb over" the surrounding region! (Virginia's, Blue Sky Laws were designed to protect the public from fraudulent exploitation by companies selling worthless stock in speculative ventures such as oil wells, gold mines, etc.)

"Do not give out any of our prospectus, UNLESS marked "stock subject to change in price or withdrawal from sale without notice!"[10]

The Colonel believed he had found a diamond and sent it to Charles Squier for verification. Squier told him,

"I have not yet had an expert examine your "diamond", but will report the result when obtained!"[11]

On November 19, Squier wrote the Colonel,

"Supplementing my former letter, please let me know the assessed value of our property, the annual state taxes, and if is necessary to file any federal or state income taxes return for this year and when the state or any LOCAL taxes are due and the amount. Perhaps you can use your local influence to have our tax assessment left as heretofore and not raised?

---

10 November 18, 1923, Letter from Charles B. Squier to Col. Thomas R. Marshall
11 November 18, 1923, Squier

"Please send by registered mail at once all vouchers for all expenditures to date to Van Tassell Sutphen, to be duly entered in the company's books; let me have as soon as practicable your detailed estimate of the expenditures necessary to completely supplement the mill machinery we have ordered from The Allis-Chalmers Co. and when the large items will have to be paid for.

"You and Mr. Runnutt have done remarkably well in the face of the greatest financial stringency, and I must again take occasion to complement you all upon the results obtained! We are now "nearly over the top" and will soon be producing, and I am really beginning to share your optimism as to the property! It is indeed fortunate that we can "swing" it ourselves, and do not have to give up "the lions share" to some outside party for capital!

"Let me know of all important developments day by day, and rest assured we are now over the worst! I would deem it wise to have you insured in the best interests of the company for at least $10,000, if you can effect such life insurance at a moderate rate with a strong company-you might look into this when you next visit Richmond."[12]

Squier reminded the Colonel, on November 20,

"It is imperative that we have all your vouchers and receipts for all expenditures to date at once, as we can not otherwise open the books in the regular way and make our statement to the government for the current year! Please send them at once by registered mail insured to: Van Tassell Sutphen, Secretary,& Treasurer.

"We find we can insure you in the company's name at the rate of $100, less $20 dividend, or $80 net per $1000.00 through The New York Life Insurance Co. Please do not attempt to investigate this in

---

[12] November 19, 1923, Letter from Charles B. Squier to Col. Thomas R. Marshall

Richmond or elsewhere, because I am sure we can get a better rate from the head office here for several very good reasons. Sometime during the next week or ten days, it would be advisable for you to come up here for one day letting me know when to expect you, when you can be duly inspected by the company's agents! I trust you will not mind this action upon the part of our company, as it is no more than good business!

"Please be sure, at your earliest convenience, to give us written estimates for the costs of the mill house, the new steam engine, boiler and all other equipment which you propose to install in order to make our plant complete, with the mill we have ordered, for handling 50 ton per day!

"I hope to soon find out what your "diamond" is, but feel sure it is merely rock crystal, which <u>will</u> cut glass! How much will our running expenses be per day from now on for labor approximately and how many ton of ore do you <u>hope</u> to take out and stack on the dump from now until February 15th?"[13]

The Colonel informed Squier of the acquisition of a second hand steam engine and boiler on . November 30, 1923. The Colonel was especially pleased that he was able to buy the equipment for one third of the cost of it new.[14]

On December 7 Squier replied,

"Your letter of Nov.30th. is before me, and I am glad you have found the engine and boiler you exactly want at 33.1/3% cost of a modern reproduction, so you can at once send the engine's specifications required by the Allis-Chalmers Co. for their drawings I have just this morning received a carbon copy of the third letter sent to you by Denison under date of the 3rd.., urging you to forward them

---

13 November 20, 1923, Letter from Charles B. Squier to Col. Thomas R. Marshall
14 November 30, 1923, Letter from Col. Thomas R. Marshall to Charles B. Squier

at the earliest possible moment, so as to avoid all possible delay in delivery of their equipment. I, however, quite appreciate that you have been exceedingly busy hunting machinery, which you were able to get last summer, when I was in Europe and the company was out of funds temporarily!

"I had lunch with Sutphen today and he told me all about his visit to the mine with Ely and Rutherford. I am to see them early next week-perhaps something good may come of it-they are financially responsible people, and the kind we want to be associated with. I would suggest you send Sutphen at once the small gold button, which you made while they were there which was not quite fused or completed-such things have a very good psychological effect!

"It will be alright if you send all the vouchers and receipts up to us very soon-but we must have them soon, as we are soon compelled to show a statement of some sort in a business-like way! I am glad they had good weather-I rather regret the fact that some other businessmen have been down on a private car once or twice and got hold of the Slaton Hill property adjoining ours, it is probably not valuable but such things may well turn the head of the little town of Mineral and raise our operating costs eventually, if you see what I mean-otherwise, it was all rather funny!

"Do not give up on the options on the Walnut Hill or Luce properties, even in part until you have had a conference with me! Property down there may boom, even if not at all valuable!

"I quite approve of your request to raise the weekly pay roll from around $250 to $300, and have so instructed Sutphen, in view of the great importance of stocking up boiler fuel for the winter months in advance!

"Let me have your figures for the accessory equipment needed in addition to that ordered from the Allis-Chalmers Co., as soon as possible, and when same will have to be paid for in whole or in part at latest!

"If you can run up here for one day the latter part of next week about the insurance matter, let me know, so I can arrange for physical inspection in advance! Mrs. Squier and I would like to have you dine with us and tell us first-hand all about the mine, etc. Please bring us some definite data if you have any as to the deposit of manganese iron."[15]

A deposit of manganese ore has come to the attention of the Colonel and this may allow them to diversify their mining operation by producing another product.

---
15 December 7, 1923, Letter from Charles B. Squier to Col. Thomas R. Marshall

ONE STEP CLOSER TO MILLIONS

Construction on the mill building began with the digging of the footings on December 15, 1923.[1] The bags of cement were bought from the Walton and Wood Company at Pendleton, Virginia. Stone and sand from the nearby creek were screened to be used in the concrete In those days there were no modern concrete plants and giant mixing trucks to provide what is called ready mix concrete, necessitating all of this work be done by hand. **Photograph No. 36** The sand, gravel and dry cement used to make concrete were shoveled into the mixer and a hit-and-miss engine supplied the power which rotated the barrel as water was added creating concrete.

PHOTOGRAPH NO. 36

CONCRETE MIXER

---

[1] December 15, 1923, Hand written note by Col. Thomas R. Marshall

The concrete was then dumped into a wheelbarrow and transported to the desired location where it was emptied into a form constructed of boards. After the concrete hardened the form was removed or simply moved up and the process was repeated creating a progressively higher foundation. The concrete mixer was purchased from Parker Adams for thirty dollars plus one dollar and forty eight cents freight. This little mixer was used to mix all of the concrete needed for the construction of the mill foundations. In 1924 a bag of cement cost $.85; one cement order consisted of 128 fifty pound bags which were purchased from the Walton and Wood Company at Pendleton, Virginia.[2]

PHOTOGRAPH NO. 37 MAN IN A SUIT SHOVELING

Pouring concrete in December of 1923 was a very time consuming and labor intensive process. **Photograph No.37** A man wearing a business suit can be seen shoveling material while another operates the mixer. **Photograph No. 38** The same man appears to be overseeing the work in the trench where the footing will be poured. The footing will later support another foundation.

The foundations ranged from 12 inches to more than 5 feet in height. When one examines the foundations that exist today, lines in the concrete are still visible, showing the thickness of each successive pour. **Photograph No. 39** The men construct what will be one of the last forms to hold concrete for the mill founda-

---

2   Bill from Walton and Wood

tions. **Photograph No. 40** Pits were being dug for the concrete piers which will support some of the beams.

PHOTOGRAPH NO. 38

MAN IN A SUIT SUPERVISING

PHOTOGRAPH NO. 39

DIGGING LAST OF THE FOOTINGS

ANATOMY OF A GOLD MINE

PHOTOGRAPH NO. 40

CONCRETE PIERS

Progress was being made at the mine, work on the foundations was progressing at a good pace, most of the footings had been dug and more of the forms which were to hold and shape the concrete into a wall had been built. Much more work still had to be done on the foundations for what would be the processing plant and fortunately the weather in December had not been not cold enough to delay the construction of the foundations.

Colonel Marshall was supposed to move quickly to secure options on as much of the property adjacent to their mine as possible, but the Colonel had not been moving as swiftly as Squier advised and this cost them the option on the Slaton Hill Property. He had recently acquired an option on a property known as the Luce Gold Mine tract consisting of approximately 252 acres, which they agreed to purchase for $6,000, if they need it. The wheeling and dealing continued as they attempted to gain control of the surrounding, gold rich properties. An option for $10,000 on the Walnut Grove tract which consisted of an additional 250 acres still eluded the Colonel. The Walton Hill tract consisting of 100 acres more or less, was taken under option, with the actual purchase price being $15,000. These options included all mining, water, and forest rights.

The Colonel asked Squier if he might be insured through the company. Squier arranged for the Colonel to take the train to New York and meet with the insurance agent around the 16 of December.

Squier tells the Colonel on the 25 of December.

"I received your letter of the 17th., and was glad you returned to Mineral safely! I was also glad to hear all was going on well at the mine!

"I have been exceedingly busy, and have perhaps interested several GOOD parties in buying the balance of the Twin Vein Stock, plus a position as a director, and perhaps a maximum of 1,000 shares of my stock (personal) thrown in as a bonus! I will keep you advised as to what transpires!

"I trust you have sent in the specifications required to the Allis-Chalmers Co. to avoid all delay in the delivery of the machinery, also that you will let me know at least ONE WEEK IN ADVANCE of the sums that will be required to pay for the supplemental machinery, such as the engine and boiler, etc., and work for the completion of the millhouse to house the new machinery. Mr. Sutphen sent you a $350.00 check for the pay-roll last week, which I trust was duly received! I received the gold button, which I will return to Mr. Ely, at the first opportunity, also the vial of free gold, which will be useful in selling stock!

"I enclose herewith a draft of the agreement between you and me personally, as per our recent understanding, covering other options in the Louisa district which my attorneys drew up at my order, as loosely, and at the same time as definitely, as possible to protect both your heirs and mine. The $10 agreed upon as "consideration" I will pay you when I see you next!

I must impress upon you the EXCEEDING IMPORTANCE LEGALLY OF HAVING YOUR OPTIONS READ IN WRITING, LEGAL FORM, THAT THEY ARE GRANTED FOR SOME CONSIDERATION. THIS CONSIDER-

ATION SHOULD NOT BE LESS THAN $10 in hand paid to those granting the option! Otherwise, your options may not be legally good! Please send up exact-duplicates of your options in writing for my lawyers to inspect! I suggest article "5" in the enclosed written agreement, in fairness to both parties be omitted. If you think well of the agreement, please sign both copies, having them witnessed and sworn to by a Virginia Notary, and forward them back to me, and I will complete them here at once, returning one copy to you for your files!"[3]

The Colonel finally had been able to get an option on the Walnut Grove property which had been so elusive. The terms were not what he wanted, but were all he could get. Strootman had agreed to a six months option for $500 and the total purchase price was $10,000. The purchase price for the Walton Hill property was an additional $15,000.00. This would have allowed them to finally control all of the adjoining, potentially gold rich land.

A contract Squier had his attorneys draw up would insure that the Colonel could only sell the options on the Luce, Walnut Grove and Walton Hill tracts to him. The contract had another angle protecting Charles Squier-it specified that if all of the property was bought not exceeding $30,000 Squier would not advance the money unless the present mortgage of $15,000 held by Dolan had been paid off. The contract had one more small detail in it; Squier would receive dividends in cash from the stock he owned in the Twin Vein Mining Company equal to the amount expended in the development of the properties acquired.[4] A small insurance policy perhaps?

Photograph No. 41 Work on the mill continues, as a man can be seen screening sand and gravel for use in the concrete. The larger stone was used as the aggregate after being separated from the sand. The sand and gravel are added in specific proportions to produce a good grade of concrete, the components are not just thrown in randomly. Winter is not the best environment for pouring the concrete founda-

---

3 December 25, 1923 , Letter from Charles B. Squier to Col. Thomas R. Marshall
4 Contract between Charles B. Squier and Col. Thomas Marshall, by Seibert and Riggs, New York, unsigned

tions, because if the concrete freezes it will be compromised and have to be redone. The foundations have been poured, and some forms are still in place which will have to be removed before the heavy framing can proceed. The photograph was taken by the Colonel from the creek looking at the rear of the mill.

PHOTOGRAPH NO. 41
SCREENING GRAVEL

On January the 4, 1924 Squier told the Colonel,

> "I have received your gift of December 27th and hope you have succeeded in keeping the men working well during the always rather demoralizing holiday season. I fully appreciate the great need of getting the concrete foundations in before freezing weather arrives and of having them very well made and also laying enough wood to operate on at least three months for fuel."[5]

---

5   January 4, 1924, Letter from Charles B. Squier to Col. Thomas R. Marshall

ANATOMY OF A GOLD MINE

Charles Squier again asked the Colonel if he has "gotten the options on the three properties sewed up in the usual written, legal form; signed, witnessed, and with the provision that they were granted for the consideration of $10.00 in hand paid?

"I regard these matters, of THE MOST VITAL IMPORTANCE, and hope to hear from you about them soon. Also, did you receive the papers which my attorney prepared about the options, were they satisfactory to you, and if so, will you please sign and return them to me for my signature because both signatures must be witnessed by a local NOTARY! If you are not sure the options to you are in legally secure form, I suggest, for the protection of both of us and the heirs that you send them to me for my inspection, or even let my lawyer draw them up for you, in which will guarantee them to be in legal order.

"In regard to the $2,500.00 to be used for machinery, etc. in two weeks and bills for any large expenses must be sent here to Mr. Sutphen in advance, so he can pay them with the company's checks. It would not be in order for us to do it any other way, since we are a company which everyone now knows exists. You must get us the receipts, so we know how much cash we must hold in hand here verses bills to be mailed to us. Mr. Sutphen also reports that the vouchers and receipts for some of the small items not over $100 in all, are missing in your last accounting up to December 15 ,1923-I presume you have these in hand, which may have come in late. Will you please send us AT ONCE, all receipts and vouchers and full a statement of all expenses incurred from Dec.15 up to and including Dec. 31, 1923, so we can close up the years accounting? THIS IS ALL VERY IMPORTANT!

"If you can get any good samples showing naked bits of gold in the rock send them with a good sized specimen of the manganese iron ore for us to have assayed. Did you receive the old copy of the Canadian mine report and the new one? I thought you might like to have them, I had several photostatic copies made and mailed them to you several days ago under a separate cover.

> "Tomorrow we are getting in $500.00 for the sale of 100 shares of stock to Mrs. Frazier, a friend of Perry's. He will have to come up with $500.00 which I expect will come out of his own stock holdings so he can liquidate his part of the debt he still owes to Mr. Ball for mining reports on the property which were no good to us, and which I refused to have the company stand for at all! It is for this reason that I must ask you to leave the rest of your salary, if possible, in abeyance a little longer, because I am carrying all of the expenses of the company and no more stock has been sold."[6]

The Colonel receives notification around January 6 that the steam engine is ready to be shipped. This catches him off guard because he was not expecting it this soon and will cause more financial complications for Squier, because it will have to be paid for when it arrives at the station. The Colonel fires a telegram off to Squier advising him of the situation.

On January 8, 1924, the Colonel received an answer to his telegram from Squier,

> "Your telegram regarding the immediate transfer to Mineral of $1,200.00 to pay for the steam engine sent to you sooner than anticipated and also your letter following of the 7th. received and its contents carefully noted. You must appreciate that we are now a company, that Mr. Sutphen lives in Montclair, New Jersey, and comes to the city only Monday, Wednesday, and Friday. All the company checks must be countersigned by the President or one of the Vice-Presidents and it is very necessary that we do everything in strict order because it takes more time for the company checks to come to you than if I were sending you personal checks."[7]

---

6   January 4, 1924, Squier
7   January 8, 1924, Letter from Charles B. Squier to Col. Thomas R. Marshall

Photograph No. 42 The Steam engine arrived aboard a railroad flat car at Pendleton on January the 7, 1924 and was unloaded and hauled to the mill site at a cost of $40. It is easy to see just how large the machine was because one man is holding the connecting rod which is longer than he is tall.

Photograph 43 The flywheel can be seen on cribbing as one of the men stands in front of it which gives a better idea of just how large it was. The cribbing, which will eventually support the engine's bed is to the left of the flywheel.

Photograph 44 The bed of the engine is on a truck at the mill site prior to being unloaded onto the cribbing at the left side of the truck.

Photograph 45 The engine bed rests on cribbing and the crankshaft is below on the ground.

PHOTOGRAPH NO. 42
STEAM ENGINE ON RAIL ROAD CAR

ONE STEP CLOSER TO MILLIONS

PHOTOGRAPH NO 43

ENGINE'S FLYWHEEL ON CRIBBING

PHOTOGRAPH NO. 44

STEAM ENGINE BED ON A TRUCK

ANATOMY OF A GOLD MINE

PHOTOGRAPH NO. 45

STEAM ENGINE ON CRIBBING

The steam engine is a Number 7 Tangye Bed Throttling Engine, which was built by The Erie City Iron Works in Erie City, Pennsylvania. The Erie City Iron Works was started in 1840 and was a very large manufacturer of all sorts of machinery, including steam engines and boilers. The complete engine is shown in **Illustration No. 12**.

ILLUSTRATION NO. 12: "TANGYE" BED THROTTLING STEAM ENGINE

A Number 7 was capable of producing 180 horsepower at one hundred and thirty five revolutions per minute. The fly wheel measured ninety six inches in diameter and was twenty four inches across its face, the entire engine weighed in at 17,500 pounds. Its cylinder was 18 inches in diameter and had a 22 inch stroke, or the length of piston travel. A steam engine of 180 horsepower is actually more powerful than a diesel engine of the same horsepower rating. Steam power was very common in the 1920's but was eventually replaced by diesel engines, gasoline engines and electric motors.

The Number 7 was available in sizes ranging from 45 to 300 horse power.

The Tangye was a well known slide-valve engine according to the 1913 Erie City Catalog. A slide-valve allows steam to enter and exit the steam cylinder. Steam engines produce power as the cylinder fills with steam and the resulting pressure pushes against a piston similar to that of an internal combustion engine. The piston moves back and forth inside the cylinder as the slide valve allows steam to enter and exit the cylinder creating reciprocal motion which is converted to rotary motion by the crankshaft. This crankshaft shaft was 8 ½ inches in diameter and it ran through the center of the flywheel and was supported on both sides by massive bearings. The fly wheel had a flat belt around the outside of it and as the flywheel rotated the belt transmitted mechanical energy through another flat belt pulley to a large diameter steel shaft running through the plant called a jack shaft This shaft was several inches in diameter and had smaller flat belt pulleys attached to it. These pulleys were connected to smaller flat belts which were, in turn, connected to the machines in the plant and as the shaft rotated, all of the machines in the plant received power.

The 1913 Erie City catalog stated that these lists of equipment were, "The outcome of an experience of sixty years, the development of higher practice, advancements in technology, more perfect materials, knowledge and skill, and the work is intelligently put together by a high class of workmen, as the reasons for the production of a superior product line."[8] This was an example of the pride that manufacturers had in their products which made The United States the envy of the world. **Illustration 13, Erie City Iron Works**

---

8   Erie City Iron Works Catalog

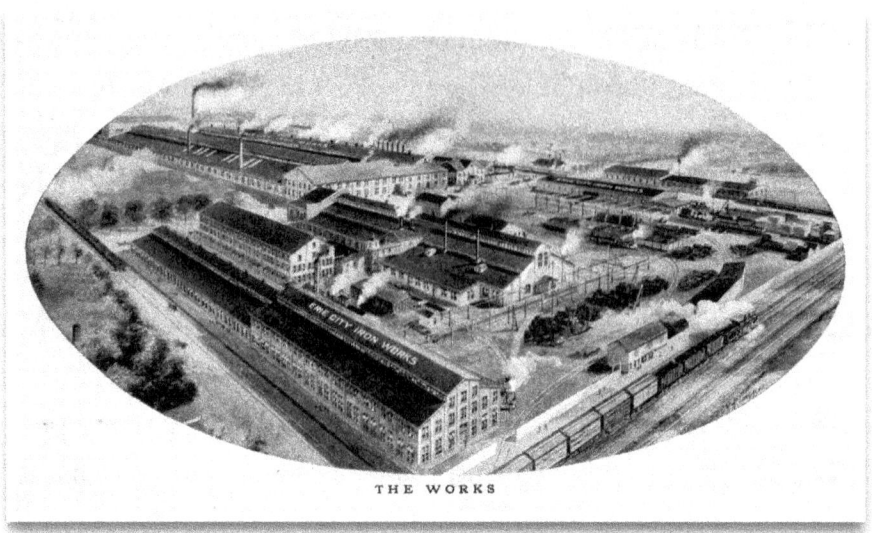

ILLUSTRATION NO. 13: ERIE CITY IRON WORKS
ERIE CITY IRON WORKS, 1909

Squier advised the Colonel in a letter on January 8, 1924. "Enclosed is a company check to your order as the General Manager for $1,200.00, which is to pay for the steam engine sent to you recently which I think can remain in the railroad or express company's custody quite safely, pending your payment in full of the bill of lading! I understand your other chief cost will be the boiler, which will come later, exclusive of labor and the machinery already ordered from the Allis-Chalmers Company. By the way, I received a letter this morning advising that all of the machinery will be delivered around February 1st., allowing 10 days for transport from Milwaukee to Mineral. Do you think you will be able to complete the set up of the equipment and have it operation within two weeks as long as the weather is favorable?"[9]

The machinery had to be stored outside under tarpaulins to protect it from the weather because the mill building was incomplete. The mill building is going to take much longer than two weeks to complete, after all it is January, the weather can be terrible and, unfortunately, money problems continue to hamper progress. The Colonel should have taken these variables into account when telling Charles Squier the building would be completed so early.

---

9   January 8, 1924, Squier

Squier responded to the Colonel's question of where is the check. "I sent you a telegram last night , advising you why the check will be somewhat delayed and I hope this will not seriously inconvenience your operations or <u>credit</u>.

"In regard to the second paragraph of your letter, I am glad to note the paper drawn up by my attorneys in regard to the operations of various properties is quite satisfactory to you, but "don't you think the paragraph, forbidding the resale of a part of said interest should be omitted for the best interest of our heirs? I trust you will hurry up the recording of the sale of these options <u>for a consideration of $10.00</u> as I have suggested twice already, and that you will forward them to me when they are ready.

"I'm sorry to hear the weather has been so unfavorable at Mineral and hope it has not greatly retarded our work or caused any serious delay therein!

"I will let you know shortly which vouchers are missing in your last statement, they were for small amounts, but please send us at once all vouchers or receipts from December 15 to the 31st. inclusive!

"In regard to the funds for the extra labor of carpenters, etc. for the construction of the mill- house, please let us know at once by return mail or night letter telegram how much they are running per week, how much has already been expended and how long they will continue IN ADDITION TO the $350.00 per week allowed for the usual labor. Also how much extra will be required for laying in a three months stock of cut timber fuel for the boiler, in advance of bad weather. We will remit a check at once, these matters must be handled in the regular way as in all companies!

"Mrs. Squier wishes to thank you herself for the Holly, etc., and is writing you separately as she has been in St. Louis on a vacation-glad the whiskey did good service!"[10] (Oops, another tiny violation of Prohibition, but it's Christmas!)

On January the 13th. Charles Squier informed the Colonel,

> "Your letter of the 8th. arrived and I trust you have received my telegram of the 11th. The large envelope containing your original copy of the pamphlet about the Canadian Gold Mines, as well as a new copy you might like to have in reserve, the blue print of the mine and other adjoining properties over which we now hold the option, the check for $350.00 for this week's payroll and $1,200.00 to pay for the steam engine which was delivered a bit ahead of what you had anticipated. You should also receive, not later than tomorrow morning, an additional check for $1000.00 which Sutphen sent you Friday for the increased payroll for carpenters, masons, lumber, concrete and other construction expenses of the mill house. The remaining $1,500.00 makes up the total $2,500.00 you asked for and it will be sent as soon as we hear from you it is required! How has the concrete foundation set during the adverse weather conditions, and how is the laying up of the good stock of wood to feed the boiler preceding so we will have no shortage in bad weather?"[11]

Squier is still not convinced that the mine will produce as the Colonel has contended and asks,

> "Have you taken any more assays lately? Are you sure you will easily be able to feed the completed mill as much as 50 ton of ore per day?"[12]

---

10   January 8, 1924, Squier
11   January 13, 1924, Letter from Charles B. Squier to Col. Thomas R. Marshall
12   January 13, 1924, Squier

Hundreds of cords of wood would have to be cut to fuel the boilers if they are to run for twenty four hours a day. A cord of wood is a stack 4ft wide, 4ft high, and 8ft long equaling 128 cubic feet. The boilers installed at the Twin Vein Mine burned a piece of wood 4ft long without the necessity of it being cut to shorter lengths. The Colonel has several men whose only job is cutting the wood to fuel the boilers.

The miners were constantly adding to the ore dump which was supposed to contain 1,500 to 2,000 tons prior to the completion of the mill. An ore dump of this size would not last long once the mill was up and chewing through 50 tons of gold ore per day. This was a respectable rate for a small mine of the day employing state of the art equipment, but pales in comparison to processing plants located in the American West which were running at a rate of 300 to 1,000 tons per day.

Squier again reminded the Colonel about the missing options, "I hope to soon receive from you the two signed, witnessed and notarized copies of the agreement I sent you regarding the options on the three properties."[13] From all appearances the Colonel is stalling the transfer of the options he holds.

---

13   January 13, 1924, Squier

MANEUVERING

Charles Squier asked Colonel Marshall if he would have any objection to him, "giving Jim Coghill a 1/10 interest in his half of the options, or 5% of the entire options, without voting rights, in lieu of certain valuable services? This would be the only part of my options I would thus or in any other way dispose of at any time! Also, let me have certified copies of the three original options that you have filed in the County Courthouse-I presume at Louisa? Have you been successful in securing the option on the outlying Walton Hill property?

"I note what you say about writing Dolan-are you sure he still holds the trust deed against our property, for you told me before he had sold it at a discount to some man in New York City? If so can we buy him off, and save some money! Is it true that such a trust deed is the same thing as a mortgage in your state of Virginia, and allows thirty days of grace to pay it off, without the right of the holder to foreclose sooner? THIS IS EXTREMELY IMPORTANT! Do you know exactly when the trust deed falls due and on what date? I have written Battle for information in this regard.

"Coghill and Bennett will come down very soon and Bennett may very likely take all of the remaining treasury stock also, Gene Perry and Frank Frasier, who has bought 200 shares will come down soon thereafter-please show them everything very fully! More people are now commencing to get genuinely interested in our little enterprise , which I hope, will be really very BIG!"

MANEUVERING

"Let me hear from you real soon about the above important matters, and, trusting this finds you in good health and spirits, for we have now almost 'pushed the ball over the hill.'"[1]

Quail hunting was a very popular activity in the 1920s and a bird dog called a pointer was a necessary component of this activity. Eugene Perry was apparently an avid bird hunter and had great appreciation for the assistance these dogs provided the hunter.

Eugene Perry told the Colonel on January 15,

"I am informed that the dog is going forward to you today (Wednesday} by express and hope you will meet her or have somebody else do so. She is costing me a lot of money but I personally know the party I am buying her from and he is a great dog man. If we should breed her, pick out something with a good pedigree so her pups will be worth something for there is a big demand for them up this way at fancy prices. I hope to get down the end of next week so we can have a try at the birds (quail)."[2]

The Colonel sent Charles Squier a letter advising him of the many difficulties he had encountered with the 3 ton mill's meager production. The Colonel had also asked Mr H. P. DePencier, General Manager of the Dome Mines in Ontario, Canada for help, hopeful that he will be able to solve the problems with the operation of Dolan's old mill.

Squier replied on January 16 to the Colonel's letter of the 5th.

"Your letter of the fifth was received and the contents noted. We should have some sort of written statement from you weekly as the amount of gold recovery you get from the plates, and you should have plenty of time to make such short reports now. I do not

---

1 January 13, 1924, Squier
2 January 15, 1924, Letter from Eugene Perry to Col. Thomas R. Marshall

think we can wait for DePencier of Canada, as DELAY seems to always mean otherwise UNNECESSARY expense, as neither you nor Runnutt seems to be able, AFTER MONTHS of rudderless operation be able to make the mill work properly."[3]

The small 3 ton per day stamp mill was on the property when it was bought by Charles Squier and the Twin Vein Mining Company. For some reason it is not catching gold as it should.

Squier continued,

"Send us up AT ONCE the written report of the assay of our ore by the Dome Mines just as it was sent to you. I'm sorry to hear the illness of the five men-we have many ill here also, as the weather is very bad here and I do not doubt the weather has been very bad at Mineral. I am sure you have had trouble cutting the wood, and it seemed to me on my last visit to Mineral that your statement that we had enough wood for seven years operation of the present mill seemed to be very exaggerated, in as much as so much of it had already been consumed! I sent you yesterday by parcel post, insured, the fine gold specimen, which I carried away with me from Mineral the last time and I hope you received it okay and will turn it into the mint with the other gold you have recovered!

"Replying to your letter of the 14th this A.M., the $1,000.00 sent you on December 3rd after our last visit to Mineral should have been quite sufficient for operating the property for one month in a small, trying-out way, enough to get the average results from the plates-to do more is a waste of money under the circumstances!

"I am by this mail instructing Sutphen to send you the balance of a check for $1,000.00, enclosed, to the company's order, after paying Perkins and Battles' account totaling $499.75, for the bond

---

3   January 16, 1924, Letter from Charles B. Squier to Col. Thomas R. Marshall

issue and other legal services; leaving $500.00. Our taxes of $125.00 need not be paid before March 1st. You may use this $500.00 toward your salary as an advance. Your accounts will soon be in quite satisfactory shape.

"One reason I have not written sooner is that I have not had the opportunity of having a desired interview with Mr. Howe, who is a very busy man and he has arranged to see me for an hour on Monday morning the 19th., after which talk I will know much better what to do. I will ask Howe to get me a good man to go down there and help straighten out intelligently the matter of getting as nearly as possible 100% gold recovery from our present mill!"[4]

"Ernest Howe, a Geologist was educated at Yale University (class of 1898) and at Harvard University, where he earned his M.A. (1899) and Ph.D.(1899). In 1900, Howe joined the United States Geological Survey (U. S. G. S.) as an assistant geologist. Most of his early work was done in Colorado under Whitman Cross. Although he served with the U. S. G. S. until 1910, in 1906 Howe was appointed geologist of the Isthmian Canal Commission. After 1910 he went into private practice as a consulting geologist. In 1916-17 he joined the Royal Geographic Society of London's expedition, headed by Hamilton Rice, to the upper Amazon and in 1920 he was hired by the Mexican government to reorganize their geological survey. Throughout his career, Howe published scholarly papers, and from 1926 until his death in 1932 he served as editor of The American Journal of Science."[5]

---

4 January 16, 1924, Squier
5 Ernest Howe Papers. Yale Collection of Western America, Beinecke Rare Book and Manuscript Library, Yale University.

Charles Squier continued,

> "Additionally, I appreciate the difficulties of the situation and hope you quite understand I am sympathetic thereto, but amount of financing for the company {to which I am not PERSONALLY obligated} has proven much greater than your original figures, due always to DELAY, which is always very costly, and I am getting very "fed up" with the financing continually and for the benefit of other people, who should contribute proportionately thereto, the apparently EXPERIMENTAL development of an as yet unproven property. Your salary must be allowed to lapse temporarily, in view of the fact I personally have to carry all the company's expenses, as I simply cannot stand the strain much longer, and will, otherwise have to close down the property entirely, unless some hopefully concrete results are soon forthcoming from the actual operation. The only expense justified at present is the operation of the mill on a very slim basis to try to discover just what is the matter that causes us to recover so little gold."[6]

The miners were operating the equipment remaining at the Dolan mine in an attempt to turn a profit while the new mill was being constructed.

Charles Squier wrote the Colonel a second letter on January 16.

> "We had our directors meeting today-it lasted over one hour and a half, but very little transpired, except to formally act on several routine matters, and discuss future policies, etc. Mr. Chappell, also Battle, who came to town on other business for one day were here so we had a full meeting, except for yourself. There are two things I must ask you to do at once: 1. Sutphen reports there is an amount of over $1,000.00 for which you furnished no vouchers in your statement

---

[6] January 16, 1924, 2nd. Letter from Charles B. Squier to Col. Thomas R. Marshall

up to December 15, and that his clerk Mr. Barker, had written you twice, stating just what they were-we must have these vouchers and receipts, or else our books are not in order, and this is highly important. Also, any large expenditures must be billed here, except labor charges which you must get receipts for and send on from time to time. We must have all vouchers from December 15 to the 31st so we can finish up the year's accounts. All the above is very IMPORTANT!

"I'm delighted to hear the concrete suffered no damages and that all is going well have you yet received any machinery from the Allis-Chalmers company or notice of shipment thereof? I'm glad all three of the checks aggregating $2,550.00, also my letter a large envelope of pamphlets and map etc. reached you O.K. We are now temporarily short of funds, but hope to have some in hand very shortly from the sales of the stock!

"Jim Coghill and Mr. David Bennett will arrive at Mineral next Saturday morning for the day, so please show them all you can, as Bennett is likely to buy a lot of stock!

"Haven't you gotten the papers about the options on the various properties in good shape legally-I have been expecting to receive them any day now for my signature to be affixed-if you want any legal advice always consult Battle. About the Dolan matter, Battle had better draw up some legally correct paper, and we must know at once just what Dolan is willing to do-six months extension would be better than three!

"Also, Dolan must sign some legally drawn up paper as to just what he agrees to, all of these things must be very carefully handled. I think the present "trust deed" for $15,000 falls due on Feb 1st, do you know the exact date thereof? On account of some features in the trust deed, Dolan will probably be only too glad to accept the $5,000.00 on account and let the balance stand for another six or nine months! (This delay in paying may cause complications for the Colonel later.)

"Jim Coghill will show you a paper, which he wants me to sign in re to the options on the other properties, but which I would only do with your written consent thereon, as per our verbal agreement when you were last here."[7]

Squier wrote the Colonel on of January 20.

"You probably enjoyed showing Mr. Coghill and Mr. Bennett the latest developments at the mine on Saturday last. Mr. Sutphen has just submitted to me the following list of expenditures, as to which you did not submit vouchers for in your last statement as of December 10, 1923. The steam hoist with the freight $1077.90, the L.A. Coleman water tank $12.50, J. C. Randolph for hauling $20, R. B. Harley blacksmith $5.05, fire insurance $175 and workers compensation insurance $149. We _must have_ these vouchers at once, especially those for the steam hoist and insurance before we advance _any_ more funds, as this is very IMPORTANT for placing the company in good order!

"I trust you will soon send me the papers regarding the options on the three adjacent properties, for my signature, which I have not yet received. Let me have the latest report as to how the mine is progressing-also we must have the detailed report of how much gold you have actually extracted from Dolan's little, crude, 3 ton mill, since we bought the property-this is highly IMPORTANT!"[8]

Two days later Charles Squier updated the Colonel in another letter,

"I lunched with Jim Coghill and David Bennett today fresh from the mine and I was so sorry to learn that they were only in Mineral from about three to five in the afternoon due to the stalling of Battle's

---

[7] January 16, 1924, Squier
[8] January 20, 1924, Letter from Charles B. Squier to Col. Thomas R. Marshall

motor (car) on the road from Charlottesville, certainly motoring is not reliable! However, I'm sure they saw a good deal.

"I signed the paper today, which you had signed as O.K., giving Jim Coghill, in return for his services when demanded, a one-fifth interest in half of my options closed with you, or five per cent of the entire options-this will be a good thing, and I'm glad you approved, as I would not have felt in duty bound to sign without your consent. However, I am disappointed to hear from Jim that you have not yet gotten the three options in good legal order- I trust in view of the developments in our property, it is not too late to get the options, that is, that the owners of the properties will try to back down! I hear the Slate Hill property is being worked full blast, with more men than the Twin Vein Company-what do you make of this, in view of the fact that the property is small and nearly worked down to the sulfite ore-they certainly are not going to the expense of putting a modern mill for so small a property on such small prospects. Is there any way of getting an option on the mining rights, at small cost, on the small strip of the Proffitt property, which apparently cuts our twin veins, as Battle called our attention to this as a bad feature.

"Bennett, who controls the "say-so"of a large estate, may invest some considerable sum with us, he especially asked me several questions; why is it, that the crosscut south from the 75 foot level, you have not really struck the second vein which I understood had been done? (The ore on the 75 foot level had already given out and the Colonel did not tell Charles Squier.) Also, he thinks the property cannot be operating before March 1, as the mill house and other accessory equipment is not far enough advanced. What is your idea as to the probable date of commencement of operations? I understand some of the Allis-Chalmers machinery has already been delivered to the property? With the present "skip"do you plan to be able to raise 50 ton of ore per day in twelve or twenty four hours? It would seem to be hard to do in the twelve usual hours?"[9]

The skip they were using at the time would not hold enough ore per trip to raise 50 tons per day. If they could have run 24 hours a day the skip would have had to deliver 2 tons per hour to the surface for processing at the new mill. The miners would have had to work at a breakneck pace to accomplish this almost impossible task. First, they would have had to drill a number of holes in the hard quartz rock using one of several methods of drilling. The first method involves one miner holding a short piece of drill steel while striking it on the end with a three or four pound hammer to create a hole. This is called single jacking, a very slow process in quartz rock The second method employs two miners, one miner holds a section of drill steel over his shoulder while the other stands behind him, striking the end of the steel with an eight to ten pound sledge hammer; this method is called double jacking. The steam powered drill which operates on the same principle as a modern jack hammer was the third method for drilling holes in those days.

Before dynamite, the only explosive known was black blasting powder. The blasting powder was wrapped in a container made of blasting paper, a very long fuse was inserted and the charge was placed in the back of the hole. The hole was filled with mud or dirt to contain the explosion, the fuse was lit and the charge was ignited. When using dynamite, the sticks of dynamite had a fuse type or electric blasting cap inserted into one end. The charge was positioned in the back of the hole with material being placed in the hole to contain the explosion.. Blasting caps were only used to provide the shock needed to detonate dynamite.

When the very long fuse was lit, the cap at the end of the fuse would explode, providing the shock that in turn caused the dynamite to explode. Electric blasting caps had the same purpose as the fuse type did, but were connected to a detonator by wires which allowed the miners to retreat to a safe location before detonating the charge. A dynamo inside the detonator produced an electric current when the plunger was pushed down that caused the cap to explode and detonate the charges.

---

[9] January 22, 1924, Letter from Charles B. Squier to Col. Thomas R. Marshall

MANEUVERING

After the shot the miners had to load the broken ore into mine cars which were pushed to the shaft where it was loaded into the skip. The ore was sometimes dumped into the skip from a holding bin above, but the miners at the Twin Vein had to load the skip by hand using shovels and other hand tools. The hoist operator was signaled, and the skip was raised to the surface where the ore was dumped into a chute at the top of the head frame. From the top of the head frame the ore slid down into the back of a wagon or truck that transported it to the mill or ore pile.

Squier continued,

> "How many men at approximately what labor cost per day do you propose as necessary to operate at full tilt, bringing up and milling 50 ton each day, including all shifts within the 24 hours?
>
> "Please let me know about all these things at once, Because they are very important! Also please let me know what to do about the trust deed or mortgage of $15,000.00 on the property, which Dolan holds, and is due on Feb1st, next! What will the local banks loan vs. the property, including machinery and other equipment as a first mortgage it would be better to get Dolan out of it, unless he accepts a partial payment of $5,000.00 cash, and lets the balance run for six months at least-we must have time- because a clause in his "trust deed" really gives him only $10,000 and not $15,000 <u>rights under foreclosure</u>!
>
> "We must also have the missing vouchers and bills for the $1,000.00 I wrote you about and have some statement as to how much gold has been recovered from the operation of the little crude three-ton mill since the company took possession. How about your specimen and the insurance?"[10]

---

10   January 22, 1914, Squier

On January 23, 1924 the Colonel responded to Squier's letter.

"Your letter of the 20th was received in the late mail yesterday afternoon in which you very positively demand that certain vouchers be forwarded at once and coupled with the statement, before we advance any more funds. I have the honor to report that the vouchers for the steam hoist, fire insurance and compensation insurance are in the Treasurer's hands and have been for some time."

"Categorically-the steam hoist was bought for cash and the conditions were that this hoist was to be shipped at once, and that a sight draft with a bill of lading attached would be sent to our bank for collection. This draft was presented and paid by check. The freight bill was paid by check also. As soon as these two checks were paid I attached them to the paid sight draft, bill of lading, and the freight bill which was receipted. The five papers were pinned together to make a full and complete voucher for the money expended, these papers were sent to the company with the first statement and were acknowledged.

"The two policies of insurance were put in force two months before I received the money with which to pay for them, as soon as the agent was paid the two policies were delivered to me. I in turn delivered them to the Secretary and Treasurer of the Company. No other papers were issued to me, and in the eyes of all public accountants, possession of the policy itself is considered a good voucher. The vouchers for the water tank and truck hauling I will at once proceed to obtain. The blacksmith, unfortunately does not have sufficient education to write, so I will get the district magistrate to prepare the voucher and have it signed. As soon as I am able to obtain these papers I will at once forward them together with all of the papers that I may have to Mr. Coghill the first Vice President who has lately visited the property and has no doubt made a report of the conditions as he found them here. I informed Mr. Coghill that I was paying for the lumber and the cost of the concrete work. I will be glad if you will write me if you think the company can buy the materials at the same price and I am mailing you some photographs of the work being done."[11]

Perry advised the Colonel in a letter dated January 23.

"I expect to be in Charlottesville next Saturday the 26th and want to run down to see you either Sunday afternoon or Monday morning, spending the day and if possible trying the dog out. I hope this will be agreeable to you. I am also bringing down a very fine camera which will permit the taking of good interiors as well as outside views of the different workings at the mine, with the idea of having some enlargements made for the officers of the company. Coghill and Bennett returned very favorably impressed with the work to date and I am keen to see it and also to have a visit with you."[12]

Squier replied to the Colonel's letter of January 26.

"I have before me your letter of the 23rd. I immediately communicated with our Secretary and Treasurer, Mr. Sutphen, and he has reported that he did not think we had the receipts for the insurance policies, or had ever had them, but would make quite sure and let me know at once-which means Monday morning, as he does not come to the city on Saturdays. In this connection, it is quite usual to send insurance policies to reputable parties with the bills for premiums attached, before they are paid, as often happens to me, but if not paid shortly, it is usually mentioned in the indenture of the policy that the insurance lapses! Mr. Sutphen also reports that the sight draft and checks for the steam hoist were sent up by you

---

11 January 23, 1924, Letter from Col. Thomas R. Marshall to Charles B. Squier
12 January 23, 1924, Letter from Eugene Perry to Col. Thomas R. Marshall

last summer, but you demanded their return, after our due inspection, and so they were sent back, they should be returned to us. The other items are of small importance.

"I quite appreciate that one has work done by ignorant people who cannot give receipts; but the payrolls should be handled either by checks or company stamped receipts, which each man could sign or mark, if he cannot write. Otherwise, we have no redress against any possible claims. I think you will agree with me that, in the case of a valuable property, one must be protected against any eventualities of human nature particularly! Also, please do not forget we are now an incorporated company, subject to the usual investigations upon the part of Federal, State, and County authorities, and we must have our books, receipts, expenditures, income, and outgo duly audited-This is very important!

"In this connection, I must again reiterate my request for vouchers, receipts, and statement in full up to and including Dec. 31st. 1923 (from Dec.10,1923}, so that we can make up our annual report as soon as possible, as required by law!

"Let me say right here I fully appreciate that you operated under very unusually and trying financial conditions last summer and fall during my absence in Europe, that you have done remarkably well in the matter of costs of construction, and I know you are very diligent and active at all times, perhaps more than is good for your own health (!), and that I know you are buying our lumber, concrete, and other accessories very low in price, and that in general, you are carrying a very great and complicated load, until the mill is actually assembled and set up and working, when I , myself, want to make my next trip to Mineral!

"Mr. Perry, our second Vice-President left last evening for Charlottesville, where his aged mother is ill, and he plans to come to Mineral Sunday afternoon, and remain until at least Monday evening, as I was not satisfied with the somewhat cursory, three hours visit Mr. Coghill made recently!

MANEUVERING

"I have given Mr. Perry a little memoranda in my own handwriting to ask you some questions, which he will probably show you, and you can orally answer to him for transmission to me. In this regard, about how much ore have you raised and placed on the dump to date which is ready for the mill?

"Answering your letter of the 24, I received the very nice photos of the mine etc. for which I am very much obliged to you! I trust the weather conditions will not prevent our milling gold ore by March 1st.-do you anticipate that the plant will work at once or will it have to be tried out for some time? I am sorry to hear of your long, cold uncomfortable ride in quest of lumber but you must not take such chances with your health!

"I'm glad to know you have arranged with Dolan about the mortgage, and I'm writing Battle asking him to represent us, because we want to make sure everything is in good legal order. I will have in Battle's hands company funds for $5,000.00 and he will pay it off at once. When Dolan has signed the necessary papers ask him to extend the balance due for SIX months not three, which you mentioned at first, is not long enough to be safe. We're not selling any more stock, except two or three small lots already contracted for, as I am making a new agreement with the company, whereby I can have the first call on the 6,000 remaining shares through convertible notes issued to me in lieu of cash advances for expenses!

"We can surely be operating around March 1, and do you think that the first months operation should yield about the product of say 50 ton per day, allowing 20 days which would be 1,000 tons, or around $20,000-$30,000 gross? This is important for our finances! Also Mr. Sutphen asked me to ask you how much longer the payroll would need to stand at $350.00 for the expense of cutting wood, before it automatically dropped back to the former rate of $250.00? If you would personally be greatly in need of an advance of $500.00 on the portion of your salary now in arrears, we could arrange it around

February the 1st., but, of course we have to consider every dollar until we are finally pushed over the top of the hill, so to speak."[13]

On January 29, 1924, Charles Squier updated the Colonel.

> "I have just received a wire from Eugene Perry saying he is remaining over until tomorrow on important business and I suppose it is on account of your insurance, the part payment of the trust deed to Dolan, and other important matters. When he arrives here tomorrow, I will be glad to get the latest news from the mine. I was talking to a practical man here yesterday who is managing a successful silver mine in Ontario, formally belonging to the Milliken interests in St. Louis, Missouri. His superintending engineer sends him a short letter each week as to how the ore is showing up in the stopes or headings; if you could arrange to do this briefly, it would help us to sell stock at this end!"[14]

The term stoping is defined as "to excavate ore in a vein by driving horizontally upon it in a series of workings, one immediately over the other or vice versa. .. Stope (probably a corruption of step), because when a number of them are in progress, each working face being a little in advance of the next above or below, the whole face under attack assumes the shape of a flight of stairs."[15]

Charles Squier continues his letter of January 29,

> "We have the two insurance policies in the company safe-deposit box number 1259 in the Farmer Safe-Deposit Company, 475 5th. Ave., New York. I have asked Sutphen to very carefully go over all the papers and records he has in regard to the mine and he will report to me at lunch tomorrow, when I will let you know the

---
13   January 26, 1924, Letter from Charles B. Squier to Col. Thomas R. Marshall
14   January 29, 1914, Letter from Charles B. Squier to Col. Thomas R. Marshall
15   Raymond, R. W., A Glossary of mining and Metallurgical Terms, from Vol. IX Transactions of the American institute of Mining Engineers, Easton Pa., The Institute pg. 84

result-if he has no record of the checks, vouchers, receipts or sight drafts for the insurance and steam hoist it will probably mean they were returned to you, in which case we must have them back here at once to be put in the safe-deposit box. Sutphen is sending you the usual week's payroll check for $350.00 to reach you Friday or Saturday morning surely! Can this go back to the old rate of $250.00 per week, when the wood is all cut, and if so, how soon? I will have a check for the $5,000.00, with interest of 6% on the $15,000.00 for nine months in Battles' hands on February 1st. or 2nd-he will hold us in escrow in the bank at Louisa, until the Dolans' attorney satisfies him with furnishing the properly endorsed and signed releases."[16]

The Colonel sent Squier some photographs of the mill house construction by special delivery on February 2. At this stage they are still in the process of pouring concrete for the foundations and are a long way from bring operational..

Squier replied the next day,

"Your letter of the second with the latest interesting photographs was received this morning on account of the special delivery stamp, and I hasten to reply.

"First, I received a long letter from Battle yesterday and it seemed to show conclusively that we have settled the matter of the trust deed with the Dolans and have three months more to pay off the balance of $10,000.00, with interest. I am deeply satisfied it was paid this way. I appreciate from what Eugene Perry told me when he came back that it may annoy you somewhat to have Dolan hanging around Mineral specially on account of the options on the adjoining property, which you may not yet have signed up in legal form; but perhaps you will agree with me that Dolan might be _more_ troublesome with $15,000.00 than with $5,000.00, and the

---

16 January 29, 1924, Squier

chances of his going away might be that much less; also, we must conserve all our financial resources in cash to finally push this whole enterprise "over the top of the hill", since we are so nearly there. Within another month now, your ambitions should prove a reality.

"While I fully appreciate that you are doing all possible to rush the work to completion as soon as possible, <u>please</u> do not overtax yourself or your usual good health. We would appreciate your full statement with all vouchers and receipts up to February the first or as near that date as possible at once!

"The directors meeting tomorrow is a special meeting called by me for the only purpose of voting to convert the $20,000.00 advanced by me to date, into a 6% one-year company note, @$5.00 per share (which leaves about $1,500.00 still in the treasury here!) into a 6% one-year company note, convertible @$5 per share! This gives me a call on 4,000 shares of the treasury stock as an option, which will have to be set aside during the life of this note! This will only leave some 2,500 shares for sale, and probably this will be likewise tied up by me by some other advances necessitated before we are on a paying basis, as I shall have to pay the Allis-Chalmers Co. $3,750.00 on March 15, and a like amount on June 15, but before then we ought to have some "earnings" in hand! Also, you will probably need some more funds for completion of mill house and for a new boiler, in addition to the funds already advanced!

"Please do not overlook the <u>indisputable</u> fact that every day of development on the Twin Vein property makes it increasingly difficult to get your options on the adjoining properties on the original basis you mentioned to me, unless you have them securely tied up legally in writing. I suggest you call Battle at my expense to look over or write up any papers you may have signed subsequently regarding the closing of these options!"[17]

---

17   February 3, 1924, Letter from Charles B. Squier to Col. Thomas R. Marshall

MANEUVERING

One possible explanation for the Colonel's delay in getting the options for Charles Squier could be that he has plans for them himself, in the event the mine produces millions in gold and needs the extra land.

The Colonel again asked the company to provide insurance for him. Perry told the Colonel that he would have to provide a medical specimen before they would grant it. The specimen was sent to the lab, however it spoiled on the way. Unfortunately, the biggest problem standing in the way of the Colonel being covered was his advanced age of 64 years. The Colonel's foot dragging in turning over the options continues, in spite of the continual prodding from Squier.

On February 6, 1924, Charles Squier informed Colonel Marshall of the "Special directors meeting which was held last Monday, where it was duly voted to fund my advances to the company, of $20,000 into a one-year, 6% note, convertible into stock @$5, and to issue similar notes for any future advances! I had hoped to have your vouchers to exhibit to the directors, as per your last letter, promising them, but none have come even now! I'm having lunch with Mr. Sutphen Friday, day after tomorrow, before which I hope to have the vouchers and receipts to date, to give him for auditing and you will appreciate that it makes it _very awkward_ for us to have our receipt so long overdue for making up our books!

> "I duly instructed Mr. Sutphen to send you last week $300.00 for the payroll, instead of 350.00, as you say the wood cutters (except two) are laid-off, and this is still $50.00 more than the former payroll, on account of the new construction in progress, in addition to the $1,000.00 formerly advanced for this purpose!
>
> "I received from you yesterday A.M. a small package containing a small specimen of quartz, showing gold formations-it looked is if some parts had been picked out, but perhaps this was due to my ignorance of such matters-I will show it to some expert for his opinion! Please send us up a fairly large specimen of the Ferro manganese ore by freight or express, so I can have it assayed!
>
> "Mr. Perry reported he thought you would not be granted insurance on account of your age, even considering your good

health and robustness-however, we are trying out some other companies, you must take good care of yourself. If you have more you can do, would you like us to send down some reliable young man, whom we can get cheap, to help with the accounts? We <u>must</u> have the vouchers and receipts in full at once-<u>also</u> your <u>canceled checks</u>, and <u>bill of lading,</u> etc. covering the steam hoist and the other expenditures mentioned in former letters! Is Dolan giving you any trouble with labor, your options or other matters? This is <u>vital</u>!"[18]

Squier was still worried that Dolan may try to buy some options out from under the Colonel because they were still not under his personal control, although they may well have been under the Colonel's control.

---

18   February 6, 1924, Letter from Charles. B. Squier to Col. Thomas R. Marshall

THE CARROT AND THE STICK

Squier's letter of February 11 brings bad news for the Colonel.

"I trust you have by now duly received Mr. Sutphen's letter, containing a check for $1,250.00, of which $1,000.00 is advanced for the mill construction, machinery and related expenses, and $250.00 is to be applied to your salary, as requested-I regret I cannot make this salary advance larger, but you must remember that I am <u>entirely</u> financing the company at this time, and I have already loaned the company $20,000.00 (in addition to the $10,000.00 I put in when we bought the tract!), which has all been used now, except for $200.00. We still have to pay the Allis-Chalmers Company $3,750.00 on March 15th. next, and a like sum on June 15th.next, that we are not yet "out of the woods" as to the mill construction, accessory machinery etc., and the $10,000.00 still due Dolan must be met on May 1st. Surely-these are <u>serious</u> items, when I have to take care of them <u>entirely myself</u>, and when the other stockholders contribute absolutely <u>nothing</u>! Outside of the above sums, we have gotten in all about $9,000.00 through the sale of stock @$5.00 per share, of which I sold $6,500.00, Mr. Perry sold about $2,500.00, and no one else <u>any</u> at <u>all</u>! I have learned that I cannot depend at all upon Mr. Perry or Mr. Coghill selling any stock , except in a very desultory, uncertain, and small way at best-Mr. Coghill has never sold a single share! I must admit it is very difficult to sell any, except to close friends and relatives, who will buy on account of their faith in you personally, I.E., I mean the seller himself, for no one thinks a gold mine in Virginia is anything but a joke! From what is set forth previously, you must be patient and let your salary lapse as much as possible, as I am the company's only financial hope and my resources are far from <u>IN-EXHAUSTIBLE</u>! If you are sure the property will produce handsomely, then we are all right, and you can afford yourself to be indulgent in the matter of salary. Also, you will understand <u>absolutely nothing else</u> has been paid out in salaries or other emoluments to anyone in the company except yourself, except for the large sum of $25.00 so far paid to Mr. Barker, the young accountant Sutphen has to help him with the books, and that Sutphen paid and not the company, and about $350.00 paid to Battle for expenses and legal fees! If I had known I was to receive practically no financial help, neither Perry or Coghill would have gotten as much stock at first. Besides I have also bought for $7,000.00 cash from several stockholders 5,060 additional shares of stock, and I now hold a company's convertible note for $20,000, which carries the option to convert into stock @$5, thus setting aside 4,000 shares more, and I shall only advance further sums, as set forth, in the agreement we ratified at the last directors meeting vs. convertible notes @$5 per share , which will be discounted to 80% of par value, which is perfectly legal, and frequently done, thus setting aside stock @<u>$4 per share equivalent</u>. This means I now control entirely to date 43,060 shares of the total "75,000 shares <u>EXCLUSIVE</u> of the 3,750 shares of your stock , upon which I have the voting right for five years, and the remaining 2,720 shares in the treasury set aside for sale, and not yet control by convertible notes, but which I will probably have to take up also against the advance of working capital. All the above will show you just how we are being financed, and in fact it was the only possible way, for <u>outsiders have no faith in gold mines in Virginia</u>!

"Now I come to the <u>VERY IMPORTANT PART</u> of this letter, I have endeavored to tell you in other previous letters, but perhaps less fully and in less detail.

THE CARROT AND THE STICK

"FIRST, I quite appreciate that you are doing several men's work at the present, and that your knowledge, industry and touch with local conditions is saving the company considerable expense, and you are working at great stress at this time on account of the construction of the mill and the assembling of the machinery. I am aware that you are extremely busy and doubtless bothered with many exasperating details, of which we know nothing up here, as is always the case when one has to deal with that humanly untrustworthy quality known as labor, and you are doing all possible to rush the job to an early completion-we all appreciate these things! I also appreciate that you were greatly "up against it" last summer during my absence in Europe, due to the absolute failure of Perry and Coghill to raise funds, which was <u>not my fault</u>! BUT, since I have returned from Europe, funds have been furnished as required by you-if not always exactly on time, because you have not let us know far enough in advance-I have also asked you to keep the advances in abeyance until actually needed as it has <u>embarrassed</u> me somewhat to meet such heavy expenditures myself alone-I knew you needed about $2,500.00 for the mill-house etc. as per your estimates, but you only asked for $1,000.00 at first, so no more was sent until you requested it in your last letter of February 4th. inst now before me-we sent this just as soon as possible-you know Sutphen is only in New York on Mondays, Wednesdays and Fridays, we must have longer advance notice than you gave us for the money to reach you the following Saturday, for the mails sometimes take two days from New York to Mineral, including all delays in delivery at either end!

"Now the only thing I must complain about is this: we cannot in the future go any such length of time as nearly two whole months-our last vouchers were up to Dec.10th, 1923 <u>only</u>!-without a single receipt for expenses! You promised the vouchers for the meeting last Monday-I saw Sutphen this morning and <u>still no vouchers</u> had been received by him-now a full week afterwards. You must realize we are now <u>a company</u>, <u>not</u> a partnership or syndicate, and our books must be kept up to date and the receipts kept, as Sutphen with Barker's assistance (paid for by him) has done well and concisely up to Dec.10th. ultimo. Properly, all bills should be sent up here for audit and payment directly by our treasurer, but this is impracticable in the case of second hand machinery bought from individuals and shipped with a sight draft attached or in the case of labor-of course. When we are running regularly, we should have a regular pay- roll which should not vary at all from week to week of full operation! The $1,000.00 just sent to you will keep the construction going some time, but in the meantime we <u>must</u> have the following. The sight draft for $1,000.00- plus the bill for the $77.50 in freight charges for the steam hoist, with your cancelled checks for vouchers. We also must have the receipts for the three or four small items that were sent up here which you demanded be returned to you. They should be permanently on file here, to complete our records up to the 10th of Dec.1923.

"All of the vouchers, receipts and checks you can furnish <u>at once</u> to the date of Feb. 1st 1924, are to be followed by any missing ones as soon as possible, including your receipts for all salary advances since your last statement and any important labor receipts you have thought important enough to demand!

"I know you are an excellent, experienced, practical engineer, have built everything very well and much better than many would have done, and at a much smaller cost. You are probably not accustomed to keeping accounts and demanding receipts for all expenditures, which is a very <u>UNSAFE THING</u> to do, considering the unreliability of human nature, which has taught me this young in life: that nothing stands verbally, and is not worth a damn, except in rare instances, unless signed and set down legal fashion! If you do not get receipts for all the expenditures, except the daily fixed wages of the laborers, parties delivering materials may later come back at us and claim they were only paid "on account" and not in full etc.! This is very <u>DANGEROUS</u> and might produce liens vs. the property. I do not believe in making any practice of trusting people unless their interests are bound up with yours and are identical! Of the wisdom of this I could mention many cases in my experience and that of others in the past!

"I have written numerous letters in the past but I have endeavored once and for all to make this one very complete on this subject, so no more will be necessary. Therefore, I must reiterate that we <u>will positively further no more funds to Mineral of any kind, from now on</u>, <u>except</u> the usual weekly payroll of $250 to keep the pump, etc. running, <u>until</u> all of the vouchers, are in our hands, and found to be duly satisfactory-any other line of action would be <u>unfair</u> to the company and all concerned, including yourself. If you find it too much to keep such an accounting with your other work, we will send down Barker or some similar person to Mineral at least every two weeks, if not more often, for several days to make up the accounts on the spot, so please <u>do not hesitate</u> to ask us to do so. Some few vouchers of small amounts may be delayed, and sent later, but all vouchers must be <u>finally</u> sent and they should be sent up regularly <u>each two weeks</u>.

"Furthermore, when the mill gets at operation, we will send down a company representative to check the gold as it comes off the plates at the mill-preferably a very honest young engineer, with some mining experience, whom we are on the lookout for now, and who must be duly <u>bonded</u> for a considerable sum by the National Surety Company! It would be most unfair to you and to all concerned to expect you to be there continually watching and it is a responsibility no one man can entirely assume! Furthermore, I well know the gold mining in Virginia runs very irregularly, so that some days the output would be very large and others very small!

"Eugene Perry, after due consideration, showed me your letter he received today-I am not provoked at it, and I quite understand your view point as to telegrams and the future will <u>only</u> use them <u>when</u> very suddenly and urgently required to save time. Still, there is no reason why your telegrams should not be kept strictly private, and if they are not so treated in the future, a complaint should be made to the head office in Richmond and the local operator replaced by someone less curious about other people's business-I trust you received my telegram sent last night to reassure you about the money being sent! You should shortly rent in the company's name a safe deposit box in Mineral or Louisa, and keep everything of value therein! We have a company box here-it only costs $7 per year!

"Evidently you have still not gotten those options duly signed up-I strongly urge you to get Battle to draw them up for you, and not let some local country lawyer take the chance of bungling it all up-also if, as I suspect, you have not ever gotten them signed up in legal form, which will <u>hold</u>, delay further is most <u>DANGEROUS</u>, in view of our daily development of the "Twin Vein" property, which will soon change the owners minds as to the adjoining properties' potentialities. Unless the options can be closed on the basis of the figures you mention when last here, and as set forth in the papers in duplicate drawn up by my attorney and mailed to you some weeks ago, I cannot consider any other agreement! Delay in this matter seems <u>vital</u>. You will easily agree with me that whenever any agreement is made, the only safe way, is to "<u>cinch</u>" it in legal form <u>at once</u>-then neither party can drop out at will, if he chooses-there is <u>no other sure way</u>! I sincerely hope you have not delayed too long to get the options "sewed up" legally- if so, we will probably not get them on a low basis, and I should not consider them <u>on any other</u>, on account of my considerable outlay in the Twin Vein Company to date!

"I, of course, quite appreciate that in the "Twin Vein" to date, we have a very large property, with very considerable developments at comparatively very small cost, when one considers other properties-there can be no doubt of all that, but I did not figure on

THE CARROT AND THE STICK

<u>financing the whole thing</u> myself-otherwise I would have demanded much more stock!

"Has Dolan left Mineral, or is he still hanging around-and, if so, has he bothered you in any way? Do you suspect he is tried to meddle with the options on the other properties? He is shrewd and not to be trusted all!

"Also, has all the Allis-Chalmers machinery arrived in good order, and how about the mill-house boiler, and when will you have to pay for that, and how much?

"Trusting you will appreciate this letter's importance, as I cannot write again at such length and in such detail, and that it is written <u>for the best interest of all concerned.</u>"[1]

Three days another letter brought additional prodding from Charles Squier for the missing vouchers and receipts.

"I must again call your attention to the fact that I saw Mr. Sutphen personally yesterday, and he had received absolutely no vouchers from you to date since December the 10th.-although you promised same for the 4th. inst.-ten days ago! Mr. Barker, our accountant, has signified his willingness to go down to Mineral any week-end and audit the accounts to the date February the 1st. of, or later, if possible. This is extremely DANGEROUS and UNBUSINESSLIKE and in every way INADVISABLE for a <u>company</u> to have its accounts over two months behindhand, and I must impress upon you the danger of LIENS etc.!

"I have instructed Mr. Sutphen to send you down regularly the weekly pay-roll @$300.00, but <u>under no conditions</u> to send any further sums, no matter how urgently requested, until the matter of the vouchers is satisfactorily adjusted, at least to Feb. 1, 1924,

---

1   February 11, 1924, Letter from Charles B. Squier to Col. Thomas R. Marshall

including the missing checks, vouchers and the sight-draft covering the accounts up to Dec.10, 1923, as described in former letters.

"Trusting to hear from you shortly in regard to this important matter at once-otherwise Barker and I will have to come to Mineral shortly, although I had not planned to go down until March.15th. when the mill should be assembled and set up."[2]

This was the last thing the Colonel wanted to hear at this point because he is running way behind and the mill will not be finished as he had said it would be. Meanwhile the Allis-Chalmers Company notified Charles Squier that they planned to ship the last of the machinery on February 11.

To the Colonel in a letter dated February 18 Squier wrote,

"Your letter of the14th. inst. was received and contents carefully noted! I saw Sutphen yesterday noon, and he reported he had received the vouchers and receipts and turned them over to Barker, our accountant, who will duly report to me tomorrow, Wednesday, as to how he found them.

"The manganese ore specimens were duly received by Perry, and we had them sent to the best assayers here, Ledoux and Company and I will report to you the results of their assay, and if sufficiently favorable will have photostatic copies made of them! {Manganese is used in the manufacture of certain types of steel).

"I'm glad to know you received the last two checks from Sutphen, for $300.00 and $1,250.00 respectively, the last one for the sum of $250 is to be applied to your now somewhat overdue salary! I'm so glad to hear that good progress is being made with the mill-house construction-when it is completed and in running order, let me know at once, as I will make it a point of coming down to Mineral with several important friends!

---

2   February 14, 1924, Letter from Charles B. Squier to Col. Thomas R. Marshall

"Letter received today from the Allis-Chalmers Co. states final shipment of machinery left West Allis, Wisconsin on the 16th.inst.- this can hardly reach you before the 25th., if not much later-winter deliveries are not so good! The freight thereon can hardly exceed $200.00. You may now order the boiler, which is to be $1100.00, F.O.B. and can hardly be delivered to you before three days after your order goes forward, even if it comes from some near or neighboring town in Virginia! If the vouchers, etc. are found to be O. K, as I presume, we will have in your hands additional funds for $1,500.00 by the first mail next A. M., the.25th.inst.-I trust this will be in good time!

"After many disheartening delays and tribulations, especially, I doubt not, upon your part, we are nearly "over the top". I really feel somehow, in an uncanny way, that there are really some good clean millions (no matter how general business is) in the old Twin Vein Company's property! Am I right? Are you quite sure? Are we wrong in placing all our faith in your personality, energy, endeavor, and technical knowledge?

"Do you know anything definite as to whether the other gold mines discovered in Georgia, Gold Hill, North Carolina and other parts of Virginia, than ours, as well as even up here in New York State, were VEINS, and were ever worked by MODERN MACHINERY? Has such machinery as we are putting in ever been practically tried out before in Virginia? It is all very interesting in the extreme!

How are the options coming on and have you got the legal papers signed in good order? Again let me suggest the advisability of calling in Battle, at my expense, to draw up your final, "clinching" agreements! Have you pushed any further toward the second vein and, if so with what _actual_ results?"[3]

At this point the concrete foundations were complete and ready for the installation of the heavy framing which would form the skeleton of the mill building.

---

3 February 18, 1924, Letter from Charles B. Squier to Col. Thomas R. Marshall

GOING UP

On February 22 the heavy framing materials and other lumber for building the mill were bought from Walton & Sugg at Pendleton, Virginia. All of the lumber was specified to be white oak due to its resistance to breaking under the weight and stress of the machinery it was to support.

A partial materials list begins with the heaviest of timbers, 1, 10 inch by 12 inch oak beam 23 feet in length, which could easily weigh 1,000 pounds, 99 pieces of 10 inch by 10 inch oak measuring from 6 feet to 23 feet in length, 23 pieces of 8 inch by 10 inch oak measuring from 12 to 17 feet in length, 59 pieces of 8 inch by 8 inch oak measuring from 4 to 21 feet in length, 25 pieces of 6 inch by 8 inch oak measuring from 16 to 18 feet in length and 18 pieces of 6 inch by 6 inch oak measuring from 7 to 22 feet in length. There were 12,453 board feet in the heavy timber order. An additional order for pine lumber to complete the balance of the building consisted of lumber having dimensions of 3 inches by 6 inches; 3 inches by 8 inches, 2 inches by 8 inches; 2 inches by 4 inches and 17,636 board feet of sheeting boards. The total cost of the lumber was $581.34.[1] Some of the posts which once supported the ore bin are still standing today.

This was a potentially busy day for the Colonel because the 35,800 pound rod mill had arrived at the C & O Railroad siding at Pendleton and it would have to be unloaded and hauled to the mine.[2]

Photograph No. 46 Some of the first posts which are to support the upper levels have been installed giving one a clear view of how a mill was constructed. Men who specialized in this type of work in those days were known as millwrights.

---

1 February 22, 1924, Bill of Materials from Walton and Sugg
2 February 22, 1924, shipping Bill for Rod Mill from Allis-Chalmers

GOING UP

Photograph 47 provides another view of the mill construction which includes the Colonel's car and the Tangye engine in the background.

PHOTOGRAPH NO. 46
BEGINNING OF HEAVY FRAMING

PHOTOGRAPH NO. 47
FIRST LEVEL INSTALLED

ANATOMY OF A GOLD MINE

In another letter to the Colonel on February 23 Squier wrote the following

"Letter received this A.M. under date of the 21st.inst. from Mr. Sutphen states he has mailed you a check for $1,100.00 which has probably already reached you, and which is to cover the payment for the boiler, which may not arrive right away due to the usual freight delay. He also sent you the pay-roll of $300, as usual. We have paid at this end the bill for the pump also the Virginia State taxes and we will send you down an additional $1000.00 the middle of next week-Sutphen will see me Monday and have the necessary funds in hand then! This will enable you to pay the freight charges on the machinery from the Allis-Chalmers Company in West Allis, Wisconsin, which they estimate will be about $200.00 for the larger shipment sent out the 11th.inst., and $25.00 for the final shipment sent out on the 28th. inst-and you will have $775.00 left to apply to the final payment for construction of the mill building, for which we have advanced some $2,000.00 to date, and which was to cost $2,500.00 in all, I believe, as per your former letters. If any amount around $250 remains, you can apply that toward your overdue salary-I am getting a report from Sutphen as to just how much your salary will be overdue on March 1st., and then we will make all possible efforts to make some further substantial advance thereto, unless you are satisfied to let it run for the present. Will you have to have the two Ford trucks for the moving of the ore to the mill at once to commence operations or can we get by with several one-horse wagons?

"What will the Ford trucks cost each? Also can you buy them better second-hand? If we had our own trucks, one of them could be used to transport you back and forth from the property in the morning and evening and at other odd times. Second hand cars are always a gamble, unless used really very little, and must be purchased through someone you can quite trust as to not misrepresenting them!

"I recently had dinner with Sir Archibald Mitchelson, his wife and daughter of London-he is a prominent British banker and colliery-owner-coal mines in Wales and is taking a cruise to the West Indies-they sailed yesterday with some other friends on the C.P.R. "Empress of Britain"-when they return in March they are going to Toronto and then northward to the Porcupine-Davidson gold district of Ontario, where they are heavily interested in the Porcupine-Davidson mine."[3]

At this point the Porcupine-Davidson mine shaft was 600 feet deep with an additional 1,425 feet of tunnels and associated workings. New development consisted of a new main shaft that had been sunk to a depth of 1,000 feet and they planned to construct a 500 ton per day mill. The ore reserves were estimated to be worth approximately $4,000,000 and diamond drilling had proven gold ore to the depth of 1,725 feet. The Porcupine -Davidson Mine was an English operation with issued capital of $3,000,000 and it was producing over $3,000,000 in gold annually.[4]

Diamond drilling is a form of exploratory geology employed to prove the existence and value of ore thought to be in place. The drilling process involves the use of a hollow drill which was studded with industrial diamonds allowing a core of the earth to be extracted for analysis. It is still a very professional method for the verification of mineral deposits. Usually after the ore deposits are verified, then, and only then, will a mine will be opened and a mill to process the ore be constructed.

Squier continued, "I gave him our Twin Vein data, he was very much interested, but had never heard of gold in the state of Virginia, which is the usual criticism, which we encounter everywhere-he said their veins in the Porcupine-Davidson ran twelve feet thick, and went down very deep, over 750-feet already, I think!

---

3   February 23, 1924, Letter from Charles B. Squier to Col. Thomas R. Marshall
4   Gold Mines of Ontario, 1923 Edition, Toronto, Stobie, Furlong & Co.

"Let me know if you have explored any further in the direction of the second vein, how far your galleries have been extended on the different levels near the shaft, and how the vein ore bodies are proving up and if they are up to your expectations so far?"[5]

On February 28 Charles Squier advised the Colonel that

"Barker, our accountant, who is a nice business-like young man, will arrive at Mineral Saturday morning, the 2nd. of March at 9:28, and return that evening. He will go over with you the various small items, which were not included in the vouchers you last sent and will want to see the sight-draft, freight bill, and the checks, which were missing in the vouchers furnished up to Dec. 10, 1923, which were duly returned at your request and which you may prefer to hold, but which should be kept in a strong box. I am seeing Barker tomorrow P.M. before he goes down, and if you can show him anything concretely interesting around the property, he can bring us back a verbal report of how things are going!

"Sutphen is sending you another check for $1,000.00, which is to be applied as follows: $750.00 for mill-house construction, freight charges, etc. and $250.00 to go toward your salary, which we figure was $1666.34 in arrears, not including the last $250.00 sent-let me to know if this tallies with your figures! A Mr. Brickford I talked to some time the other day, has had considerable experience in the Porcupine District, Ont., and asked why we had put in so large a plant as a 50 ton mill, and not 10-ton units to start with, unless we had our reserves of ore more definitely proven with the usual diamond drilling process. He also stated that free-milling quartz ore frequently ran out of gold values; I offer this criticism merely to get your ideas as to the answer to these queries!

---

5   February 23, 1924, Squier

"Brickford, who is the Canadian representative of the Sir Archibald Mitchelson, London interests in the Porcupine Davidson Mine, regarding which I wrote you before, expressed doubt as to your being able to feed the mill 50 tons of ore per diem (24 hours?), with the present workings we have? I explained you are storing up some ore on a dump for the start. How much ore approximately have you so far "up"?

"Your letter was received this morning and I am glad the vein is running as thick as 6-ft. and proving up to your expectations-we are all naturally very interested indeed. Just as soon as you are all set to commence operations, which will be, I presume, around the 15th. of March, let me know and I will come down at once to see it all going.

"Are you quite right about the $5,000.00 for the mill house with foundations? It could hardly be done for less-we will send down the additional $2,500.00 when you ask for it. I know you have had considerable trouble moving the equipment in such bad weather, and I hope March will be less severe in our vicinity-it was certainly too bad we had all of that delay last summer!

"I shall be pleased to have your report about the ore bodies which are now in sight. We will shortly have Ledoux's assay of the ferro-manganese! Please let me know also, if you feel reasonably sure we will produce enough gold before May 1st, to pay off Dolans $10,000.00 mortgage? Also, how are the options on the adjoining properties coming on-don't you think they ought to be duly signed up in legal shape before our "Twin Vein" spouts gold!!!"[6]

---

6   February 28, 1924, Letter from Charles B. Squier to Col. Thomas R. Marshall Squier

Photographs 48 and 49 are the first two in a sequence of four photographs taken by the Colonel which show the beginning of the second level of the mill as a beam is being set into place using a gin pole to accomplish the task.

Photograph No. 50 The men continue to work on the installation of the cross beam, a crude ladder on each of the uprights can be seen which would not be considered safe today. The ore bin supports are located on the left as the workers climb on the ladder while the beam is still secured to the gin pole.

Photograph No. 51 The Colonel has moved to the rear of the mill building and the back side of the ore bin can be seen on the left.

The progress was slow, and March 15 is closing in. The building is nowhere near complete, and it may take months longer to finish the plant than the Colonel had expected due to another serious problem which has the potential to shut them down until it can be resolved.

PHOTOGRAPH NO. 48
BEGIN SEQUENCE OF 2ND LEVEL, 1 OF 4

GOING UP

PHOTOGRAPH NO. 49

INSTALLATION OF 2ND LEVEL CROSS PIECE, 2 OF 4

PHOTOGRAPH NO. 50

SIDE VIEW OF 2ND LEVEL, 3 OF 4

PHOTOGRAPH NO. 51

ORE BIN SUPPORTS, 4 OF 4

A SQUABBLE

On March 1 the General Manager of the Slate Hill Gold Mine placed a sign on the road which connected the Slate Hill and Twin Vein Mine properties with the main road. The sign said that the road would be closed on March 19. This road was the only way in or out of the Twin Vein Mine property. The Colonel was expecting more of the heavy machinery to arrive by rail at Pendleton, and it would have to be hauled to the mine over the existing road or sit on the cars until another road could be built.[1]

On March 6, Charles Squier wrote to the Colonel,

> "I have been expecting to hear from you about the promised report on the ore body showings, etc. I had a long talk with Barker Tuesday P.M., and he told me about all he had seen at the mine while at Mineral, and said he thought you and he had established a better understanding for the future as to the company's accounts-this was our sole reason for sending him down-we have the utmost faith in you and your ability to make a go of the whole enterprise but you do not always take into account that we are incorporated company and not a syndicate, and that our accounts must be in order. We appreciate that you had been under the unusual strain of assembling the machinery, setting up foundations, buildings and I thought Barkers coming down might save some time and trouble!
>
> "I understand the mill house with complete machinery and equipment will not be ready to operate before April 1st., but we had

---

[1] March 1, 1924, Letter from Col. Thomas R. Marshall to Charles B. Squier

anticipated this delay of two weeks on account of the bad weather you have had. Do you think the machinery should all work well from the start? Barker said some small pieces from Allis-Chalmers Co. had not yet come-do you want me to stir up Denison about this? Barker says some of the upper 40 foot gallery in the shaft had caved in somewhat, but that you planned to take this ore out from the lower level by "stoping"-what does that mean?" He said you had recently definitely found the second vein-how much further did you have to cut to find it and have you taken any assays therein?"[2]

The gold-bearing quartz vein was running about six feet wide according to the Colonel and it can be seen in the photograph taken at the 135 foot level. **Photograph No. 52**

PHOTOGRAPH NO. 52

UNDERGROUND VIEW OF GOLD BEARING VEIN

---

2   March 6, 1924, Letter from Charles B. Squier to Col. Thomas R. Marshall

A SQUABBLE

Squier's letter continued.

"Barker said you had four men working in the mine shaft, taking out ore, and you were a little disturbed at first about not being able to feed the mill, as you would only have enough ore on the dump around April first for one months operation, which I take to mean 1500 tons? How much ore have you on the dump now? Barker says you took a photo of him on the dump! Wouldn't it be better for you to put on a larger gang in the mine levels to take out ore more quickly? How much per day would this increase our pay-roll account if we doubled the present output? Are you pleased with the machinery, and does it all seem good in every way, and quite up to specifications?

"Barker says the mill-house, to his inexperienced eyes seemed only half-done, but I told him I thought the foundation was much the slower part. Will the machinery suffer no damage from the weather by being out in the open? Barker said the boiler had to be tested in Richmond, and so had not come yet and that you would not need any more money for the present, but would let us know in advance, so Sutphen will only send the pay-roll, or $300.00 down this week. I think we had better take out at least $5,000.00 more in liability insurance, covering the employees, or per-haps $10,000 more AT ONCE. Let me know when it will be advisable for me to come down to see everything in working order.

"Also, how about your options-you say nothing about them, and I feel they are more uncertain each day with the progress on our plant, etc!

"ALSO, Do you think if the mine will produce sufficient earnings, net, during April to pay off your salary in arrears to date, as well as Dolans' mortgage of $10,000 due on May 1st., as I can stave off the Allis-Chalmers payments of about $7,500.00 until June the 1st. This is very IMPORTANT, as the entire financing falls on me, and I must arrange things well in advance."[3]

On March 9 Colonel Marshall wrote Charles Squier concerning the bad snowstorm that they recently had here in Virginia and the effects on the construction it had.[4] On March 13th Charles Squier responded to the Colonel's letter.

> Your two letters of the 9th. And 11th. insts. (came this A.M.) are before me, and before receiving your second letter I had anticipated trouble from the severe storm, which caused the train upon which my mother was bound to Virginia Hot Springs, to be twenty hours late in arrival there! Of course, such unavoidable storms cause big delays, but we must do all possible to push the work along to operation, that time which interests me so very much, when I will come down for several days to see the 'wheels go round." I'm also worried as to the $10,000.00 mortgage due Dolan on May 1st., which I understand he will not extend, and the approximately $7,500.00 still due the Allis-Chalmers Co. which cannot be staved off much beyond June 1st., so we must get some good EARNINGS soon, as we have not yet been able to sell much stock-except for a $2,000.00 sale pending this week. I will personally have to bear all of the brunt of the financing, however, we should soon be "out of the woods" at last, don't you think so?
>
> "Regarding pay-roll increase, the $300.00 at present paid is, as I understand it, the $250.00 we pay regularly, as for over six months past, and $50.00 toward laying up more wood even than the 300 cords we now have stocked- is it as much as 300? As I regard the storing up of a large ore dump to feed the mill as quite necessary and very vital, so please arrange to put on, commencing Monday next, five extra men in the mine, taking out ore, which will cost $75 more per week of

---

3   March 6, 1924, Squier
4   March 9, 1924, Letter from Col. Thomas R. Marshall to Charles B. Squier

six days more-I thought we had to pay $2, but your letter says $2.50, so I trust the labor has not gone up yet. Ledoux's manganese assay; It is not good- how do you account for this-commercial ore runs 40 to 45%. (The assay showed manganese at 26.09%) Please send us up another box of gold samples from as widely separated places as possible for Ledoux's assay, which will be interesting to have and only cost a few dollars to assay-also send us some sort of written report as to the quality of the ore bodies in sight-that is, what we have so far <u>definitely blocked out-as</u> this will help us in selling more stock, which we need <u>badly</u> to do shortly! Do you think the two Ford trucks will answer our purpose until such time as we have accumulated enough surplus to put in a tram line from the shaft to the mill house? It is too bad about the storm-I hope it does not give you too much trouble or delay matters much! I will instruct Sutphen to send you the weekly payroll from now on @ $375.00, so please do all possible to increase your ore dump to a good size!"[5]

Tram is shown in Illustration 14

ILLUSTRATION NO. 14: BLEICHERT WIRE ROPE TRAMWAY THE ENGINEERING AND MINING JOURNAL, VOL. LXVI NO. 20, NOV, 12, 1898, PG 35

---

5   March 13, 1924, Letter from Charles B. Squier to Col. Thomas R. Marshall

On March 19, Van Tassel Sutphen sent Colonel Marshall a check for $375 which was to cover the increased weekly payroll due to the extra miners employed in the shaft taking out ore. Sutphen told the Colonel, "I trust you have dug out of your snowbank. Curious, that we did not get any of it up here in New York."[6]

Work on the mill had stopped due to the snow and as it melted work once again resumed. Snow can be seen on the roof of the mill building and ice sickles hang on the small covering protecting the piece of machinery on the left. **Photograph No. 53**

Photograph No. 54 The road is closed as McSween had threatened. This will cause the Colonel a lot of trouble because the boiler and other equipment from Clarence Cosby is not at the mill site.

PHOTOGRAPH NO. 53

SNOW ON THE ROOF

---

6   March 19, 1924, From Van Tassel Sutphen to Col. Thomas R. Marshall

A SQUABBLE

PHOTOGRAPH NO. 54
ROAD CLOSURE

The Colonel has Gordon, Gordon and Crank file a lawsuit to reopen the road on March 20, 1924. The Colonel claims the road has been in continuous use for 50 years and this could affect the employment of 36 laborers when closed and they plan an increase to 60 or 75 within 30 days. An injunction was awarded enjoining and restraining the Ricswan Mining Company Incorporated, from obstructing or in any way blocking the road which would interfere with its use by the Twin Vein Mining Company. This injunction was to be in effect for 60 days from the 20th of March 1924 and would allow all parties to prepare their case prior to going to court.[7]

With the lawsuit and other concerns the Colonel has not contacted Charles Squier for a lengthy period time.

In a letter on March 23, Squier asks,

> "How are things getting along at the mine? I have not heard from you in some time, and wondered if all was well? Sutphen sent $375.00 to you this week for the newly increased pay-roll and will

---

7   Louisa County Court Chancery Case No. 1924-005, Box 155

continue to do so, until further notice from me. I trust you have put the extra five men to work getting ore out as fast and in the largest quantities possible to feed the new mill!

"Will everything be in fine working order by April 1st., as Mr. Perry and I will come down as soon as possible thereafter to see it all working? We are naturally very anxious to be there on the day we have so long awaited!

"How are the options coming on-have you gotten anything definite in writing, covering same? It seems to me most VITAL to get this all closed up legally before the "Twin Vein" mine starts to produce!"[8]

Things continue to drag along and April 1 is right around the corner. They had better hustle if they hope to be operating by then.

According to court records, McSween's response to the Colonel's lawsuit to reopen the road was filed on the 24th of March. McSween claimed it was never a public road and that he cut it out of the woods, and had allowed the Twin Vein Mine to use it for awhile.[9]

J. M. McSween was a 49 year old mining engineer with 30 years of experience who had been sent to the Arminius Mine in 1910 by the S. F. Pearson Co. to get the property in shape. Before he came to Mineral, he worked for the McIntire Gold Mine Company in the Porcupine District in Ontario, Canada. He then went with Harrison Pain at the Ally Cooper {Allah Cooper} mining property located near Mineral and he worked there until the mill had been set up and was operating in 1915. He developed under option the Virginia Lead and Zinc property {Valzinco mine in Spotsylvania County, Virginia} and eventually sold it to the Williams Company of Richmond, Virginia. In 1925 the Valzinco mine went into receivership.

In 1919 McSween developed the R. E. Dolan Gold Mine which did not show enough gold to continue with work. One witness said that R. E. Dolan and J. M. McSween had a "fallen out"and in 1920 McSween went to work for the Ricswan

---

8   March 23, 1924, Letter from Charles B. Squier to Col. Thomas R. Marshall
9   Louisa County Court Chancery Case No. 1924-005, Box 155

A SQUABBLE

Mining Company out of New York City on the property known then as the Slate Hill Gold Mine which he developed and operated.[10]

The Slate Hill Gold Mine originally opened in 1849.[11] It was still in operation in early 1854 according to a stock certificate dated May 3, 1854 from the Slate Hill Gold Mining Company. The Company stock consisted of 20,000 shares of capital stock worth $12.50 each, with a total value of $250,000

The mine was described in an 1892 mine report by D. F. Earnest who at that time was the Mine Superintendent. He examined and took charge of the Slate Hill Mine property about 1890 and found the main shaft had filled up to within 20 feet of the top with water and mud. He cleaned out and repaired the 120 foot deep shaft with heavy timbers.

At the depth of 80 feet he found a level that had been driven about 20 feet. The vein at this point was about 4 feet thick and he encountered a riser (an interior mine shaft} of unknown height 25 to 30 feet from the shaft. At the 120 foot level there were two levels {tunnels}, the east level was 80 feet in length with a well defined vein of gold-bearing quartz which averaged four to four and one half feet thick. About 40 feet east of the shaft there was another riser which connected with the level 30 feet above and he could see some of the ore had already been stoped. Here the quartz vein had perfectly defined solid walls which were visible overhead in the level for its entire length of 80 feet. He reported that A vein of ore like this is rarely encountered and is admired by those who have the opportunity to see it.

> "Two blasts were made into foot (the wall under the vein [16] }of this level, proved to be of the same thickness and character as it is overhead. The west lower level is about one hundred and fifty feet in length. At about 90 to 100 feet from the shaft there is a riser 40 feet high connecting with a level that was driven from shaft number 2 west. The vein in this riser is from 5 to 9 feet thick and the ore much the same character as in the East level.

---

10   Case No. 1924-005
11   Sweet, Palmer C. And Trimble, David, 1983, Virginia gold Resource date: Virginia Division of Mineral Resources Publication 45, 196 p.

> "The report stated the ore samples taken assayed on the average $18.00 gold per ton in 1890. One of the samples selected from the mine by J. J. Weicher showed a large amount of free gold and it assayed above $3,000.00 gold per ton or processed ore.
>
> "Professor J. F. Carll of Pleasantville, Pennsylvania examined the vein at the 120 foot level and exclaimed "I unhesitatingly pronounce that a true fissure vein." (A fissure vein was an old term used to describe a crack in the rock which had been filled with mineral or gold bearing material).

Mr. Earnest said, "In my opinion the Slate Hill Mine is very valuable, there are three other veins in a zone 200 feet wide and the mine would produce handsome returns."[12]

Things at the twin Vein Mine are still moving at a snail's pace and on March 27 the Colonel advised Charles Squier that the mill will not be operating until at least April 23 due to the illness of their head carpenter.[13]

This development could jeopardize the payment of the $10,000 mortgage which could result in the loss of the property through foreclosure by the Dolans.

On March 28, Clarence Cosby delivered the Boiler, a Duplex pump and some other related items which weighed a total of 41,710 pounds to the C&O railroad depot in Richmond. The machinery was loaded onto flatcar No. 300237. Without road access the machinery and materials cannot reach the Twin Vein Mine; unless they can find a new way through, since the road was closed. The machinery was held in Richmond pending the resolution of the dispute. For some reason the boards had not been removed since the injunction was issued on the 20th of March.[14]

On March 29, Charles Squier told the Colonel,

> 'I received your letter of the 23rd and I have been too busy to answer sooner. However, I yesterday placed sufficient funds in our treasurers hands, verses a company convertible note, to permit him

---

12 Slate Hill Mine Report by D. F. Ernest, 1892
13 March 27, 1924, Note from Col. Thomas R. Marshall to Charles B. Squier
14 March 28, 1924, Freight Bill from C&O Rail Road

A SQUABBLE

to send you an additional check for $1,500.00 toward the mill house construction expenses, which leaves approximately $1,000.00 you will need before completion, according to your former estimates-this $1,500.00 will reach you by letter not later than next Monday morning, and the increased weekly pay-roll of $375.00 was sent in time to reach you today or sooner.

"I regret to hear of the matter of the roadway obstruction upon the part of the Slate Hill People, and presume this is merely in the nature of what we call blackmail! I hope you have no further trouble in this regard! This is one of these matters, which should be definitely legally fixed (as to the public status of the road)-shall I ask Battle to go over and fix it up? (Charles Squier was apparently unaware at this time that the Colonel had hired Gordon, Gordon and Crank a local firm to represent the Company}.

"We have not yet sold the 200 shares-business has turned bad here again with all of this political rubbish in Washington! Let me know your Richmond dealer's best figures on the"Ford"trucks, before ordering them.

"I am much disappointed to hear you will not have everything all ready before April 23rd., as we had figured to be operating by the first-I appreciate the two bad snow-storms delayed us some, but did not think it would set us back that much. It is indeed too bad about the valuable head-carpenter! I had the first Allis-Chalmers note for $3,750.00 for machinery extended for another 45 days-it was due yesterday! They are both now due May 15th.,do you think Dolan will re-extend the $10,000.00 loan on May1st.?[15] Foreclosure by the Dolans loomed on the horizon as Charles Squier, pressed for cash, searched for a way to save the mine.

---

15   March 29, 1924, Letter from Charles B. Squier to Col. Thomas R. Marshall

On March 30 Squier acknowledged a small amount of good news from the Colonel.

> "I am pleased to have your latest letter of the 28th.inst., that you are now encountering lovely spring weather, and that the mill-house construction is proceeding very nicely! The matter of the public right of way of the road to our property from the concrete highway should be settled for all time in due legal form-do you wish me to request Battle to assist you therein?
>
> "I am glad to hear the100-foot level has been opened up an additional <u>211</u> feet, and trust the ore bodies are proving up satisfactorily! Do you think it at all likely that the fissure veins such as we have, might soon run <u>all quartz, without</u> any paying gold values-this is very IMPORTANT, and I should like to have your personal opinion!
>
> "We are sending down next week merely the increased pay-roll ($375.00), and trust you have been able to put on the extra five-men who will be able to pile up a lot of ore on the dump in a short time! Let me know the quotations on the "Ford"trucks? Are you absolutely sure that we shall be operating <u>not LATER than May 1st</u>? Also, will Mrs. Dolan give us another extension of the mortgage of $10,000.00 for six months more from May1st-if you can get her to do this, I will give the loan<u> my personal</u> <u>endorsement</u>, as additional security of the principal and interest!"[16]

On April 2 Eugene Perry wrote the Colonel. "I should have written you before and have no excuse except the usual one, laziness. C. B. S. has shown me several of your letters and I am glad that our proposition is now nearing completion. I am glad you got the chickens and hope they are going to produce some good stock and give us a chance to have a good scrap. (This possibly is a reference to an activity known as cock fighting, which has been illegal in Virginia since 1887.) A

---

16   March 30. 1924, Letter from Charles B. Squier to Col. Thomas R Marshall

A SQUABBLE

letter from my dog man tells me that the puppy has had a bad attack of eczema. It is not contagious but in some cases means losing the dog. He later wrote me that the puppy had improved to such an extent that he believed she was out of danger but suggested that I send her to some dog hospital in Brookline, Massachusetts. Since it is not contagious, don't you think it would be wise to have her sent to Mineral? He tells me that in spite of her youth she stood a perfect point this fall and he thinks that she is the best dog he has raised. Let me know what you think. When I come down I am going to bring you some very delightful stuff that grows in Scotland and which I have only recently fallen heir to."[17] **Photograph 55** shows what the pointer looked like. They are called pointers because when a quail is found they position their body so it actually points to the bird's location and this helps the hunter bag the bird It is also possible that Eugene Perry's reference to delightful stuff is code for Scotch whiskey which was known to be smuggled into northern cities during prohibition.

PHOTOGRAPH NO. 55

THE POINTER

---

17   April 2, 1924, Letter from Eugene Perry ro Col. Thomas R. Marshall

Construction on the mill continued with all haste possible as they awaited the results of the court battle over the road. On April 4 Charles Squier instructed the Colonel to telegraph to him at once the names of the parties in New York who own the Slate Hill property. He also advised the Colonel that Battle would represent them if Gordon was not there when the case came up on Monday the 7th.[18]

Three days later the Colonel sent a telegram to Mr. Richardson of the Slate Hill Mine at 11 Broadway, New York,

> "Have two car loads machinery at Pendleton station. Please wire me at Mineral permission to haul it through Slate Hill property to our mill. No inconvenience or damage can occur to your property."[19]

On April 8, news from Charles Squier arrives regarding the road closure.

> "After receiving your telegram last Saturday, I communicated with Mr. Richardson on the telephone, and ascertained that he is the Vice President of the Richman Co. owning the Slate Hill property- he seemed inclined to be friendly, and said as far as he knew, Mr. McSween, had not been instructed to try to block our access over the roadway but that he thought the roadway should be made a regular public highway, with which I agree, PROVIDED there is an agreement between the parties owning the three properties which the road traverses, that they shall each and all have access over same-this is another of those matters that is better to have <u>definitely</u> covered in legal form. I wrote Battle to look out for the matter Monday at Louisa-it is better to always get Battle for all legal work, and not to bring in Gordon or any other lawyer, as that complicates matters and may be more costly."[20]

---

18 April 4, 1924, Letter from Charles B. Squier to Col. Thomas R. Marshall
19 April 7, 1924, Telegram from Col. Thomas R. Marshall to Charles B. Squier
20 April 8, 1924, Letter from Charles B. Squier to Col. Thomas R. Marshall

A SQUABBLE

On April 10 the case was argued by counsel, during which witnesses stated it was never a public road. This was bad news for the Colonel. The injunction was vacated by Judge Alexander T. Browning. McSween wins, the Twin Vein Mining Company had to pay the court costs and buy a right of way from H. H. Walton.[21] There is no evidence that a road was ever built on the right of way purchased from Walton and today the 50 foot right of way is fenced and cows graze there.

Squier had more questions for the Colonel in his letter of April 8.

> "Do you know if the Dolans would extend the loan another three months? Battle reported to me he thought you could not be operating before the 1st. of May, and perhaps somewhat later-I do not quite understand why we are delayed nearly two months longer than your estimates made in January, even if bad weather and the head-carpenter's health threw you out some weeks, unless the machinery has not come, and is not up to specifications, and I thought all of the Allis-Chalmers material and equipment had been delivered complete, and that the boiler was being tested in Richmond, and would be delivered very shortly. Please let me hear your latest at once as we have not heard from you in a long time."[22]

Squier was in a financial squeeze and the Colonel did not seem particularly interested in providing the information he desperately needed.

---

21 Louisa County Court Chancery Case No. 109-1926-013
22 April 8, 1924, Letter from Charles B. Squier to Col. Thomas R. Marshall

ROLLING ALONG

In a letter to the Colonel dated April 11 Squier wrote,

> "Please let me know at once if the Dolans are willing to give us another extension of three months on all or half of the trust deed of $10,000.00 due May1st.- or, if not, do you think it can be procured through some local bank or individual in your district, with all the machinery, buildings, etc., as a straight mortgage for one year? The delay in our recovering gold puts an additional expense strain on me. You had better get the two "Ford" trucks ordered from your local agent- it will be much better and just as cheap. Let me know the exact amount you will want deposited, and I will instruct Sutphen accordingly. Mr. Richardson informed me over the telephone that he had instructed McSween to let you have the right of way over the road for the machinery, etc., so I trust. you will have no more trouble in that line- but, if you do, wire me at once, and I will get in touch with the owners who seem to be friendly. I called their attention to the undeniable fact that the development of our property would tend to benefit the value of theirs- I would not have any words with McSween about it if possible.
>
> "Mr. Coghill, who has been in North Carolina for several weeks, will come to Mineral some time soon now, and then you can let him see how you are progressing."[1]

On April 14th., the Colonel traveled to Richmond after having removed the barriers from the road. The voucher for the trip shows he charged the company

---

[1] April 11, 1924, Letter from Charles B. Squier to Col. Thomas R. Marshall

$11 which seems to be a bit excessive. The trip was necessary so he could inspect the loaded machinery and verify the completeness of it prior to it being sent to Pendleton.

On April 16, the 41,710 pound load of equipment from Clarence Cosby of Richmond, Virginia finally arrived at the railroad station on car No.300237.[2] From there it was transported to the mine by an early example of a modern tractor and trailer in **Photograph No. 56**. The fight with McSween over the road added 18 more days to a project already running seriously behind.

Photograph No.57. The boiler had been unloaded as close to where it will be set {installed} as possible. The Dorr Classifier is located in the rear center, behind the boiler. Some of the smoke stack is stored on the ground to the right and the some of the Tangye engine parts can be seen in the rear. The installation of this machinery will take more than a week to complete.

PHOTOGRAPH NO. 56

THE BOILER FOR THE MILL ARRIVES

---

2   April 15, 1924 Freight Bill from C&O Rail Road

ANATOMY OF A GOLD MINE

PHOTOGRAPH NO. 57

MACHINERY PARTS

Colonel Marshall sent a telegram to Charles Squier on April 17 of saying,

"I have removed the barriers across the roadway."[3]

On April 20, Squier told the Colonel,

"Replying to your letter of the 17th. inst., I think you were quite justified in removing the barriers across the roadway, in as much as I had telegraphed you several times that Richardson, the officer of the Richman Company with whom I have frequently talked over the telephone, told me he had instructed McSween to cooperate with you and to allow the roadway to be open for our use, although it must not be declared a public highway, which also has its advantages to us in a certain protection caused by a private road.

---

3 April 17, 1924 Telegram from Col. Thomas R. Marshall to Charlse B. Squier

Richardson informs me McSween is one of the officers as well as a director of their company which gives him a bit more leeway.

"I feel sure your check for last week's payroll arrived O.K., as Sutphen is very reliable and had the necessary funds in hand- we will try to send you the $500 advance toward your salary in arrears next week, although you will appreciate that our two months delay in commencing operation has considerably embarrassed me financially, as it has meant the payroll had to be continued, or over $2,500 more than we had planned to have to put up, before some income came in. You were originally to have things running by March 15th., now I feel sure it will not be before May 15th.! Of course, the spring has been bad, and you had trouble with the head carpenter's illness- but these could hardly account for two months delay- did you have any trouble assembling the machinery- how long did McSween set you back? PLEASE LET ME KNOW AT ONCE IF THERE IS ANY CHANCE OF DOLAN EXTENDING THE LOAN DUE MAY FIRST?"[4]

Progress toward installing the machinery continued and the boiler has been moved toward the area where it will be installed. The rod mill will have to be moved out of the way so the boiler may be moved to the rear of main structure. **Photograph 58** The rod mill is just to the rear of the boiler. **Photograph No. 59** The pile of bricks at the left marks the future location for rear of the boiler. **Photograph No. 60** The rod mill has been moved out of the way so the boiler may be moved further to the rear of the building **Photograph No. 61**. The boiler is in position and has been suspended by links which are attached to the I-Beam frame above it. This boiler installation is different from that of the shaft house because the shaft house boiler was supported by the wall which surrounded it. This boiler is suspended from the I-beam frame and will have a wall surrounding it which will not bear the weight of the boiler. **Illustration 15**

---

4   April 20, 1924 Letter from Charles B. Squier to Col. Thomas R. Marshall

PHOTOGRAPH NO. 58

ROD MILL AND BOILER

PHOTOGRAPH NO. 59

MOVING ROD MILL

PHOTOGRAPH 60

RELOCATION OF THE BOILER

PHOTOGRAPH NO. 61

BOILER INSTALLED IN FRAME

ANATOMY OF A GOLD MINE

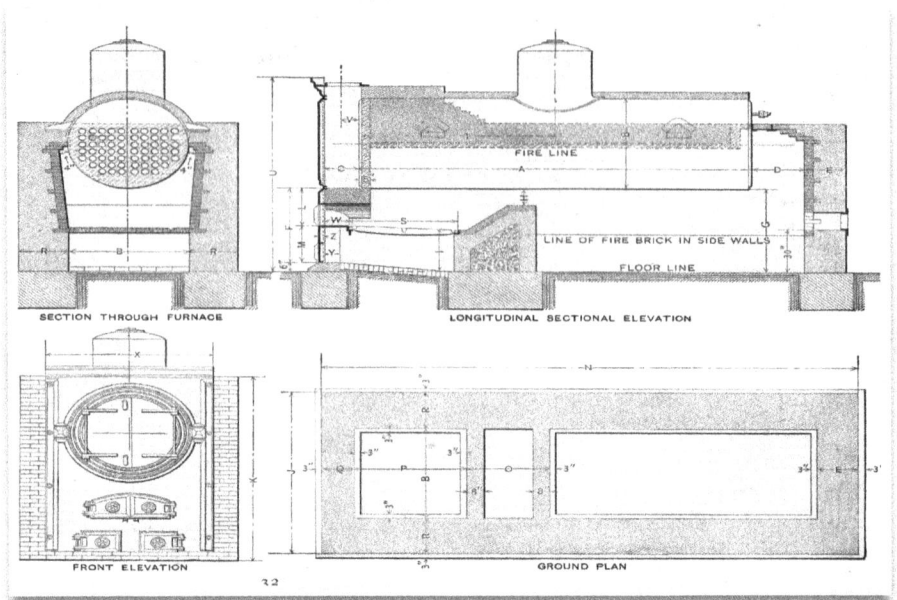

ILLUSTRATION NO. 15: BOILER INSTALLATION
ERIE CITY IRON WORKS

Colonel Marshall ordered the two Ford trucks on April 19 from Mr. Frank Reynolds of the Louisa Hardware Company in Louisa, Virginia. The Colonel sent Charles Squier the financial details of the purchase. The two trucks with dump bodies, seats and extra transmissions cost $645.30 each for a total cost of $1290.60. The Louisa Hardware Company agreed to sell them on the basis of a $690.60 down payment in cash, with the balance divided into four $150.00 installments of 30, 60, 90, and 120 days. The company was responsible for interest, fire, and accident insurance. They also offered alternative terms of a cash payment of $462.60 and eight monthly installments of $115.00 each.[5]

Sometime during the week of April 14th, the Colonel had written to R. E. Dolan in Brooklyn, New York concerning the extension of payment on the bond. On April 22, Dolan indicated his inability to come to Mineral on May 1st, and suggested the Colonel have John Battle prepare the necessary papers and send them to him at 1076 East 17th Street, Brooklyn, New, York for his signature.[6]

---

5 Price quotation for Ford trucks from Louisa Hardware Co.
6 April 22, 1924, Letter from R. E. Dolan to Col. Thomas R. Marshall

Time was becoming a critical factor for Charles Squier, a $10,000.00 mortgage was coming due and there was still no money coming from the mine with which to pay it. The mine and all of the equipment could be lost to the Dolans if they decided not allow them more time to pay and foreclose.

Around April 27 Colonel Marshall received a reply from R. E. Dolan concerning his second letter which was written on April 25nd asking if they would be coming to Mineral on May 1. Dolan said,

> "Yours of the twenty fifth was received late yesterday afternoon. It was the first and only communication I have had from you since we left Mineral in February"[7]

There appears to be a game afoot here and the Colonel may pay the price later, he is in jeopardy of losing the $5,000.00 commission promised him by Mrs. Dolan, because the payment date stipulated by Mrs Dolan has passed. There is the ever present clause, "on or before maturity" which the Dolans believe will allow them to avoid paying the Colonel.

Unfortunately, the mill is still not operational. The value of the gold ore they have stock piled has not been proven and the Colonel was for some reason trying to convince Charles Squier to install a second 50 ton per day plant. This is a very strange request considering the financial difficulties and conflicting assay results which have plagued the project from the beginning.

Charles Squier replied on May 8.

> "Your letters of the 25th. Of April ultmo, and the 6$^{th.inst}$., duly received. I did not come down this last time, as I want to go down when all is ready to have the wheels go round, and when my friend; Mr. Ernest Howe, who is a mining engineer with great experience in California with gold mines, will come down with me, and perhaps several other gentlemen, and I knew it will be soon now. I think I

---

[7] April 27, 1924, Letter, from R. E. Dolan to Col. Thomas R. Marshall

wrote you of this in a previous letter. I am going to the country to my small summer home in Vermont for the summer season, and am closing my apartment here for summer on the 28th.inst., I shall probably come down on the 16th. or 23rd. inst. even if the property is not a working proposition. You will appreciate that all of these delays and large expenditures have been very embarrassing to me, as I have had to personally fork up over $50,000.00 to date. It is for this reason that we must begin to produce gold as soon as possible and some considerable sums of money will have to be duly returned to me, before I will consider advancing money for the additional fifty-ton unit, which would also probably mean sinking another shaft at considerable expense to feed out as much as 100 tons per day!"[8]

PHOTOGRAPH NO. 62 REAR VIEW OF THE BOILER

Could the Colonel have been trying to sucker Charles Squier into sinking another $50,000 into a mine he knew would never produce any gold so he can take control of it all? From the evidence in the photographs the mill will not be finished for another month, construction continued and they begin bricking the boiler. **Photograph No. 62** The rear of the boiler and the fire

---

8   May 8, 1924, Letter from Charles B. Squier to Col. Thomas R. Marshall

tubes through which hot gases flow can be seen. The fire tubes are surrounded by water which is heated by the hot gasses inside them thereby producing steam.

Squier continued on the 8th.,

> "Perry and Sutphen seemed pleased with what they saw, but said they did not go down in the mine as you said it was very wet there- I trust this does not mean you are often unable to continue taking out ore on account of water, etc. To feed the mill is the great problem! Mr. Coghill seemed to think you then had not over 400 tons <u>on</u> the ore <u>dump</u>.
>
> "I am glad to know the insurance is in force on the mill house and trust you are also covering the 5 extra men in the mine workings under owners liability for workman's compensation! We will send you the last $1,000.00 due on the mill construction next week- will that suffice? Also what is still due on the Ford trucks, and when will that be due?
>
> "Has Dolan yet turned up to be paid off- Battle has the funds in hand as you know for immediate payment? What has happened in re the options you mentioned so long ago, and the covering agreement drawn up by my attorneys which I sent you so long ago- it seems to me strange it has been delayed so long- these things are always better signed up and delivered!
>
> "I trust you will make every effort to actually locate the second vein before Mr. Howe and I come down. Have you taken any assays lately, and how is the vein running in dimensions as you open up!
>
> "If the Allis-Chalmers people do not arrange to send a man down to instruct you on how the mill should be run- please let me know at once- there ought be no delays on this score, if you give them some advance notification, and let me call up Denison to expedite matters.
>
> "I shall be very anxious to come down and see how our plant looks- the other officers seemed to think it appeared to be very well done- if we later have to sink another shaft, how much would that

cost approximately? Please forward at once <u>all</u> <u>vouchers</u> to Barker or Sutphen to make up the books at least up to May 1."[9]

The Colonel and John Battle were concerned that the Dolans had not come to Mineral and wrote to them in Brooklyn, New York on the 6th. and 7th. asking why they did not come to Mineral to be paid on the first of May. Once again, this was serious because the payment to the Dolans had not been made on time and the Twin Vein Mine was in danger of foreclosure.

R. E. Dolan replied May 8.

"Yours of the seventh and also one from Mr. Battle dated the 6th. was received in the last mail this afternoon. Mr. Battle states he was surprised that we were not in Mineral on May first and you state money would have been paid had we been there. Now Marshall, you know I gave you ample notice, for on April 22nd. I wrote you that it would not be convenient for us to get to Virginia by the first and suggested you advise Mr. Battle to send papers here for execution. I have your letter where you say you have advised your board and will have Mr. B. send the papers here, now why was it not done? Surely it was no fault of ours when you had ample notice. Here is nearly a third of a month gone by since maturity and nothing done.

"You are doing Mrs. Dolan an injustice when you further state that she owes you three hundred dollars. I am surprised that you would make such an assertion to Mr. Battle.

"We had fully expected to be in Virginia when the bond matured (May 1st} but matters here compelled me to postpone the trip, however, we hope to be down there before long."[10] The Dolans have the Colonel right where they want him.

---
9   May 8, 1924, Squier
10 Allis-Chalmers Manufacturing Co specifications, June 2, 1923

The men continued to work on the installation of the engine which will bring the mill closer to operation. Some of the engine's components can be seen in **Photograph No.63.** The engine had to be moved into the mill building and then onto the concrete foundation where it was bolted down employing bolts approximately one inch in diameter.

The next big job was the installation of the crusher. **Photograph 64** The crusher on the left, sits on boards to keep it off of the wet ground and the grizzly still leans against the white oak tree.

Photograph No. 65 The 7inch by 10 inch Standard Style "B" Blake Crusher is about to be hauled up to the third story of the mill building where it was installed. The body of the crusher can be seen as it is pulled by ropes up a ramp constructed of heavy timbers. The flat belt pulley and fly wheels have been removed to lighten the load. The worker standing at the bottom of the ramp was directly in the path of the crusher's iron frame and risked very serious injury if anything went wrong.

PHOTOGRAPH NO. 63

CLOSE UP OF ENGINE PARTS

PHOTOGRAPH NO. 64

BLAKE CRUSHER

PHOTOGRAPH NO. 65

INSTALLING THE CRUSHER

The Colonel sent a check on May 3 to Clarence Cosby in Richmond, Virginia. for a Worthington Duplex 6 inch by 4 inch by 6 inch steam powered water pump which would be used to supply water for the boiler and the mill while processing ore.[11] The pump was designated as a 6in by 4in by 6in. The 6 inch measurement referred to the 6 inch steam cylinder which provided power, the 4 inch measurement described the 4 inch water pumping cylinder and the second 6 inch measurement referred to the stroke of the cylinder. **Illustration 16** The mill plans specified a 2 inch pipe as the main supply line and a 2 inch boiler supply line. The 25 horse power boiler used a great quantity of water and a small pond was built to impound what the Colonel hoped would be a sufficient water supply for the boiler and mill. If the water supply was inadequate the mill would not be able to run at full capacity which will have a negative impact on production.

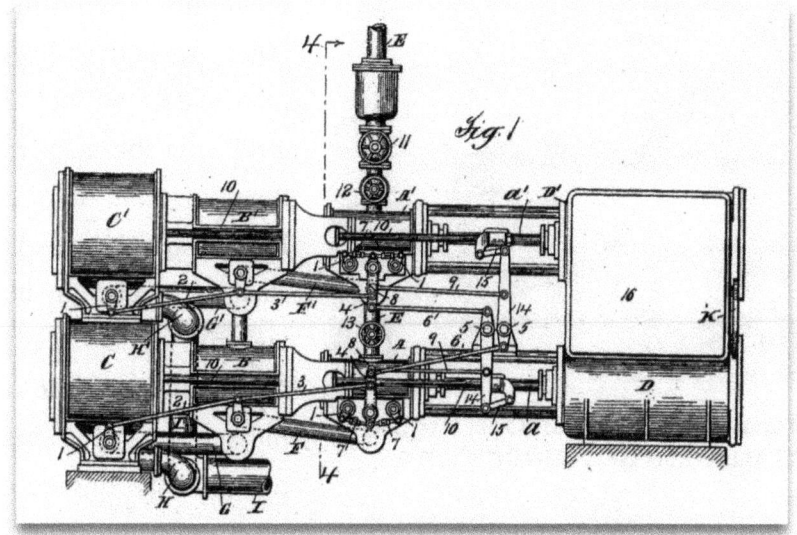

**ILLUSTRATION NO. 16: WORTHINGTON 6 X 4 X 6
DUPLEX STEAM PUMP
UNITED STATES PATENT AND TRADEMARK OFFICE**

The bricking up of the boiler was completed on May 9 and the labor for the work cost $90.00.[12]

---

11 May 6, 1924, Receipt .from Clarence Cosby Co.
12 May 9, 1924, Hand written receipt

ANATOMY OF A GOLD MINE

On May 10 the Colonel purchased 215 feet of 30 pound per yard railroad rails and 225 feet of 50 pound per yard rails from the Sulfur Mining and Railroad Company. These rails would be used as track for the mine cars and skip. Railroad rails are listed as weighing a certain number of pounds per linear yard, the heavier the rail the more that can be transported on them.[13]

After the boiler bricking had been completed the smoke stack was installed on top of it This operation required the use of a taller gin pole to hoist the approximately 50 foot tall smoke stack over the existing wall and then lower it onto the boiler. **Photograph No. 66** The smoke stack is resting on the ground and the miners are preparing to hoist it up while one of the miners makes some adjustments to the rigging of the gin pole. **Photograph No. 67** The miners have succeeded in raising the stack and it now rests against the roof while one of them moves the attachment point on the stack so it can be lifted higher. **Photograph No. 68** the smoke stack is suspended from the rigging and the miners have achieved some advantage, so, they celebrate. **Photograph No. 69** The stack has been raised a bit more on its way to its proper location at the top front of the boiler

PHOTOGRAPH NO. 66 SMOKE STACK INSTALLATION SEQUENCE 1 OF 5

---

13   May 10, 1924, Receipt from The Sulfur mining and Railroad Co.

PHOTOGRAPH NO. 67

HOISTING STACK, 2 OF 5

PHOTOGRAPH NO. 68

CELEBRATION, 3 OF 5

PHOTOGRAPH NO. 69

ALMOST THERE, 4 OF 5

PHOTOGRAPH NO. 70

STACK INSTALLED WITH SMOKE EXITING, 5 OF 5

Photograph 70 The smoke stack is in place and the guy wires are tight preventing it from toppling. The gin pole is still attached and the position of the hoisting rope location on the smoke stack should be noted. The most important aspect of this moment in time is there is smoke emanating from the top of the smoke stack; the boiler is being fired!

May 12 rolls around and Squier told the Colonel,

> "I lunched with Sutphen today- he will send to reach you not later than Saturday next a check for $1,375, being the final payment on the mill-house construction, and the weekly pay-roll of $375. The only other item we have to meet is the final payment on the "Ford" trucks, and if you can stave this off three months, so much the better!
>
> "You will appreciate that I have personally put in virtually the entire money for the mine except some $2,400 raised by Mr. Perry and $6,500.00 raised by me, while the balance of nearly $50,000.00 I have put up myself! Therefore it is vitally necessary to show substantial profits as soon as possible, as I will most certainly not put up anymore for development, until some considerable amount is returned!
>
> "Also, we must have our vouchers for all expenditures from Feb.1 to May 1st. As soon as you can possibly arrange, which is very IMPORTANT! I expect to be in Mineral on the morning of June 6th., with Mr. Howe, a man of large experience on such matters, of whom I have written you before, and then we can go over all the details, and we will hope the entire plant will be ready to operate! Where are the papers covering the options on adjoining properties, which I sent you for the signatures some months ago?"[14]

---

14   May 12, 1924, Letter from Charles B. Squier to Col. Thomas R. Marshall

On May 18 Charles Squier told Colonel Marshall,

> "I am in touch with Mr. Ernest Howe, M. E.(Mining Engineer) , of Litchfield, Conn., and am expecting to come to Mineral about June 5th. with him, at which time, I trust the "wheels will be ready to turn."
>
> You will, of course, appreciate that I have taken much of the "Twin Vein" on faith in you, and that any present or future financing depends very largely upon me, at least until we run into large "paying" values! It is for this reason that my better common sense tells me that we must now, with our present equipment, actually show very considerable returns to me, who hold the company's notes, before any more money goes into development of the property!
>
> "Please put off as long as possible the final payment for the "Ford" trucks- we are now almost "over the top" and should soon show results, which will concretely justify our faith in the property! I will notify you by telegram exactly what day Mr. Howe and I will arrive at Mineral."[15]

Unfortunately, the Colonel had still not done as he said he would do and Charles Squier prods him,

> "Have you duly sent the long promised vouchers and receipts up to May 1st. to Barker or Sutphen? How about the options on the adjoining properties? They are long overdue of legalization!"[16]

Charles Squier informed the Colonel on May 24 of his future plans.

> "We are closing up our apartment here, and removing to our country estate on the 4th of June, Wednesday, after which date

---
15 May 18, 1924, Letter from Charles B. Squier to Col. Thomas R. Marshall
16 May 18, 1924, Squier

please address me: 24, Monument Avenue, Old Bennington, Vermont: send telegrams to: C. B. Squier, BENNINGTON, VERMONT. We are leaving there August 6th (leaving Bennington the 4th.) and sailing for Paris on the "Aquitania", to remain in Europe until around November 1st. when we will return to New York for the winter months.

I talked to Mr. Howe this morning- he is the great mining (especially gold-mine) expert engineer I mentioned, and he is holding himself free to come down with me the 6th. of June, Friday, which afternoon I shall come down from Bennington, and join him here for the 8:45 P.M. train to Doswell, we will arrive in Mineral on Saturday morning, June the 7th., about 9:09. We want to make a thorough inspection of the entire property- Mr. Howe will remain over until Sunday evening, if necessary, but otherwise we will take the 4:55 P.M. train back to Doswell the same day, reaching Washington that night, where we will investigate the history of the District about Mineral.(Howe would have gone to the United States Geological Survey in Washington, D. C.)

"It is most IMPORTANT that Mr. Howe have every opportunity of going down the shaft and examining thoroughly the ore bodies on the various levels, and I trust, in this connection, that you will by that time have definitely located the second vein to his entire satisfaction! I am naturally much interested in this trip, which I have so long anticipated, and shall be much interested to see all you have accomplished under, in many cases, most trying weather conditions!

Squier again asks,

"How about those options on the adjoining properties? You never mention them, and they should be quite safe before we commence production without, any possible hitch!"[17]

---

17 May 24, 1924, Letter from Charles B. Squier to Col. Thomas R. Marshall

PHOTOGRAPH NO. 71

A FEW MORE PARTS

Photograph 71 As the mill nears completion there are fewer and fewer machine parts to be found sitting around the mill building. The Dorr Classifier is still crated up and is positioned behind the front of the Colonel's car. The main gear for the rod mill is supported on boards until it can be installed..

On May 24 Squier continued,

> "Mr. Sutphen received your vouchers up to May 1st , and has turned them over to Barker to audit, and I expect to hear the results Monday noon next. Now that all the extra work of setting up the mill and equipment is over, and the expenses per week will be mostly labor, we must have our receipts or vouchers at the end of each month, and a statement of the weekly pay-rolls for each class of men.
>
> "Mr. Sutphen turned over to me your letter of the17th.inst, regarding the vouchers, etc. In regard to the matter of the deficit of $2,575.35, if everything for the mine equipment is not fully paid

ROLLING ALONG

without any outstanding claims or liens of any sort, any such must be paid at once to give us a clean "bill of health", so to speak, as a company. Your overdue salary of approximately 50% for the past year must wait a while for the following reasons: I have personally had to put up practically all the capital (some $45,000 to $50,000 over the less than $10,000 obtained from other sources}, and this had been much more than I reckoned on and there is no other way for us to get funds at this time except by advances from me personally which I can not keep up much longer. I had recently to borrow on good bank collateral some $15,000 to secure the money to pay off the Dolan loan, and for working capital, and I am not in a position to put up much more than the few hundreds we will need for operation before we are actually producing. I have found I can not rely upon anyone to raise money for us. We must produce very soon, and I feel your optimism regarding the property justifies your allowing your salary to lapse a bit longer! None of us here have received any emoluments whatsoever, nor do we expect any, and while you have done your work very well and saved us much money, it is all to your advantage as well as ours on account of your large block of stock, and your living expenses at Mineral is so very small that you must have saved for your family's expense much of the $2,500 approximately paid you so far! I have been carrying a big load and only my money and attendant faith in you have made the whole undertaking at all possible! It is for these reasons you must see the justice of my argument. We are running a pay-roll of $375 per week (or over $1,500 monthly), as I will not put up much more without results, justifying the quick return of the money invested!

"We will talk this all over when I come down. I am willing as we produce to go "50-50" with you in making up your salary right up to the date together with paying off the money advanced by me to the company vs. its notes and bonds I hold- this seems most reasonable to me, as it should only be less than one month for such production to catch up your salary to date that way, after which it would not be allowed again to run into arrears!

"Battle informs me the trust deed was duly paid off and has sent the cancelled papers here to me to place in the company's strong-box. I trust you have had no more trouble with McSween or any-one else- did Richardson come down to settle McSween, as he intimated he might do?

"What do you think of the danger that much of our ore is good quartz, but has never mineralized into gold in the process of time and nature? This is the one serious objection I have heard experts mention in regard to gold in Virginia in paying quantities!"[18]

During the month of May the Colonel bought a great deal of used parts from the old Sulfur Mine which were purchased at junk prices. Some of the items he acquired were valves which were used in the mill to control the flow of steam and water. One 5- inch valve cost $2.50, 400 pounds of 1 1/4- inch pipe were bought for $5.00, and 50 pounds of "junk'24- inch smoke stack cost him $.75 for a grand total of $30.15.[19]

On May 29 Clarance Cosby shipped the two iron boiler doors which weighed 125 pounds each.[20] The doors allow the fire tubes to be cleaned periodically to remove the ash or soot.

The ash acts as insulation which interferes with the transfer of heat to the water thereby reducing the efficiency of the boiler.

Additional items were purchased on May 31 from the Sulfur Mining and Railroad Company. The list included a 30- inch sheave for $2.00, similar to the one at the top of the head frame. Some scrap shaft for $.50 and two pillar block bearings which would have supported the sheave.[21]

---

18   May 24, 1924, Squier
19   Receipt from Sulfur Mining and Railroad Co.
20   May 29, 1924, Shipping bill from Clarence Cosby Co.
21   May 31, 1924, Receipt, Sulfur Mining and Railroad Co.

One small steam hoist which cost $50.00 was purchased from Walton & Wood.[22] While these parts do not seem important separately, together they could be used to construct a small version of a headframe which would have been attached to the side of the mill building. It would have operated as its larger cousin at the mine shaft. Ore from the trucks would be loaded into a small skip which was hoisted to the top of the mill building where it was dumped onto the grizzly and then put through the crusher. This method was one of the possibilities available to accomplish the task of feeding the ore into the mill without using a conveyor or a tramway. The tramway or conveyor would have cost Charles Squier even more money at a time when funds were short. The mill was nearly finished but all of the unforseen delays were costing Charles Squier a lot of money and the mine was still not producing ANY gold.

---

22 May 31, 1924, Receipt, Walton and Wood Co.

GETTING UP STEAM

Charles Squier wrote the Colonel on June1,1924.

"Your special- delivery letter of the 29th of May ultimo received Saturday A.M., and I am very sorry to hear of the weather bring so bad- it has certainly been the same here, and the weather bureau claims this is the Coldest May ever recorded since its founding in1871!

'We will arrive in Mineral on the A.M. train from Doswell on the 7th .inst. next Saturday, surely, and please be sure to have everything opened up and running well, as I particularly want to get Mr. Howe's expert opinion of our plant, ore reserves etc.

"I understand the man sent down from the Allis-Chalmers offices gets $15 per diem, plus his traveling expenses, at least that is their charge, so I trust he did not have to stay long! I believe this charge will be billed to us here by the Allis-Chalmers people, so you will not have to pay it, but let me know what it should be! I am sorry to hear the $500.00 sent you on account of your salary has been used for the company's needs, but you do not state for what, so how are we to know what to set down! I thought everything had been paid for, except the two "Ford" trucks, which you have paid part on, and arranged for time payment on the balance! Also, you say you have increased the force of men getting out ore, and that the $375.00 weekly pay-roll is not sufficient, but you do not say how much more is needed, so we are again in the dark!

"I will bring a check for $500.00 when I come down and Sutphen will send you the regular weekly check this coming week. (Colonel

Marshall's handwritten notation on his copy of the correspondence said,"did not do so.")

"I trust you have received my last letter as to the vouchers- We POSITIVELY MUST have this question of the expenditures more carefully tabulated and kept and must now have monthly statements. Our books are now only up to February the 1st., until you furnish us with the data missing in your last statements, and this places the company's books in very bad condition- we must know what the various kinds of labor items are, as you could easily kept track of on the slips Barker gave you when he was in Mineral. You do not seem to appreciate that a company can not be run in the loose manner of a partnership, which is entirely different, and not subject to the same laws! When the mill commences to run regularly, you will have a fixed number of men on exactly the same job all the time, and this will be much easier to keep track of, but we must have the figures to put down on the books as to what labor charges were for the different following items: 1) Shaft-house construction; 2) Mill-house construction; 3) Mining of ore for the dump; 4) Transporting machinery to site; 5) General or miscellaneous: items you cannot exactly charge to any of the other four headings!

"Regarding your overdue salary, it seems to me this can wait on the production of the mill, which according to your own frequent estimate, should bring in upwards of $20,000.00 net per month, depending on how the ore runs and figuring on 1,500 ton mined per each 30 days- one more month and your deficit can be easily paid off in full! Otherwise, I will personally have to put it up, which is extremely inconvenient on top of all the other amounts I have already advanced! I think you will appreciate the justice of this point of view, as it is financially an awful strain on me, and I get no help!"[1]

---

1   June 1, 1924, Letter from Charles B. Squier to Col. Thomas R. Marshall

On June 2 roofing material was being applied to the mill building to make it weather tight. The small inclined track way up the side of the mill building had to be completed before the gold ore can begin its journey through the state of the art gold processing plant. The day Charles Squier had waited for so long was nearly at hand, his financial embarrassments would be cured by the millions in gleaming yellow metal the Twin Vein mine held.

On June 4, Colonel Marshall sent the Dolans a letter threatening a lawsuit if the $5,000 fee for selling the Dolan property to Charles Squier and associates is not paid.[2]

Dolan replied on June 7, 1924.

> "Your threatening letter of the 4th of June was received yesterday and note the stand you say you will take. If you want the court to decide on any portion why not let them decide the whole thing? The writings speak for themselves. I was willing to go over the proposition with you in a friendly way but as you would have the courts settle a part we would be glad, if you so decide, to have the court go over the whole transaction. Mrs. Dolan now says she will adhere to the writings and on what they say and mean.
>
> "It is not necessary to have a "quarrel or fight with a woman" or anyone else because the papers, records and facts answer for themselves. It has been our desire to go over this thing in an amicable way and try to straighten out the differences of viewpoint, but apparently that is not your attitude.
>
> "I wrote you that I was and am still under the doctor's care but can go next week, therefore we are preparing to leave for Mineral as early as we can the coming week."[3]

---

2   June 4, 1924, Letter from Col. Thomas R. Marshall to Charles B. Squier
3   June 7, 1924, Letter from R. E. Dolan to Col. Thomas R. Marshall

GETTING UP STEAM

The Colonel took delivery of the two special order Ford trucks on June the 7. The extras included pneumatic tires for an additional charge of $415.38 for each truck, spring seats for an extra $15.00 each, Jumbo Transmissions installed for $75.00 each and H. B. 1 Man Dump Bodies with a 1 ton capacity for $139.50 each. The new trucks were powered by a 22 horse power engine. The total cost for the two trucks was $1,289.76. The Colonel paid $650.00 by check and the balance of $639.76 was financed on a 4 month note. These trucks would take the place of wagons.[4] The delivery of the trucks came in the nick of time, allowing them to finally feed the mill with gold ore the Colonel said would make them all very rich **Photograph No. 72**

PHOTOGRAPH NO. 72
STUMP REMOVAL 1920'S STYLE

June 7 continued to be a busy day for the Colonel because Charles Squier and Dr. Ernest Howe arrived in Mineral and had to be given the grand tour. Dr. Howe examined the mine and mill thoroughly. Squier was still not convinced that the mine would produce the millions in gold the Colonel had said it would. Dr. Howe

---

4   June 7, 1924, Delivery receipt Ford trucks from Louisa Hardware Co.

planned to examine records in Washington that described the characteristics of Virginia Gold deposits. When his investigations were complete he would render the findings concerning the mine based on the information obtained at The Bureau of Mines and Geological Survey.

Dr. Howe may have found that the characteristics of the gold deposits of Virginia and Louisa County particularly may have consisted of the following:

> "The Gold-bearing rocks of Louisa traverse the central portion of the county, in a southwesterly direction, in the form of a narrow but well defined belt. Near the center of the county and in the gold belt, 2 to 5 miles northeast of Mineral, Virginia, are the famous Louisa County pyrite mines. These large bodies of pyrite are probably contemporaneous in origin with the gold veins."[5]
>
> "The gold-bearing veins are quartz, which vary in texture from large crystalline masses to very fine saccharoidal (sugary) grains. In structure they vary from massive to thin platy or schistose bodies, both usually penetrated by closely spaced irregular fractures. The principal metallic content is auriferous pyrite which at times, is copper bearing and contains more or less admixed chalcopyrite. Within the weathered zone, which extends from the surface down to the local water level and accordingly is variable in depth, the quartz is rendered more or less porous or cellular and discolored or stained with iron oxide from the oxidation of the sulfide minerals, and the liberation of free or elementary gold. The degree of porosity and staining is proportional to the amount of the sulfide minerals present and the stage of oxidation. Below the local water level the veins are fresh, the sulfides are unaltered, and elementary gold is less frequent in occurrence."[6]
>
> "The vein structure is irregular lenticular, varying in width from a few inches to as many feet. Often the lenticular stringers are discon-

---

5   Watson Thomas, L., Mineral Resources of Virginia, Lynchburg, Virginia. J. P. Bell Company. 1907 pg 557
6   Watson Thomas L. Pg 551

tinuous. One stringer may dwindle to a thread or disappear and is replaced by another or by others."[7]

"The ore lenses of pyrite and the quartz veins carrying gold observe similar strike, (the direction of a horizontal line, drawn in the middle plane of a vein or stratum not horizontal[8]) dip (the inclination of a vein or stratum below horizontal[9]) and pitch (the inclination of vein, or of the longer axis of an ore body[10]). Traces of gold are found in the pyrite and small gold-bearing quartz veins which, according to W. H. Adams, formerly the manager of the Arminius Mines, are gold-bearing to the extent of from $4.00 to $15.00 per ton, are reported encountered in the mines on the hanging and foot-wall rocks."[11]

In 1924 gold was worth $20.67 per Troy ounce and at the time of this writing gold is worth approximately $1,300.00 per ounce. By June of 1924 Charles Squier had invested $50,000 in the mine which would buy 2,418.96 ounces of gold that would be worth $3.15 million today.

Squier told the Colonel on June 12,

"I have given Sutphen funds and instructions to send you $1,600.00 verses $2,000.00 face value bonds of the company discounted to him at 80% off face value. He will also send you this week a check for $400.00 for the pay-roll, after which I presume from your letter, as you say the pay-roll can be cut down $175.00 weekly, and has been running $525.00, it can be reduced to $350.00, which I will instruct Sutphen to send from now on- both of these checks will reach you by the end of this week, and I trust will tide over any difficulties. These two checks aggregating $2,000.00, should clear up the outstand-

---

7 Watson Thomas L. Pg 552
8 Raymond, R. W., A Glossary of Mining and Metallurgical Terms, from Vol. IX, Transactions of the American Institute of Mining Engineers, Easton, Pa. 1881 pg 85
9 Raymond, pg 29
10 Raymond, pg 65
11 Watson, Thomas L., Mineral Resources of Virginia, Lynchburg, Virginia. J. P. Bell Company 1907, pg 557

ing bills of $1,310.00 and pay back almost all of the amount you advanced for additional labor charges last week- we must go easy now on expense, as I am under considerable strain in this regard!

"I have before me Howe's written report on the mine, and he says as to the character of the veins: "At the depth to which mining has extended, the one hundred foot level, no fresh rock or vein matter occurs"- what do you make of that? He told me his one criticism of the whole undertaking was that we had not opened nearly enough ore bodies to justify us putting in such a mill, before we had done much more sampling and exploration work! Have you gotten any written assay reports, since the one Tainter took last year? How about the new skip- have you been successful in getting one at once, so we can immediately commence operations? Also, have you received the $750.00 from the sale of the small, old mill to the two gentlemen? This would help us along some!

"In regard your letter of the 8th. inst., the figures you furnish in respect to the labor items are what we want, but they must go back far enough thus separated for the different items to let us enter on the ledger just what were the labor charges for the shaft house, transportation, and other headings complete- please send this in at once, and give us now monthly statements, which you will find yourself much less trouble!

"When you commence to operate, please be very careful to check up on the output, and to send same in just as soon as possible, so let me know when final payment on the two "Ford" trucks comes due.

"Allow me to congratulate you upon the good job at the mill, economically done, and fine in arrangement and construction. It might be good policy to improve the road in a little. Please let me know the actual cost of the little electric light plant you mentioned, and if you can get same and assemble it at short notice!"[12]

---

12   June 12, 1924, Letter from Charles B. Squier to Col. Thomas R. Marshall

GOING FOR THE GOLD

With the mill now complete, the quest for millions in gold can begin in earnest. Charles Squier told the Colonel on June 16,

> "I am wondering if you secured the skip last week, and if same is set up and is the mill now really working? Have you been able to extract any real values from the ore? I will endeavor to send you through Sutphen this week $800.00 more, which you can place to the credit of the weekly pay-roll, at the rate of about $375.00 per week, as per your estimate of cutting it from $525.00 to $375.00 in view of the mill being now all finished.
>
> "Sutphen writes he has had no further statements or vouchers from you. Won't you <u>please at once</u> send him your separate labor items, i.e., the exact amount for labor to charge to date to the (1) mill-house; (2) shaft-house; (3) transportation of machinery; (4) cutting and stacking wood; (5) miscellaneous. All these items must be entered separately to show our exact costs for the various important items! Also, can't you get a complete receipted bill for the lumber! I presume this was all used for the mill house?
>
> "Have you sold the small mill yet for the $750.00 agreed to with the Philadelphia syndicate? I shall be in New York tomorrow night and will see Sutphen Wednesday at Horton's office- I return here Friday."[1]

---

1   June 16, 1924, Letter from Charles B. Squier to Col. Thomas R. Marshall

Squier wrote the Colonel on June 24.

> "Your last letter of the 17th.inst. received at the Ritz-Carlton Hotel New York- I returned here from New York Friday and expect to be in New York again at the same hotel from next Sunday, the 29th.inst., to Wednesday following the 2nd. of July. I plan to go down to Mineral about the middle of July, to see everything in full working order which should be accomplished by that time and to hold the stockholders meeting which will be called to authorize the funding of the companys notes to me vs. cash advances into a first mortgage lien vs. the entire company's property in lieu of the present outstanding convertible notes!
>
> "Sutphen sent you last week in time to arrive in Mineral Saturday, a check for $750.00 which was to be for two full weeks of pay-roll @ $375.00 which was the amount we mentioned, after the extra work of erecting the mill-house was terminated! According to my figuring, if no money is sent down this week, it will leave the company with only $350.00 to keep on running, unless not enough so, I shall arrange to hand Sutphen another, new check for $1,000.00, with which the company can carry on as best it may! WE MUST, HOWEVER, pare expenses to the bone, as I cannot continually advance these large sums promiscuously! I am glad you sold the little mill for $700.00, and hope you now have the cash in hand which will give us nearly two weeks pay-roll! I trust I will not have to advance much more money. I shall not instruct Sutphen to send you anymore this week, but will send you at least $1,000.00 next week, which should reach you not later than Friday, the fourth of July. Perhaps you can commence to assemble the material and machinery for the installation of the little hydro-electric light plant, which would seem to be very necessary for the continual operation of the mill by night, and which you said you could set up complete for under $1,000.00.

"Regarding vouchers, it is MOST VITAL that our company accounts be kept in the best order and quite up to date- you too appreciate the wisdom of that. You showed me such lists and papers in Mineral, which I neglected to take away, which would seem to show you have all the receipts and accounts and bills we want- the originals of all these MUST be kept here in New York or in Morristown, as Barker elects to be the most simple and convenient for him, as he is paid very little at present! Why can you not send us at once the vouchers for the $1,300.00 of additional bills for the mill-house construction which you showed me at Mineral, and which have since been paid for the mill-house construction, etc.,. and also get the LONG MISSING and as yet inaccurate account for the mill-house lumber? I will instruct Sutphen to return to you any vouchers you have sent regarding labor to separate into the various headings indicated in my last letter, but I know there are no detailed ones! We must have these matters in business-like shape before sending down more funds!

"Nothing was done at the recent directors meeting, which was not held, as we must have a stockholders meeting for the purpose, which will be held at Mineral the next time I come down."[2]

On June 26 Squier asked the Colonel more questions.

"Have you gotten real results in values yet? Also, have you gotten a suitable skip, have you done anything about assembling the little hydroelectric plant for lighting the mill, and have you gotten the cash in from the sale of the Dolan's little hand mill for $700.00? Sutphen reports I have advanced to the company so far the sum of $53,400.00, a large amount to be paid off, and the reason why I cannot continue to put up much more without definite earnings! This is over and above the $10,000.00 I originally put into

---

2 June 24, 1924, Letter from Charles B. Squier to Col. Thomas R. Marshall

the syndicate to buy the property! We have now in hand enough for two weeks pay-roll, and that is all- I am hoping by then the mine will carry itself at least.

"I received a letter from Mr. Howe today, asking how we were getting along, and also for a map of the property, which I will send to him when I am in New York next week. I will be at the Ritz next Sunday night, the 29th. inst until Tuesday, the 2nd. of July in the A.M. at the Ritz.

"Sutphen has instructed Barker to send you all the vouchers we have covering labor charges-you probably have them by now- we must as soon as possible have your full statements made up therefrom, showing the various labor items, as set forth in my former letters, also send the vouchers back, together with all other ones you may have, and be sure to get a complete bill to date from the lumber company for our files. I do not think you realize how behind-hand our books are here and how imperfectly they have necessarily had to be kept to date on account of lack of important data! This is a very SERIOUS LACK and must be remedied at once.

"Sutphen and I will come to Mineral some time in July to hold the directors meeting and the ensuing stockholders meeting, which should have been done long ago to ratify and legalize the bond and note issues to me covering the funds advanced to date and in the future, if need be."[3]

On June 27 Colonel Marshall traveled to the Powers & Taylor Drug Company in Richmond, Virginia in order to pick up two five pound jugs of mercury at $1.50 per pound and two pounds of cyanide potash at $1.10 per pound which were to be used in the mill.[4]

---

3   June 26, 1924, Letter from Charles B. Squier to Col. Thomas R. Marshall
4   Receipt from Powers & Taylor Drug Company

The mercury was applied as a coating to the copper amalgamating plates so they would catch gold, and once the gold was captured by the plates it was necessary to separate it from the mercury. The miners conducted what was called a clean-up During the clean-up the gold and mercury amalgam was scraped off the plates, and the gold was later separated from the mercury using a mercury retort. The process consisted of first placing the amalgam into an iron retort that has a top which can be clamped on to prevent the mercury vapor from escaping. The top has a metal tube attached to it, sometimes with a piece of wet burlap wrapped around it. Water is poured onto the burlap which provides the cooling necessary to cause the mercury vapor to condense; The retort is heated until mercury begins to drip from the condenser, the application of heat continues until mercury ceases to drip from the outlet. The gold remains in the bottom of the retort because the mercury will vaporize long before the gold reaches its 1,945 degree melting point.

Another technique used to separate gold from mercury is called the baked potato method. The miner takes a potato, cuts it in half, scoops out a small cavity in the potato and places the amalgam inside. The potato halves are put back together and secured with wire. The potato is placed on the hot coals in a fire, it is left there until it is very well done.

The mercury vaporizes and is trapped inside of the potato, leaving clean, bright gold behind. Warning: The potato is now quite poisonous, do not eat it.

On July 2 the Colonel completed the sale of a bar Mill for $750.00 which he said he had put in good condition. It is not clear where this mill came from or who ended up with the cash, but it was purchased by the Gold Rock Mining Co. Inc., located at 234 West Johnson Street Philadelphia, Pennsylvania. The owner was Mr. William Spencer and their mines were listed as being at Bumpass, Virginia and they were producing gold, silver and mica.[5]

Mica is a clear mineral which was used in place of glass for some applications such as in gauges on airplanes and as electrical insulation.

Colonel Marshall had ordered an additional mine car from C. J. Hanky in Richmond but when the Colonel inquired as to its status he was advised that it

---

5   Letterhead, Gold Rock Mining Co.

was not quite complete. The addition of another car would allow the miners to move more ore out of the mine tunnel to the shaft where it could be transported to the surface in the skip. Extra railroad rails would be laid to allow the mine car to be pushed further into the ever lengthening mine tunnels as they pursued the gold the Colonel said was there.

Charles Squier wrote the Colonel on July 6, from the Mount Washington Hotel in the White Mountains of New Hampshire.

> "Sutphen has funds in hand and instructions to send you $375.00 this week and next, after which he returns from his vacation- he is now away so I can send no further funds until his return. I suggest you start to assemble the parts, etc. for the hydro-electric plant. Sutphen and I start for Mineral next time on the 23rd. inst. and will arrive the 24th. We will bring the $1,000.00 you require for the hydro-electric plant with us then. I hope you will sell the little mill in time to "carry on" in the meantime! You said $375 weekly was sufficient after the mill construction ceased! Have you had any samples, assays, or other results lately?
>
> "I am today on my way to a friend's camp at Rangeley, Maine- I return to Bennington Friday morning early. I shall be in New York at the Ritz Carlton from Monday the 14th. inst. until Thursday morning, the 17th., when I return to Bennington until the 22nd. when I go to N. Y. again, leaving for the mine (Mineral) the evening of the 23rd. Inst."[6]

Charles Squier wrote to the Colonel from Bennington on July 13.

> "I presume you received some days ago my letter written to you from Bretton Woods, N.H., while on my motor trip, or was it from Rangeley Lake, Me.- I am not quite sure?
>
> "I have been waiting to hear from you, but nothing has come in some considerable time! I am going to New York on business

---

6   July 6, 1924, Letter from Charles B. Squier to Col Thomas R. Marshall

tomorrow evening and shall be at the Ritz-Carlton Hotel there until Thursday morning, when I return here. Sutphen and I are coming to Mineral on the 24th. to hold the stockholders meeting to formally authorize the issue of the bonds to me-I have put over $53,000 of my own funds in this property and should be covered fully, before anyone else; and, as I am not a very rich man and I am getting rather restive as to the outcome!

"Have you secured a skip of the proper size and have you attempted to put any good ore through the mill yet, if so what have been the recoveries of gold? I am very anxious to have your answers at once, and also how soon you propose to assemble and set going the hydroelectric plant for the running of the mill at night as soon as we find the $1,000.00 necessary therefore and place same in your hands or the same is otherwise arranged for?"[7]

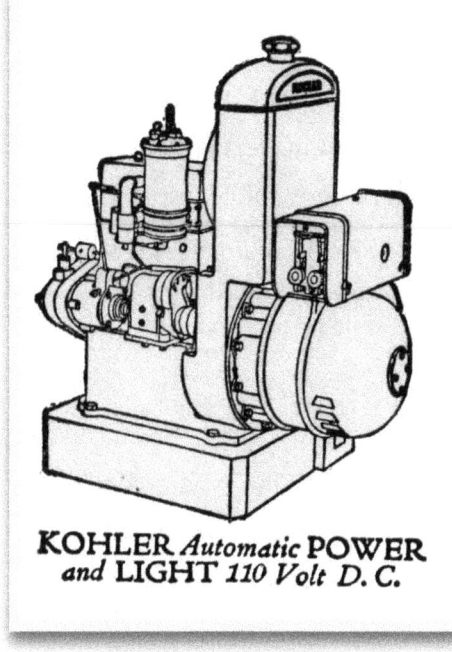

ILLUSTRATION NO. 17:
KOHLER ELECTRIC PLANT

The model K-231 electric plant was bought from the Kohler Co. of Norfolk, Virginia and was capable of producing two and one half kilowatts per hour of direct current at one hundred and ten volts. It was powered not by water {hydroelectric} but by a gasoline engine and it cost $750.00 plus rail freight to Mineral. Electric lights would allow the mill to run twenty four hours a day. Electric lights were uncommon at this time and only some of the larger towns had them. This illustrates the employment of the latest technology in the mines. **Illustration 17**

---

7   July 13, 1924, Letter from Charles B. Squier to Col. Thomas R. Marshall

Charles Squier continued,

> "I regret to have to enclose the letter just received from Barker and I must admit he is correct in his judgment of how our accounts have been kept, which is most unsatisfactory, to say the least! I have tended to be very lenient up to the present, knowing you were working under a big strain and carrying a very big load, leaving you little time for accounts. But now the mill is completed, and all is ready to run and we are getting closer to the time when the work is routine and regular I see no more excuse for _irregular_ accounts!"[8]

Barker advised Charles Squier July 11.

> "Mr. Sutphen has asked me to write you about Colonel Marshall's reports, there haven't been any. The last thing sent up by him was the one you took to Mineral with you. You must admit that's not regular.
>
> "In fact it's so irregular and unsatisfactory that I don't want to have anything more to do with the business. I think it would be a good idea if you carried out your plan to have a permanent clerk in Mineral if he sent you copies of his entries you could have a set of books in New York. I hope you make a lot out of the property but I think I've done enough for it and really can't go on, Its too informal."[9]

Squier continued on July 13,

> "Our accounts _must be kept up here_ in N.Y. City, where the company should eventually have a regular office, and where all records should be kept. The last time I was in Mineral you seemed

---

8 July 11, 1924, Letter from T. M. Barker to Charles B. Squier
9 July 13, 1924, letter from Charles B, Squier to Col. Thomas R. Marshall

to have all your accounts well in hand, but we must have copies of same, or the originals, which will be carefully preserved!

"I very much regret to have to say that we must have our accounts in fine shape and, all vouchers and data sent up for us, before we advance any more funds whatsoever- this is our only protection and is for the good of all who are in any way interested in the property.

"Sutphen and I will bring down a check for $1,000.00 for the electric-lighting plant, but we will not turn it over or go on with any more expense, until our books are in fine shape, and all expenditures classified and separated to date!"[10]

---

10   July 13, 1924, Squier

!! BLACK GOLD !!

A new commodity near Mineral had come to the attention of the New York investors and this time it is oil! Eugene Perry had contacted the Colonel in early April, about coming into possession of a small bottle of crude oil which was reported to have been found in the neighborhood of Mineral. He was keenly interested in knowing if oil has really been found, where it was located and if the people who owned it had made any attempt to sell it. Perry told the Colonel if he thought it was worthwhile, he would bring an oil man {a petroleum engineer} with him when they came down the next time. Perry had been assured that if there was anything that even looked like crude oil there, he could get the money necessary to make the preliminary investigations of the deposit. Perry suggested that he, the Colonel and Squier, form a small syndicate to develop the deposit, if there was anything worthwhile to develop. Perry believed that if they could even bring in a small well, and buy up options on all of the surrounding property, they would have a bonanza on their hands, not to mention the millions they might make on stock sales.

After waiting for several months to hear from the Colonel, Perry again contacted him on July 12 concerning the oil deposit. The Colonel had his hands full with all of the holdups at the mill, a cave in, the weather, and equipment problems. He had not had time to investigate the oil discovery. Perry advised Colonel Marshall that he had some people who were looking for an investment like this, and that he would have come down earlier to investigate if the Colonel had responded sooner. This delay had caused Perry to put the oil project on the back burner for a while.[1]

Eugene Perry took the preliminary steps toward organizing a company for the development of the properties they believed sat on valuable oil deposits. Perry told the Colonel that he had contacted Mr. Wiley, who found the big Haynes-

---

[1] July 12, 1924, Letter from Eugene Perry to Col Thomas R. Marshall

ville Pool in the northern part of Louisiana and that they were very enthusiastic about this new opportunity. Wiley indicated a strong interest in coming down to examine it as soon as possible. Perry characterized Wiley as a very knowledgeable person who worked hard and was very trustworthy. Perry believed they would have no trouble selling enough shares of the company's stock to allow them to begin drilling operations on the first well. He told the Colonel that the investors up- state were very excited and could not wait for the first derrick to be erected. Perry advised the Colonel of his plans to talk again with Wiley and see if he could arrange for him to make a trip to Mineral for a quick look. The Colonel had told Perry that the mill was up and running, Perry was excited by the apparent good news and asked how much gold they were producing?[2] The Colonel's reply could have not sustained Perry's delight for long.

With the additional project of oil prospecting on his plate, the Colonel still had the usual demands upon his time. The extra mine car was shipped by C. J. Hanky of Richmond, Virginia on July 17 and arrived in Mineral a few days later. The new mine car weighed in at a respectable 915 pounds empty and was made entirely of iron. The wheels were of cast iron and similar in design to those on a railroad car, only smaller so they would fit the rails in the mine.[3]

The car is used to transport ore and waste rock on the railroad rails in the mine to the skip which then transports the contents to the surface.

On July 20, 1924 Charles Squier told the Colonel,

> "Your letter of the 15 inst. reached me at the Ritz-Carlton Hotel in New York just as I was leaving there on Thursday, the 17th inst. to return to my home here. I also received the "Special Delivery" letter you addressed to me at the same hotel the last time before when I was in New York!
>
> "I am glad to know you expect to get the new skip made to order, shortly, and hope it will come and be working, before Sutphen and

---

[2] July 12, 1924, Eugene Perry
[3] July 17, 1924, Shipping receipt C. J. Hanky

I arrive the morning of Thursday, the 24th, inst. at Mineral about 9:30 to hold the stockholders' meeting, authorizing the issue of bonds to cover the company's indebtedness to me- Battle will come over also from Charlottesville!

"I appreciate the difficulties you are having with payroll, etc., but I have personally advanced the company to date over $54,000.00, which must be covered by prior lien bonds and convertible bonds covering the remaining treasury stock, and I am very much displeased with the fact that our accounts are in very bad shape and considerably in arrears, and these statements and vouchers to conform to Barker's (or any other certified public accountants) demands must be made up and furnished by you before any more funds are advanced! We have written you so many times about this that there is no use going into it again here!

"We will bring down with us $1,000.00 to cover running expenses and the part payment for the hydroelectric plant equipment, but, unless you can furnish us with all your statements of expenditures to date or nearly so, we will close down the property, until I come back from Europe- I sail August the 6th and return in November.

"We have GOT to keep books and they have GOT to be kept in order in the most modern way, and they have got to be kept up here. You can hardly be as busy now, as when you had the assembling of complicated machinery and the erection of the mill-house in hand, all of which were done when I was last in Mineral around one month ago! There is no excuse for not furnishing proper accounting of all expenditures to date and it will be much easier in the future, as out expenses will be fixed and regular with the mill running! You are the only person who can furnish us the proper receipts and statements for all work done, we want particularly the itemized labor items and the completed lumber bill for the mill-house as mentioned. I am sorry to be so decided, but the plant either stays

!! BLACK GOLD !!

idle for lack of funds until I return from Europe in November, or we have proper statements and accounts to date as due!"[4]

There had been a lot of activity at the Twin Vein Mine from July12 to July 21. The miners had used four, 50 pound boxes of dynamite at $13.50 each, 1500 feet of fuse at $2.00 per 100, nine boxes of blasting caps at $2.25 each, and 3, 100 pound cans of carbide for the miner's lamps at $6.50 per can. They had also purchased one box type exploder (detonator) for $3.75 which would allow them to use electric blasting caps instead of the older fuse type. The total for the listed and other items from these bills was $314.09.[5]

Squier and the members of the Board of Directors arrive in Mineral, hold the board meeting and tour the mine and mill. Squier also brought Frank Cannady, a guest who was not known to the Colonel at the time, but is later introduced as his future assistant. The Colonel was dissatisfied with the bond issue, the lack of income from the Company and his future assistant. As a result he arranged a private meeting with Charles Squier at his home in Bennington to discuss it all.[6]

On the July 31 the Colonel decided at the last minute to cancel the meeting in Bennington and he sent Squier a telegram notifying him of the change. Squier told the Colonel,

> "I was pleased to talk with you over the telephone yesterday, and glad you received my wire, before you actually left Mineral, so that you knew I was tied up here, closing our house for the summer, and packing to go to Europe which means quite a lot of work. I am sorry you decided not to come up here today, as I could have had a nice talk with you and we could have settled everything up here without causing you the trouble and discomfort in this hot weather of coming all the way back to New York, but perhaps you preferred to do it that way! I really cannot imagine just what you have to talk

---

4   July 20, 1924, Letter from Charles B. Squier to Col. Thomas R. Marshall
5   July 21, 1924, Bill of Materials from Mineral Hardware Co.
6   July 31, 1924, Letter from Charles B. Squier to Col. Thomas R. Marshall

to me about, as I have just been in Mineral, but I will be very glad to talk with you in New York next Monday. (At this point Colonel Marshall's salary is $4,000.00 in arrears according to his handwritten notes.)

"If you had come up here, we could not have put you up here at the house, but we could have given you some very good meals (with the carpets all up, however!) with fresh vegetables and the best raspberries from the garden you ever consumed!

"I will reach New York Sunday evening about 8:15 City Time and shall go to my apartment- I presume you will be arriving from the mine on the night train out of Doswell at 6:15 P.M., which is due to arrive at the New York-Penn Station around 7:25. I suggest you come up town, after you have left your bag anywhere you want to go, or in the station, if you are returning that night, and meet me at the Plaza Hotel's main dining room on the corner of Fifth Avenue and 59th Street for breakfast at about 8:30 A.M. where we can have a nice long talk. Afterward my day will be pretty full with repacking in the apartment, and attending to the thousand and one nuisances that come up just before one is leaving the country for several months for a foreign address, and is not easily reachable! I sail at 10:00 A.M., Wednesday, August the 6th

"I will leave with Sutphen in the company's treasury an additional $2,100.00, which will be for two weeks pay-roll and for the hydroelectric plant to permit continuous operation at night- I shall be glad to hear from you as to how soon you can have this in operation! This will make exactly $58,000.00 cash I have advanced the company to date!

"Frank Cannaday, who was at Mineral with me last, has agreed to go down to Mineral on or about August the 7th, after he has seen his family off to the Phillippines from Seattle, and will stay right there, barring week-ends (only when you are there, though!) when he may run over to see his relatives in Richmond, Washington, Charlottesville, etc.! He will be a wonderful help to you and you can very soon break him in, so you can have a vacation, which you have dearly earned! I will tell you just this: he is the "salt of the earth" and both strictly honest and reliable and very experienced- so we are very lucky-he will stay until the end of October, and, if the mine turns out well by then, perhaps indefinitely, as sort of Asst. Manager and General Bookkeeper, or whatever we decide to entitle him! Call me Monday, from the station, as soon as you get in- 3314-Regent!"[7]

On August 1, 1924 the Colonel received a short but very official letter from Charles Squier,

"The attached letter is a true copy of one I am leaving with Capt. Cannaday, and rather explains itself! You will find Cpt. Cannaday a very courteous and interesting gentleman, who you will find will bring much interest into what must have been a rather lonely and cut-off existence for you, during the long months of your development work at Mineral! I sincerely recommend, for your own as well as for the company's, best interests, that, just as soon as Capt. Cannaday has been sufficiently "broken in" to assume control during your absence, that you take a nice, extended vacation, which you certainly deserve and must sorely need as well!

"Trusting all will soon be well during my absence in Europe, and that we will soon be "out of the woods" and on a paying basis."[8]

This does not sit well with the Colonel; he has been running the show and now he has competition.

As of August 3, payroll records showed the work force was comprised of 12 men who worked for 10 hours each day except Sunday. This will change when they hire more men to operate the mill.

---

7   August 1, 1924, Letter from Charles B. Squier to Col. Thomas R. Marshall
8   August 1, 1924, Letter from Charles. B. Squier to Capt. Frank Cannady

The enclosure from Charles Squier to Capt Cannaday of August 1st read.,

" I shall be in New York City again from Sunday evening next until I sail on the R.M.S. "Aquitania" at 10:00 A.M., Wednesday morning following. I expect to return from Europe, sailing October 29th from Southampton on the R.M.S. "Majestic", due in New York Nov. 4th My permanent address in Europe will be: National City Bank of New-York, 41, Boulevard Haussmann Paris, France, and they will forward promptly all mail; the cable address is: Charles Squier, "CITIBANK, PARIS". You can use the deferred rate messages at half rates.

"I shall hope to see you in New York before I sail, and Colonel Marshall also will be in New York this Monday next for our final discussion as to the management of the gold mine property at Mineral, which you inspected with me on the 24th of July ultimo, when you had occasion to meet Colonel Marshall, whom you will find a very experienced and interesting gentleman. He has been on the job continuously for over 14 months, his services and experience have been invaluable in the development of the property, and he needs a good vacation, for his health, as soon as you feel sufficiently "broken in" to take charge during his absence!

"I feel very much relieved that you have agreed to come to us and act {shall we say?} as the Assistant General Manager, Accountant and Bookkeeper for the company until around October 15th at least at the nominal salary during that period of $150.00 per month out of which you agree to meet your living expenses at Mineral. Your wide experience throughout the world in knocking about as you have, the fact you are a native of Virginia and understand how to manage the local labor talent and would be respected by them accordingly, together with my long experience of both your business acumen and integrity make you peculiarly suited to help us out. I only hope the Twin Vein will look sufficiently attractive to you by

!! BLACK GOLD !!

October 1st. that you will give up any idea of going back to Spain and will remain with us permanently, under the conditions already outlined to you which would give you a substantial stock interest.

"I am the ultimate and last word in the company as I own 30,000 shares of stock and one of my most intimate friends Richard D. Brixey of 420 Park Avenue, New York City owns 10,000 shares and he will always stand with me, making a total of 40,000 shares out of the 75,000 authorized. I control the directors through stock ownership, Mr. Jas. H. Coghill, of Normandie Park, Morristown, New Jersey, and of Bennett, Coghill and Company, Brokers of 2 Rector Street, New York City, is the First Vice President, and technically, although not actually in command during my absence owns 4,000 shares. Coghill is a fellow with a good, clear head for business. Eugene Perry, Jr., Manager of the uptown office of H. L. Horton & Co., 547 Fifth Avenue. New York City is the Second Vice President and is a southern boy, coming from Charlottesville, Virginia originally, although since marriage has lived at 122 East 76th Street, New York City. Either of the above men can go down to Mineral upon short notice during the summer if any matters come up needing adjustment.

"It is my idea that Colonel Marshall shall be in full charge of the mine and milling operations, as he knew more about it than anyone else, but you will learn all you can as to the properties' operation so you can assume full charge at any time Colonel Marshall shall be ill or have to go away on vacation or for any other reason. He will certainly never go away unless for some very good reason or for a sorely needed vacation!

"What I want you to do especially is to take charge of all accounting of all expenditures for materials and for pay-roll. Our Secretary and Treasurer, Mr. Van Tassel Sutphen, of 22 Franklin Place, Morristown New Jersey who is a most reliable and punctual person will have control of such funds as will be available for the company's expenses during my absence. I anticipate that the mine will very shortly "carry itself", (at least from my last conferences with

Colonel Marshall!), keep our books in good shape, with all vouchers, etc. (which Colonel Marshall has often said he has not the time to do, naturally with all his other important work in installing our plant is also, to avoid the expense of bonding anyone, I shall expect you and Colonel Marshall jointly to check up on, and render strict accounting of all gross and net returns from the mine- duplicates of everything must be sent to Mr. Sutphen monthly, to be entered in the company's books in New York. I am taking the liberty of sending a carbon copy of this letter to Colonel Marshall. It gives me great satisfaction to know two such reliable men are in charge."[9]

The Colonel's report to Charles Squier on August 5 said,

"I was at the mill this morning at 9:30 A.M. and found things in order. I have moved in the electric and will have it installed by the end of the week, and as soon as I do I will commence to run the mill day and night. I should draw your attention to the fact that running the mill at night will add to the pay-roll the wages of four men and the cost of fuel for the boiler.

"I have given the subject of Mr. Cannaday's coming down careful thought, and although it will be disagreeable for me, I am going to try it out because I see you want it done. If he makes himself amenable I will try to continue until you return. I hope you had the time today to write him the letter that I suggested that you write.

"I think that I can say to you that you need not worry about your investment in the mine while you are away and when you come back here I think you will approve all that has been done while you were away. When you return the mill will have been carrying its full load and producing what you expect."[10]

---

9   August 5, 1924, Letter from Col. Thomas R. Marshall to Charles B. Squier
10 Instructions from U. S. Mint, Philadelphia, Pa. Form 506, April 21, 1921

!! BLACK GOLD !!

The Colonel planned to meet with Charles Squier in New York one last time before Squier sailed for Europe. At the meeting he was to receive final instructions concerning the management of the gold mine and he also intended to air his complaints relative to the financial arrangements and the new assistant which he did not want.

Squier sailed on Wednesday at 10:00 AM., the mill was running and the Colonel wrote the Superintendent of the Mint of the United States in Philadelphia, Pennsylvania, telling him he expected to commence shipping gold to the Mint. Colonel Marshall asked for instructions and the regulation slips which were required. The Superintendent promptly sent him the material requested including an"Abstract of Regulations Covering the Receipt of Gold Bullion for Coinage or Conversion into Fine, Standard or Unparted Bars. "The Mint received gold in bars, lumps, grains and dust in their native state, free from earth and stone or nearly so, also amalgam with quicksilver, {mercury} expelled. Bullion unsuitable for the operation of the Mint and deposits of less value than $100 were refused. The amount of gold required to produce a value of $100 would require, in native gold, 4.838 ounces Troy weight."[11] Some gold can contain silver and other impurities, this results in a loss in net weight when it is refined..

The Colonel was still not satisfied with the financial arrangements concerning the bonds which were to be issued to Charles Squier and he consulted Van Tassel Sutphen. Sutphen told the Colonel on August 8,

> "I am sorry you had so little time with Squier. I did my best to persuade him that it was unwise to force anybody on you. At the same time I liked what I saw of Cannaday very much indeed and I venture to predict that you will be able to get along most comfortably with him.
>
> "I don't wonder in the least that you feel aggrieved at this new lien placed upon the property, but as I have already told you the initial blame rests on the two members of the syndicate who

---

11   August 8, 1924, Letter from Van Tassel Sutphen to Col. Thomas R. Marshall

agreed, at least verbally, to provide the financing up to $50,000. When it became necessary to have funds to put up mill, etc. the directors had to borrow and Squier was the only available source of supply. I, for one, never had the faintest idea that the syndicate was obligated to take care of this financing; my first information on the subject came from you when I was at Mineral the last time. So when the money was borrowed from time to time from Squier, I as treasurer was instructed to give company notes to offset the loans. These notes were a legal obligation on the company, and could have been called by Mr. Squier at their last writing. Where would we have been in that contingency? And, of course, the proper bonds are merely the same obligation in a more tangible form. The all-important thing is not to tie up the enterprise at this critical time."[12]

After Squier sailed, a special stockholders meeting was held on August 11, 1924 to approve the bond issue, but the Colonel had other plans and he used his position as a Director to stop the vote on the bond issue which would protect Charles Squier's $60,000 investment in the company. The Colonel threatened to file suit and possibly throw the company into receivership. The meeting adjourned without any results and was rescheduled for September 11, which gave Battle and the Board time to consult with Squier.

Squier was staying at the Hotel Continental in Paris, France and on August 23 of he wrote the Colonel.

"Just a few lines to say I have just chanced to meet a very charming Virginia lady here who married a U.S. Naval officer, but who was a Miss Fairfax, one of the famous family, and who knows you and your family well and was very much interested in hearing of our mine and venture in the Old Dominion state. She seems very well connected, is " in" with all the prominent people here and is

---

[12] August 23, 1924, Letter From Charles B. Squier to Col. Thomas R. Marshall

very aristocratic in bearing and appearance. Of course, Fairfax, as they say, is a fair name! "I do hope the mine is now justifying our beliefs, as it should have done by this time!"[13]

What Squier does not know is that problems with the recovery of gold continue. The amalgamation plates are apparently still not catching the gold and it is possibly being washed out onto the tailings pile.

"I hope you and Frank Cannaday are by now fast and firm friends, he is a courteous Virginia gentleman and the personification of honour like yourself. He will be invaluable to us with his youth and wide experience of the world and people. You must quite get over the idea he is to be with us for any other reasons than those outlined to you fully in our long conversation in my New York apartment before I sailed. You must admit if you think it over seriously, two people are always more of a safeguard than one in unforeseen troubles of any kind! I am sure you do not want to be bonded by The National Surety Company as this would be quite expensive to the company. Captain Cannaday is absolutely honest and reliable in every way and you can trust him at all times and under all conditions. The development has now reached the stage that it is neither fair to you nor the stockholders, which you must remember own 4/5 of the property, outside of your own personal interests, to have you solely and alone assume responsibility for the property's production. I should, in this connection, only like to mention one probability, which I have foreseen: supposing, we will say, as frequently happens in the kind of enterprise we have embarked upon, the gold production becomes very irregular, and at times shows up very poorly, and at others produces very freely and richly- don't you think it would ease your mind a good deal

---

13 September 1, 1924, Letter from Col. Thomas R. Marshall to R. E. Dolan

to have some other party's O.K. on your statements, and cause you less worry they were thus checked up to the satisfaction of all stockholders? If, for any unfortunate reason, you and Mr. Cannaday do not get along, we will only send some other party down from New York, who may be much less desirable in many ways. The plain matter of fact is: we are an incorporated company, which I have often before emphasized, we (mainly myself!) have placed a very considerable cash ($60,000.00) investment in the property, none of which you will remember you have secured by subscription, and the majority of stockholders have a perfectly just right to demand that our books be kept in the usual audited manner, and it is not right to ask you hence forth personally to assume all of these duties, which are beyond your powers and time available! If Mr. Cannaday does anything to interfere with our business (which I know him too well to think he would ever do, other than for our very best interest!), other than along the lines outlined to him im my letter sent to him in Washington, D.C., carbon copy of which is in your possession, then you would be justified in asking for his removal, but I do not feel you are justified or authorized to remove him during my stay abroad, or after my return, unless you have had a personal through conversation with me relative thereto, and I will hold you thus accountable to me, as the majority interest, which is after all the last word of authority naturally! I trust you will quite appreciate that all this is for our own personal best interests, and that is most vital that we all <u>pull together</u> for the best interest of the enterprise.

"You are at times inclined to be overoptimistic as to your own powers of work perhaps, and we, the stockholders must remember that it was not possible for you to obtain the desired insurance we endeavored to get, and that, in the event of you being incapacitated, even for a short period of time only, the property would be left <u>not</u> in responsible hands!

Also, this is, if you will think it over, as much for your own personal interest as for that of the company, only to a smaller degree, but however, to a very large one at that! It is, therefore, greatly to your own personal interest to make the mine produce sufficiently satisfactory results before Oct. 1st next at least to make Cannaday think it worth his while to remain with us permanently as <u>Asst</u>. General Manager, Secretary, or Treasurer, or whatever position we may want him to permanently assume!

> "Please send weekly written reports to Sutphen, who can notify any interested stockholders accordingly, and report same to me, when he writes as I am too far away to return them to him in time to be much good. Allow 14 days for letters from Mineral.
>
> "I shall be at the Hotel Lotti, 7 Rue de Castiglione, Paris, from Sept. 14 to October 19 and thereafter, until Oct. 29, at the Berkley Hotel, Piccadilly, London, when I sail on the R.M.S. Majestic of the White Star Line, for New York, where I should arrive on November 4th, and where I will be pleased to see you at any time thereafter."[14]

On September 1, the Colonel's attention returned to the $5,000 owed him by the Dolans in the form of a letter demanding the payment of the money allegedly owed him by Mrs. Dolan as the fee for selling her property. The Colonel pressed his old friend for the money in his collection letter of September 1, 1923.

> "I have your letters to me since the first day of May of this year before me, and I have carefully read them. I can't understand how a man in the position that I have accredited you to hold could act as you have done in regard to the money that you and your wife owe me. A full settlement was made with you, now nearly four months ago and without a shadow of excuse, you are withholding the money you should have handed me at once. You must

---

14 August 23, 1924 letter from Charles B. Squier to Colonel Thomas R. Marshall

remember how urgently you and your wife wanted me to sell the property for you (and it is proving a "pig in a poke" for us) and I put up all of the costs of making the sale. Now what am I getting in the way of treatment from you??

"I feel I have written to you on the subject as often as all reason requires, and hope that you will remit the amount that you justly owe me by return mail, and thus save me the trouble of making it, and you the cost and injury to yourselves. I shall register this letter to be sure that you receive it."[15]

The oil deal in Virginia fell apart when Perry and the others learned the extent of the deposit. The oil deposit they hoped would make them rich was only a very small oil shale deposit which was not large enough to be of commercial value. The site was listed as "W. E. Gibson Property Deposit Petroleum Oil Shale Prospect."[16]

---

15 September 1, 1923 letter from Colonel Thomas R. Marshall to R. E. Dolan
16 Virginia Rockhounder Web site

SUSPICION

On September 1, 1924 Charles Squier told the Colonel,

"I was surprised to learn recently from both Sutphen and Battle that you held up the special stockholders meeting called for the 11th of August, to vote the bond issue, so that the same has been postponed until September 11th. I can see no reason for your having acted in this way, except that you may have felt that the amount of your salary, which has been allowed to lapse to date, which is around $5,000.00 by now, was thus jeopardized, and even this would mean you had lost faith in the property's value! Furthermore, it seems rather strange to me that I have received from you no letters or reports of any kind as to the progress being made, entirely with my OWN MONEY, in the development of the property. I have written you many long and carefully worded letters in the past, which I have also noted you frequently ignored, whether purposely or through lack of time I do not know, although I now commence to suspect the former!

"I have also noted in other business dealings in other connections than this mine that a great many people do not appreciate the value of capital, its difficulty to interest, etc., particularly people who have never controlled much money of their own, nor been able to obtain capital when wanted!

"I remember that last summer about this time, when things were standing idle, on account of lack of funds, and while I was in Europe, that Mr. Perry Raised $1,400.00, Mr Coghill, $500, and you or anyone else connected with the company, nothing. Talk or promises are never satisfactory or as impressive as net results.

"You are laboring under a great and misinformed delusion, if you suppose, other than the question of salary being in arrears, which we can arrange to pay up to date, if necessary to protect the property from any lien or proceedings you might institute that you can alone prevent in any way the issue of the bonds as arranged for to me. Of the entire $60,000.00 approximately that has gone into development of the property, nearly all has come out of my pocket as you well know and the said development would otherwise not have occurred!

"The property is owned entire by the Twin Vein Company, and the company, its directors and officers must do exactly as the majority of the stockholders dictate at all times. I own 30,000 shares, Mr. Brixey, one of my very best friends, who will always act with me, owns 10,000 shares more- it is obviously true that these two holdings control the company's actions absolutely, even if directly opposed by all other stockholders! Now you are not a director, and we will simply hold the meeting at Mineral with Battle or Perkins and some sufficiently empowered officer of the company, who will have these proxies duly voted for the bond issue- if, in the meantime you care to try and throw the company into receivership, and even if such action were instituted, your only collectible lien is the amount of salary in arrears! Any accredited lawyer will affirm the above! I am very sorry to have to speak as plainly, but I have not time further for long letters, which are evidently largely ignored!

"If you have any complaint verses the former syndicate it is now much too late, as the syndicate has been out of existence for over one year! You can bring any outside action you please for fraud or misrepresentation vs any person formally a member of the syndicate, but this will not lie in any way vs. the present company or its property, but would merely be personal vs. the party or parties involved as persons! I believe you understood under what terms the syndicate was dissolved and the company formed- at least, you signed at that time the papers legally drawn up, showing your acquiescence therein, so I fail to see what ground such a complaint would have to stand upon. Your entire power with the present company or its property lies in your overdue salary, as a claim, and in your own 15,000 shares, and goes no further! If you or anyone else think that any man in his right mind is going to personally advance some $60,000.00 for the development of property held by a company, whose stockholders have put in little or no moneys, and whose stock ranks all the same as the stock of the man financing the company without protection to said advances in the shape of some sort of a prior charge on the companys assets, such as they may be. I fear you are unfamiliar with financing methods and demands! I am the one, who would stand to lose everything, while others lose practically nothing or make a good deal! This is neither just or reasonable!

"Mr. Cannaday should have arrived about Aug. 15th. I trust this finds you well and cheerful, and that the mine is working out well, which we have had ample time to see, it would appear to me under the circumstances of your unexplained and unjust action in re the bond issue, which we will put through just the same a little later, for you have only achieved a small delay of no great importance, I shall, of course refrain from advancing any further funds whatsoever to the company although I believe the funds already advanced are quite sufficient to show the property is good- or bad!

"I would call your attention to the fact that you allowed me to go to Europe, thinking you had no objection to the bond issue, which is merely a protection and not a good investment (!), and that you then held same up without "rhyme or reason" on a technicality- under the circumstances, it is well that Mr. Cannaday will be able to make reports of what is going on, and Mr. Sutphen or some other officer will attend to the matter of voting the stock, because we are going to have that bond issue just the same!"[1]

---

[1] September 1, 1924, Letter from Charles B. Squier to Col. Thomas R. Marshall

Apparently the Colonel's complaints of not having time to do the accounts and send them to the headquarters in New York were not exactly legitimate.

On September 5 Charles Squier told the Colonel,

> "I recently received from Frank Cannaday a long letter, saying he had left Mineral after some few days stay, as there seemed very little for him to do- he seemed to think you could keep such accounts as are required in several days work in each month. He also said you were extremely reticent in furnishing him with any information, which you were not justified in withholding from a very trusted and duly accredited representative of the company! He said you were courteous and there arose during his stay no discussions or misunderstanding or unpleasantness of any kind whatsoever, but that he thought he was not wanted, that you never once asked him over to your room, which, of course, is a matter of small moment, and that you had very little to say about the property. He said he would run down again in September, if I wanted him to do so, and I shall certainly so instruct him accordingly, even if for merely a week-end.
>
> "He reported the following, as to which please send me at once your own explanations or ideas, as the case may be: 1) that you had nearly finished installing the electric-light plant; 2) that you were having trouble with the supply of water, which was not sufficient at all times, and accordingly building a dam across the little pond; 3) that you were having considerable trouble with the plates, which did not seem to catch the gold from the ores put through; 4) that in the mine there are earthy streaks of considerably important size, which ran within the veins, which did not appear to be gold-bearing.
>
> "Have you ever received from the Allis-Chalmers people the new part to make the water drain off the plates quicker? Also, about how much ore have you actually put through the mill and what has been the actual amount of gold recovered so far to date?

SUSPICION

"Frankly, I am beginning to feel somewhat skeptical as to the property, and to regret having put so much money into the development of the plant, etc., without having the ore bodies more thoroughly investigated. Are you sure all the ore put through has been good-value and auriferous? Also, have you yet your assay plant in such shape that you take frequent and varied assays? It would seem to me it is about time to show now what the property actually is, and that it is certainly unwise in the extreme to put any more moneys into development of any kind, unless the ore we have piled up shows good values run through our mill- if not, we had better close down, as there are not going to be any more funds I can possibly see in sight for experimentation!

"All the above, coupled with the fact you have not made so much as the smallest kind of report to me, since I have been away, makes me feel the extreme desirability of the proposed bond issue to protect all the good money I have advanced in so far is possible!"[2]

The report said the amalgamation plates were still not catching gold as they should. This could have been caused by several conditions. It is possible that the plates were at too steep an angle and the material was being washed too quickly across them, but in this case it was believed the water was not draining off of the plates quickly enough.. Excessively muddy water could have interfered with the amalgamation process. Gold can sometimes have an irony coating which will prevent its bonding with the mercury, it will be washed off and lost on the tailings pile. The slope of the plates was specified by the Allis-Chalmers Co., if the miners had not followed the instructions, problems could be created.

Boilers, steam engines and gold recovery machinery use very large amounts of water, measured in hundreds of gallons per hour. Without an adequate supply of water, the plant cannot operate 24 hours a day. The necessity of enlarging the pond indicates an inadequate water supply which would have interfered with the plant's ability to achieve optimal efficiency.

---

2   September 5, 1924, Letter from Charles B. Squier to Col. Thomas R. Marshall

On September 1, 1924, the Colonel sent the Dolans another collection letter.

> "I have read your letters to me since the first of May of this year before me, and I have carefully read them. I cant *sic* understand how a man in the position that I have accredited you to hold could act as you have done in regard to the money that you and your wife owe me. A full settlement was made with you, now nearly Four Months ago, and without a shadow of excuse, you are withholding the money that you should have handed to me at once. You must remember how urgently you and your wife wanted me to sell the property for you, and it is proving a "pig in the bag" for us and I put up all of the costs for making the sale. Now what am I getting in the way of treatment from you? ?
>
> "I feel I have written to you on the subject as often as all reason requires, and hope that you will remit the account that you justly owe me by return mail, and thus save me the trouble of making it, and you the cost and injury to yourselves. I shall register this letter to be sure that you receive it"[3]

On September 6 Dolan responded to the Colonel's demand for payment of the $5,000.00.

> "Again I must disagree with you in viewpoint. The statements and demands made in yours of Sept. 1st. as well as statements made in some of your former letters are erroneous and not borne out by records and facts which I can plainly show you as soon as I can get to Va. which I hope and am endeavoring to do in the very near future."[4]

---

[3] September 1, 1924, Letter from Col. Thomas R. Marshall to R. E. Dolan
[4] September 6, 1924, Letter from R. E. Dolan to Col. Thomas R. Marshall

SUSPICION

Colonel Marshall replied with still more demands for payment of the money owed on September 8.[5]

Dolan responded swiftly three days later,

> "I have written to you repeatedly that the written records and facts do not warrant your demands which I intend to prove fully to you when I get to Virginia, which I am endeavoring to do at the earliest possible date."[6]

Problems with the gold recovery continued to plague the Colonel, and he was running only the best ore from the stock pile through the plant in an attempt to produce the gold. Sutphen and Perry came to Mineral to check up on the mine around September 11, most likely due to a request from Charles Squier. The report they made was not favorable to the Colonel.

On September 15 the Colonel replied by telegram to Dolan's assertions that the records would show the Colonel's claims concerning the $5,000 were unwarranted.

> "Your letter of the eleventh received- am not willing to wait your coming to Virginia. Mail check for $5,000.00 you owe me not in dispute- wire me my expenses."[7]

Colonel Marshall had hired the law firm of Gordon, Gordon and Crank in Louisa to represent him. This may have been the beginning of a very lengthy process in view of the fact the Dolans were now moving from place to place.

The payroll records for the weeks of September 20, 27 and October 4 show the labor force at the mine had increased from 14 to 34 men and they were working 50 to 60 hours a week. The costs for running the mine and mill continued to escalate without meaningful returns which added to Charles Squier's financial difficulties.[8]

---

5 September 8, 1924, Letter from Col. Thomas R. Marshall to R. E. Dolan
6 September 11, 1924, letter from R. E. Dolan to Col. Thomas R. Marshall
7 September 15, 1924, Telegram from Col. Thomas R. Marshall to R. E. Dolan
8 September 20 to October 4, 1924 Payroll by Col. Thomas R. Marshall

ANATOMY OF A GOLD MINE

On September 22 of a letter from Charles Squier arrived in Mineral.

"I am in receipt of two letters from Sutphen, and it commences to look to me, I am sorry to have to say, as though you have been mistaken as to the "ore" in our property, and that it is really not pay dirt! The plates, even if their elevation is not correct should certainly retain some good percentage of gold, if the ore is really there- there is the real "rub"! After several months of even a small percentage operation, there really is no reason for so small a net recovery, unless the ore is poor, and Sutphen's last letter stated you were using selected ore now, which we could not do for long on a paying basis, as you know, Ledoux's assay of the tailings only showed $1.54, which, if I remember correctly, is much less than you had estimated- around $5?

"My mother recently ran across a man in traveling, who was a great expert on all sorts of mines- he knew of the gold mines in Virginia. He said they were always similar to many of the mines in Australia in that the veins never ran true long, which necessitated a lot of exploration for new vein matters, and it ate up all the capital derived from the net returns. At least we will have the advantage that there is not going to be any more capital sunk in this venture so far as I am concerned!

"Cannaday stressed the fact of the questionable value of the earthy sections, which ran through the middle of our "veins might easily not be auriferous! (Gold-bearing)

"Now there is one thing for your own protection which you should understand: we are an incorporated company, and no stockholder is liable in any way <u>personally</u> for advancement of funds in any way, as the stock is non-assessable! What considerable sums of money I have advanced was done voluntarily and was not in any way obligatory! The further outlay of moneys of any kind or for any purpose are at the persons' risk arranging for same, cannot

> be covered by any sort of mortgage or lien without the majority of the stockholders consent and due ratification and MAY NEVER BE REFUNDED, INCLUDING YOUR SALARY IN ARREARS- over $5,000.00 EXCEPT FROM NET EARNINGS of the company! This should be quite clear to you, as I do not like your action at all in attempting to hold up the mortgage, which was quite justly desired to protect the very large sum of money I have personally advanced and which alone has made possible the operation and development of the property, and said action upon your part has made me somewhat suspicious of your own personal belief in the property having the value you first ascribed to it at all!
>
> "The above summed up should mean to you the following: 1) You must understand I have definitely resolved not to loan the company one cent more whether it fails or not! 2) There is absolutely no use in operating the mine any longer, until you definitely prove the ore has value for feeding the mill out of the 2,000 ton or more you have on the dump- to do anything else than feed that dump ore to the mill, while shutting off all other expense, is the height of foolishness and is only courting bankruptcy, with the company quite "broke" and no net earnings of any size in sight! I think you will agree with me in the, not only wisdom, but dire necessity of the plan of operation, until at least real values are proved beyond any SHADOW OF DOUBT!"[9]

On September 22 R. E. Dolan contacted the Colonel's attorney, R. L. Gordon in Louisa, Virginia.

> "First of all I wish to advise you that I expect to be in Virginia in the next ten days or two weeks. If in the meantime you deem it advisable to commence suit I would suggest that before doing so

---

9   September 22, 1924, Letter from Charles B. Squier to Col. Thomas R. Marshall

you go well into the matter, examine the written records, and facts including my letters to Marshall. He has them all, if not I have.

"After you have analyzed the situation, please let me know your views. You well know that I respect your opinions most highly.

"Have written Marshall repeatedly that his claims and demands are not borne out by the real facts and I intend to prove it as soon as I get there. From the past you as well as everyone in Louisa County knows I never dodged or evaded a just debt.

"Of course I do not know but will venture the statement that you have not looked into the true facts. This I ask you to do in justice to me and advise me of your findings before proceeding further."[10]

The true facts statement may elude to the "on or before maturity clause" which was violated because payment was not made on or before May 1st. This could jeopardize the Colonel's $5,000 fee.

Gordon wrote the Colonel on September 24, advising him of Dolan's correspondence.

"I had a reply to your telegram advising a letter was on the way and I am herewith enclosing you a copy of the letter from Dolan received this morning. I presume you will want the attorney who represents the company to attend to this matter for you and will therefore make no investigation of the matter unless I hear from you further. I would have to go through all of the papers as Dolan suggests to make an intelligent examination and I haven't got the time to do it unless you desire me to represent you and you make the proper arrangements for the fee."[11]

---
10 September 24, 1924, Letter from R. E. Dolan to R. L. Gordon
11 September 24, 1924, Letter from R. L. Gordon to Col. Thomas R. Marshall

Dolan sent a telegram to R. L. Gordon on Saturday, September 27,

> "will leave here Sunday night or Monday for South If delayed will wire for name of Chicago attorney. Would gladly present our views to him. Contract of June tenth was not carried out. That is but small part of story have documentary evidence to bear out my statements."[12]

The Colonel desperately sought an answer to the problems with the gold recovery and Perry used one of his connections to try and help. On October 1 Eugene Perry wrote to his friend, L. H. Timmins of the Holliner Mine in Ontario, Canada.

> "This will serve to introduce to you Colonel Thomas Marshall. Colonel Marshall is General Manager of the Twin Vein Mining Company, Inc., of Mineral, Virginia. I am associated with the company as a Vice-President. Ours is a gold mining proposition, and I understand from the Colonel that the ore we are grinding is similar to that in the Holliner and our method of extraction also identical. We are having some trouble with our plates and the Colonel is of the opinion that if he visits your property he could probably learn something that would show us where we are making our mistakes. There seems to be no question about the high grade of the ore but the plates do not catch the gold, as a recent assay of the tailings has shown us."[13]

All the while the Dolans were still in Chicago and did not come to Mineral as promised, leaving the Colonel in a financial pinch because he was still not being paid for his work as General Manager.

12　September 27, 1924, Telegram from R. E. Dolan to R. L. Gordon
13　October 1, 1924, Letter from Eugene Perry to L. H. Timmins

On October 10, the Colonel boarded a train headed for the Holliner Mine to confer with L. H. Timmins. He was desperate for information which might enable him to solve the gold recovery problems at the Twin Vein Mine. The cost to the company for the trip was $184.13, the expenses continued to mount and still there was no gold.

The Colonel returned form his trip to Canada only to find the Dolans had still not arrived and on Monday, October 20 he officially retained R. L. Gordon in Louisa as his legal representative. Gordon contacted the law firm of Musgrave, Oppenhiem, McKeever & Lippincott in Chicago, Illinois requesting a fee schedule and details for filing suit against the Dolans there. The fee for collecting the $5,000 from the Dolans in Chicago, Illinois was $221.00 provided the matter could be settled without litigation. The charge for litigation would be, "the usual moderate and reasonable attorneys' fees, but these fees will depend on the amount of time involved and the results obtained."[14] If they litigated the case, the Colonel will have to pay a legal fee approaching one third of the $5,000.

Gordon requested the Colonel advise him quickly of his intentions,

> "I reckon these terms are as reasonable as we will be able to get any city attorney to represent you for. Must we reply immediately to these attorneys or wait until Thursday the 23rd. to see if the Dolans come."[15]

The Colonel anxiously waited for the Dolans on Thursday, but the wait was not worth the time because the Dolans still did not appear as they had led the attorney to believe. The game of catch us if you can continued.

November 1 rolled around and Charles Squier sent word confirming that he would be arriving in New York on Tuesday evening, November 11. The Colonel was probably dreading the meeting because he would have had to explain why almost no gold had been recovered since Squier's departure. The number of truck

---

14 October 8, 1924, Letter from Musgrave, Oppenhiem & Lippincott
15 October 20, 1924, Letter from R. L. Gordon to Col. Thomas R. Marshall

SUSPICION

loads of ore taken to the mill was very inconsistent, ranging from 2 loads to as many as 29 loads per day.[16]

Squier told the Colonel on November 8.

> "You have had ample time and funds to definitely prove whether your equipment has been well installed and functions properly, also whether <u>the ore</u> itself is profitable or not- a very much more important question, even! I have written Mr. Perkins and Mr. Battle telling them of my return and to proceed with the bond issue. I think it no more than just that you should be given some of the same bonds in the amount your salary is in arrears, if you so elect, which would rank equally <u>pro-rata with</u> the bonds issued to me in lieu of <u>the</u> company notes I now hold against the very considerable sums I have advanced for the development and operation. All the stock held by you will still rank identically the same, pro-rata as that held by me and others- which goes naturally without saying!
>
> "Trusting that this finds you well and in your customary vigor, and that Mr. Sutphen will have a more favorable report for me than that last written to Paris two weeks ago."[17]

The November 26 clean up of the amalgamation plates yielded only $200 in gold, the bare minimum accepted by the mint. The mine was still not producing enough gold to even make the payroll expenses, not good news for the Colonel, as the mine teetered on the brink of financial disaster.[18]

On November 28 Sutphen, Battle and the other directors held a stated meeting in New York to prepare the way for the bond issue. Charles Squier desperately wanted to protect the $76,500.00 he had invested in the Twin Vein Mine which appeared to be an empty hole in the ground.

---

16 Col. Thomas R. Marshall's Hand written, daily load tally
17 November 8, 1924, Postcard from Charles B. Squier to Col. Thomas R. Marshall
18 November 26, 1924, Receipt for gold, American Railway express

ANATOMY OF A GOLD MINE

It has been said Mark Twain once described a mine as an empty hole in the ground with a liar at the bottom. It is not known at this point if the Colonel has done anything wrong, but it looks bad for Charles Squier because if the mine does not produce gold, his money is gone. That is not the worst of it. If his friends who have invested in the mine lose their money, Charles Squier's reputation will be destroyed.

The announcement of the special stockholders meeting was sent out on December 1

> "A special meeting of stockholders, of Twin Vein Mining Co., Inc., will be held at Mineral, Virginia, Saturday, December 13, 1924 at 12 PM for the purpose of ratifying the action of the Board of Directors, at their stated meeting, November 28, 1924, in voting to place a second-mortgage on the entire property for $80,000.00, in order to take up notes held by Mr. Charles B. Squier for money advanced from time to time to meet equipment charges and operating expenses and aggregating $76,500.00; the balance of $3,500.00 to be held in the treasury for future sale."[19]

On December 3, Dr. Howe told the Colonel, he had received a telegram from Charles Squier approving his plan for the mine. Howe said he would describe it to the Colonel when they met. Howe told the Colonel his schedule would only permit him to visit the mine the next week and he had asked Squier to purchase the necessary tickets for him on the train to Doswell which was to leave New York on Monday evening December 8. Howe expected to arrive in Mineral on Tuesday morning, for a stay of two or three days and he wanted the mill to be running when he arrived.

Howe asked the Colonel to wire him if anything happened that would interfere with his evaluation of the mine or mill so he could postpone his visit. Howe told the Colonel that he was very anxious to conduct tests on ore going into the mill[20]

This test would indicate whether the ore contained sufficient gold to make it profitable to mine and process.

---

19 December 1 1924, Letter from Van Tassel Sutphen to Col. Thomas R. Marshall
20 December 3, 1924, Letter from Dr. Ernest Howe to Col Thomas R. Marshall

SUSPICION

More bad news for the Colonel, the pump relied upon to keep the water from flooding the mine shaft broke down and the parts had to be ordered from The Gardener Governor Company of Quincy, Illinois. The order was placed by wire on December 5 and the parts for the pump were shipped by rail the next day, the terms were COD.[21]

This could not happen at a worse time for Colonel Marshall as Charles Squier is back and his friend Ernest Howe is coming to Mineral to correct the problems at the mine or suggest it be shut down.

On December 7 the Colonel received a letter from his friend Eugene Perry.

> "I would like to thank you for the wonderful bird you sent me and "I extend my greetings to you for this year. It starts off rather well for the Twin Vein, at least everybody up this way are happy over the prospects to date and are rooting for you. I was disappointed not being able to get down there during the shooting season. Is it over yet? If not, I can possibly run down yet so let me know what you are shooting now. Had another letter from the man I had agreed to take the dog from. He has a good bitch pointer–a trained dog–and I may get her if you think we could breed her to some real high-class dog down there and get some good puppies and have the benefit of shooting over her in the meantime. If you will write quickly I will have the dog sent down. We are having a spell of cold weather for the first time this winter."[22]

Unfortunately the pump parts did not arrive in time for them to be installed. The pump was going to take more time to repair than the Colonel had, so, Dr. Howe was wired advising him to postpone the trip.

The pump was finally repaired and Dr. Howe arrived on Wednesday December 10. He conducted his tests and took additional ore samples. Dr. Howe's report could make or break the entire project and exonerate or destroy the Colonel's rep-

---

21 December 5, 1924, Telegram
22 December 7, 1924, from Eugene Perry to Col. Thomas R. Marshall

utation with Squier. The Colonel was desperately trying to discover why so little gold was being recovered and again sought help from H. P. Depencier, General Manager of the Dome Mines.

On December 10 Colonel Marshall received the analysis of the samples he took with him to Canada in October from Mr. C. W. Dorsely, the General Superintendent of the Holliner Mine in Porcupine, Ontario. Mr. Dorsly was skeptical of the gold content in the tailings sample because it contained only a small amount of very fine gold. He suggested they treat the tailings with cyanide in order to leach the fine gold from them. Dorsley said that taking samples from the tailings is not as easy as one might believe, because fine gold could be floating on the surface of the water and from there it was being discharged onto the tailings pile.

Mr. Dorsely advised the Colonel of Mr. DePencier's intention to visit the Twin Vein Mine and that he would be leaving for New York in a few days. Mr. Dorsely requested that the Colonel wire Mr. DePencier at: H. P. DePencier, % J. S. Bache & Co, 42 Broadway New York, N. Y. and if he would arrange for accommodations in Mineral prior to his arrival.[23]

News of the opening of the Twin Vein Mine and the large expenditures of money by Charles Squier came to the attention of someone else with something for sale. After the closure of the pyrite mines near Mineral the local economy suffered and real estate prices tumbled. The Mineral City Land Company, which controlled all of the land in Mineral found themselves with approximately 1,000 unsold lots on their hands. They retained the law firm of Nelms, Colonna and McMurran of Newport News, Virginia as their representative. In an effort to unload the remaining lots, they contacted the Colonel on December 11.

The remains of the Mineral City Land Company consisted of $13,367 in out-standing stock and they were interested in selling the lots for only $10 apiece for a total sale price of $!0,000.00 cash money, plus a 10 per cent commission. Their attorney, Mr. McMurran, told the Colonel he was not sure of the exact number of unsold lots but believed it was in the neighborhood of 1,000. He emphasized the fact that none of the lots had sold for under $25 in the past years, a few had gone

---

23   December 10, 1924, Letter from C. W. Dorsley to Col. Thomas R. Marshall

for as much as $150 each. He said the price they were asking was less than $10 for each lot which meant they were losing money on the deal. McMurran told the Colonel he knew of the large investment the New York Company had made in the mine, and he was hoping they would interested in the real estate in Mineral.[24]

Apparently, however, Charles Squier and company were not interested in buying anything else in Mineral with the way things were going at the mine, because a local business man later bought all of the lots.

Squier told the Colonel on December 11.

> "I received your telegram yesterday A.M., but did not reply thereto, as you must have shortly after met Mr. Howe, who came over from Charlottesville on the train which was due at Mineral at 9:55, and the one by which Sutphen and I will arrive Saturday next morning to hold and ratify the proposed bond issue at the special stockholders meeting called for the 13th inst. We will return via Charlottesville, leaving Mineral, I believe, around 7:00 P.M. the same evening, so we will have more time with you, and not reach New York at such an inconveniently early hour!
>
> "Please go easy on the expenses, as I really cannot make any further advances at least before January 1st.. I hope Mr. Howe will be able to remain down there until we are there too- he said he might have to return before then, but would do his best- at any rate, I trust he will be justified in making a very favorable report of our property's value!
>
> "We will expect to have a copy of all the accounting in fine shape to date to bring back for Barker to audit! I received another rather pressing letter from Walton two days ago in re a bill of about $331.00 for lumber, which I returned to him, advising him it would be settled when you told us it was all right and in full detailed form!"[25]

---

24 December 11, 1924, Letter from Nelms, Colonna and McMurran to Col. Thomas R. Marshall
25 December 11, 1924, Letter from Charles B. Squier to Col. Thomas R. Marshall

On December 13 the New York investors arrived in Mineral. The stockholders meeting was held and the bond issue was ratified despite the Colonel's objections.

Squier got what he wanted in the form of five separate bonds. Bonds one thru three in the amount of $20,000 each were due by June 1st, 1925, bond number four in the amount of $16,500 and number five, a bearer bond for $3,500, were due on December 1st, 1926.

**PHOTOGRAPH NO. 73
NEW YORK INVESTORS ARRIVE**

Many photographs were taken of the mine, mill and of the members of the company. **Photograph No.73**, taken on December 13th, Shows (left to right) Eugene Perry holding a camera, Dr. Howe due to his advanced age, Charles. B. Squier and his wife, possibly James Coghill, and possibly Van Tassel Sutphen. The man attending to the car in the back could be J. S. Battle because he had a car and could have driven down from Charlottesville. The attempt at identifying the persons in the photograph is a good best guess.

Photograph No. 74 The completed head frame and shaft house welcome the New York investors.

Photograph No. 75. They are given the grand tour and inspect the mine shaft

Photograph No. 76 Charles B. Squier and his wife are pictured standing in the skip.

SUSPICION

PHOTOGRAPH NO. 74

COMPLETED HEAD FRAME

PHOTOGRAPH NO. 75

MINE INSPECTION

ANATOMY OF A GOLD MINE

**PHOTOGRAPH NO. 76
GOING DOWN IN THE MINE**

Just down the road the Slate Hill Mine was still running, but on January 1, 1925 the Ricswan Mining Company stopped sending money to pay its employees and the expenses related to the operation of the Slate Hill Gold mine. McSween the Mine Manager said,

> "The mine still operated for a time, the men working in expectation of receiving their wages, but finally the laborers quit work and have since done no further work on the property."[26]

The Colonel had hired an accountant in Richmond, Virginia to provide a professional statement of account for Charles Squier. On January 5, 1925 Charles Squier reminded the Colonel,

> "When Sutphen and I were in "Mineral last on the 13th, you were handed a check for $250.00 toward your account of salary- three days later a check was sent to you for $1,000.00 to keep the mill running, which should have lasted for one months operation, or until about Jan. 15th You were later sent a check $340.00 to pay off half of the notes falling due on the "Ford" trucks, December 23rd.

---

26 Louisa County Court Chancery Case 1926-013

SUSPICION

You must have received an additional check for $1,000.00 for one months operation, of the mill, last Wednesday, the 31st of December, which would pay for operations to around February 10th We have received no word from you, except a short note asking Sutphen for more funds!

"The certified accountants' statement of expenditures for the past ten months or year was not in order, in that it must be written on his regular letter-head paper, and all his details, such as expenditures for each listed item for each month should be given first, and then the addition thereof! You can not expect us to advance further funds without such regular statements furnished regularly at the end of each week. You have more time now than when you were constructing the mill, etc., FURTHERMORE, we must have an expert mill man's services for such time as it necessary to adjust our mill expertly to the proper refining of our ore, which we are not now procuring, and this must be done as soon as possible, and we herewith authorize such expense as may be necessary for this man's time, as per Mr. Howe's recommendations. We are positively not going to expend money in keeping the mill operating when it seems evident Mr. Runnut as well as yourself are somewhat at sea when it comes to just what the matter is- experimentation is too costly, and I think you will see the wisdom of this advice! I will send you shortly back the specimen of ore we smelted the last time I was down to send in to the mint with what else you may have recovered- I have been very busy and have overlooked this matter!

"We should have FREQUENT WRITTEN REPORTS of what progress you are making and what results you are obtaining in a very practical and concise form! Unless you see fit to comply from now on at once with the entirely reasonable demands set forth above, we shall have to close down the plant, until we can operate under some more satisfactory conditions. The time for any costly experimentation is over. I am sorry to have to be so specific, but this must be regarded, nevertheless, as quite FINAL!"[27]

On January 8 the mill stopped, the steam pump which supplied water to all of the machinery had suffered a broken piston ring, and the parts would have to be ordered from the manufacturer. This repair cost them a great deal of time and still more money.

January 12 brought a new development in the R. E. Dolan case. Sheriff Henry Von Phul, of Cripple Creek, Colorado, wrote to the Sheriff of Mineral seeking information as to the whereabouts of R. E. Dolan. The sheriff said he was trying to locate Mr. Dolan who once lived in Mineral and had a gold mine near there. The Sheriff said Dolan also owned the Caladonia Mine at Cripple Creek and he was taking care of Dolan's property for him while he was away. The Sheriff had sent several letters to Dolan at Mineral which were all forwarded to Dolan at the Alexandria Hotel in Chicago, Illinois, but he was not there and they had been returned to the Sheriff. He had important information relative to Dolan's mining property in Cripple Creek which he needed to relay to him. He hoped that someone at the Louisa Court House or Mineral might be able to find out where Dolan was so he could contact him.

Von Phul was a six term sheriff of Teller County but he had resigned on July the 3rd. due to a court decision from the Colorado Supreme Court which required Sheriffs to derive their salaries from the fees collected by their office. Von Phul did not believe the new funding measure would produce an adequate income in his county.[28]

This is bad news for the Colonel and his lawsuit because now they have to figure out where Dolan is hiding. Interestingly, the Colonel ended up with the letter that told him Dolan had skipped town. The Colonel's attorney cannot initiate legal action against the Dolans until he can locate them and hire an attorney in that state to represent the Colonel.

---

27 January 5, 1925, Letter from Charles B. Squier to Col. Thomas R. Marshall
28 January 12, 1925, Letter from Sheriff Henry Von Phul to The Sheriff of Mineral

WHERE'S THE GOLD ?

Squier sent the Colonel a telegram on January the 23, 1925 saying that he had a long conference with Dr. Howe and, he was going to secure an expert to run the mill. Howe had advised Squier to close the mine if they could not find such an expert to run the mill.[1] This put additional pressure on the Colonel who had been working with DePencier to find someone who could run the mill properly. Squier and Howe had been working out details which they thought might remedy the problems with the rate of gold recovery, but they always reach the same conclusion- the operators are the problem.

The Colonel fired off a letter to Dr. Howe in the hopes of having him intercede at the meeting with Squier on his behalf. In the letter the Colonel once again pleads his case concerning the need for more money to keep the mine running

Ernest Howe advised the Colonel on the 24th of January that he was in New York when his letter arrived and he was not able to mention the continuing shortage of money to Charles Squier. Howe assured the Colonel that he would bring it up with Squier at their meeting the next week. Squier let Howe know that the Colonel had still not been able to get a mill man from Porcupine and asked if he could find someone to fill in until they could find someone on a permanent basis.

Howe informed the Colonel that it was almost impossible to find a man on the East Coast who could run a gold processing mill, and that he had a number of Consulting Engineers who were friends of his but they would be of little help in this case. The problem with obtaining a mill man in the eastern part of the United States was due to the fact that there were very few gold mines operating there. The greatest majority of the gold mining activity at this point was in the American West, Canada and Alaska.

---

[1] January 23, 1925,Telegram from Charles B. Squier to Col. Thomas R. Marshall

Howe indicated that he would continue to try to turn up someone who could do the job and advised the Colonel to send a telegram to his friends in Porcupine and ask how long it would take for them to find a mill man and for that man to get to Mineral. Howe told the Colonel that if he got a positive answer he should advise Charles Squier immediately. Howe also gave the Colonel the bad news that if they could not find an expert mill man, he would have to advise Squier to shut the mine down until someone could be located.[2]

Charles Squier sent the Colonel a telegram saying he and Dr. Howe had just secured the services of a mill man. This news upset the Colonel, who seemed to want a mill man sent by his friend H. P. DePencier who would be sympathetic to his wishes.

The Colonel replied on January 26.

> "Your telegram was received this morning at 9 O'clock; I wired you that I had secured a good mill man which you had authorized me to do. I had taken up the matter before you had taken up the same subject with Mr. Howe. I have the greatest respect for Mr. Howe and his ability as a professional man, but I do not need him to select a man for me. Mr. Howe has told you he is not a mill man and he has repeatedly told me the same thing. I went to practical mill people to assist me in securing a good man for the position and he starts for Mineral on Sunday morning. He has been loaned to us for two or three months, and if we want him after that time we can make arrangements to keep him.
>
> "The mill has been shut down for more than two weeks on account of the breaking of a piston ring in the pump and because I did not have the money to cut fuel and keep going. The check for $500.00 that was sent to me by Sutphen had to be used entirely to pay the men, my statement showed the situation."[3]

---

2 January 24, 1925, Letter from Ernest Howe to Col. Thomas R. Marshall
3 January 26, 1925, Letter from Col. Thomas R. Marshall to Charles B. Squier

WHERE'S THE GOLD?

Telegrams continue to fly back and forth between Charles Squier and Colonel Marshall over the hiring of a mill man. Both Squier and the Colonel had hired someone and now they had to decide what to do with two employees instead of one. Squier sent the Colonel a telegram on January 29 telling him of his plans to send Mr. R. V. Yerxa who was a mining engineer with experience in running amalgamating plants. Mr. Yerxa would be arriving at Mineral on February 8 and planned to stay until Saturday, February 14. Squier asked the Colonel to

> "show him every courtesy as to the functioning of the mill and to run it at the rate of five tons per day."[4]

On January 29 Dr. Howe tried to explain what had happened during his meeting with Squier to the Colonel. Howe said he had talked with Charles Squier on the 26th and Squier had asked him to find a mill man. As a result of this conversation Dr. Howe got in touch with Mr. R. V. Yerxa, who was a Mining Engineer with experience in the operation of gold recovery mills in the American West. Mr. Yerxa had agreed to go to Mineral, have a look at the situation and possibly provide some advice.

Howe realized the trouble having two people working on the same problem would bring and he tried to explain this to the Colonel. Howe informed the Colonel that Charles Squier still wanted Yerxa to go to Mineral in spite of the fact that the Colonel had told him about his success in hiring a mill man. Howe advised the Colonel he hoped to leave on Sunday night and arrive in Mineral Monday morning.

Howe alerted Mr. Yerxa to the problems existing between the Colonel and Charles Squier. Howe assured the Colonel of Mr. Yerxa's interest in doing everything he could to help with the problems at the mill. Yerxa was planning to take samples of the heads and tails which were to be analyzed at the Columbia School of Mines in an effort to see what was going into the plant and what was being lost to the tailings pile. Howe advised the Colonel to keep the mill man from Canada when he got there, because he could be helpful to them.

---

4   January 29, 1925, Telegram from Charles B. Squier to Col. Thomas R. Marshall

The Columbia School of Mines had opened in New York City in 1864.

Howe told the Colonel he was aware of the discord between he and Charles Squier, but had no idea of how to rectify the problem, but he would try to smooth things over with Squier.[5]

The Colonel received another telegram from Charles Squier on January 30,

> "I have conferred with Mr. Sutphen today and he has mailed a check for $500.00 to cover the payroll and he expresses his doubt that you will see it until Monday. You must keep them more often advised and in more detail. Colonel Marshall is asked for the January statement and to have the mill operating on a small scale when Mr. Yerxa arrives."[6]

The Colonel responded to Charles Squier's telegram on the same day.

> "Your telegram of 3:03 P.M. Jan. Twenty- Ninth was delivered this morning at 8: AM. You had been informed repeatedly that I had asked Mr. DePencier of the Dome Mines Ltd. to lend us a capable and experienced mill man, you wired me that we could not wait for Mr. DePencier showing that you were acquainted with the fact that he was securing the man for us, so I did not think it necessary to continually repeat it.
>
> "I can't understand why you continually send me threats over the wire that you will not send any more money here, I have called your attention to the fact that in this little place that the messages are seen by anyone going into the telegraph office and are discussed by the community. To use your expression, I am "fed-up" with these threats and must request that you discontinue them.

---

5 January 29, 1925, Letter from Ernest Howe to Col. Thomas R. Marshall
6 January 30, 1925, Telegram from Charles B. Squier to Col. Thomas R. Marshall

"You have not sent the money to meet the actual expenses that you know had to be incurred, your attention has been called to it not only by me but by others, how can you expect me to accomplish anything under these conditions?? You have allowed my salary to get in arrears for more than a year and still you seem to think that I can continue to show zeal in carrying on the work and continue to allow encroachments on my interest in the property. Stop and think and try to put yourself in my place and see how you would feel.

"There was a fire at the Dome Mine and Mr. DePencier had to go back and was unable to come here as he had planned, but he allowed his Chief Geologist to take a holiday and come here. He has been with me for a week and has looked over the property fully, he was pleased and surprised with what he saw, and after he had viewed the whole, he remarked to me, that your associates should be satisfied with what you have accomplished, I had given him no inkling of how you had expressed yourself. I know that I have done my duty here and done it well and economically, so I don't feel any regrets.

"Anyone you send here will be treated with all courtesy, I could not do otherwise, and will give them the opportunity to see the property. I used the $500.00 last sent me, to pay the men last Saturday, but will not be able to do so again tomorrow, Saturday, the labor will not work if they are not paid when their pay is due, that is a commoderty (sic) that is not handled on credit."[7]

Mr Yerxa arrived in Mineral on February 9 and stayed only two days going over the mill with the Colonel. He also took samples of the heads and tails each day which were to be analyzed by Ledoux & Company. The assaying of the ore being mined could aid in determining whether or not the mine will prosper or fail.

---

7   January 30, 1925, Letter from Col. Thomas R. Marshall to Charles B. Squier

The previous assays of Twin Vein ore had not been favorable to the Colonel and the absence of substantial gold recovery only worsened his predicament.

On February 10, 1925, Mr. L. W Dowrdlty wrote the Colonel,

> "Your letter of about January 15th must have gone astray. The man we are sending down, H. W. Shoemaker, is a very capable mill man and a real hard worker. He worked on the Dome some time ago and stopped with us for some years. His experience was in mill, assay office, survey office and Mine. As soon as your sample of ore arrives, we will start on it.
>
> "Mr. DePencier is leaving the mine tomorrow, the 10th for Toronto where he may stop for a few days, but after his business is finished there, he is coming on down to see you. Mr. Wright was quite interested with things you showed him. Mr. DePencier wants to go into the business of the Zinc-Lead proposition with you"[8]

This little side deal could be just what the Colonel needs to put some badly needed money in his pocket.

On February 13 Dr. Howe told the Colonel he was happy to hear from him and that Mr. Yerxa had arrived safely. Dr. Howe was anticipating the reports from both Yerxa and the mill operator from Canada. Howe wanted them to do a careful test on the ore as it progressed through the mill so they could determine if the machines were doing their job and if the ore contained enough gold to continue operating the mine.[9]

The results from Ledoux and Company were very bad news for the Colonel. The February 18 assay report showed only .01 ounces troy weight per ton of processed material.[10] The amount of gold produced amounted to a paltry 62 cents per ton, which seemed to confirm that the mine was an empty hole in the ground after all.

---

8   February 10, 1925, Letter from C. W. Dowrdlty to Col Thomas R. Marshall
9   February 13, 1925, Letter from Ernest Howe to Col. Thomas R. Marshall
10 Assay certificate from Ledoux and Co.

WHERE'S THE GOLD ?

Charles Squier wasted no time in firing off a scathing letter to the Colonel on February 23.

"This letter has been very carefully thought out, (as have many others in the past to which you have paid little or no attention!), and I trust you will read it carefully and reply thereto after equal consideration in the spirit in which it is written with an eye to the good of all concerned as we are at the point in the development of the mine, where it will shortly be unavoidable to show if our property has really considerable value, or if it is a "fake" pure and simple!"

"It is not my intention to spend much more money foolishly to show this, in which I shall be guided entirely by the advice of Mr. Howe, who is friendly, unbiased, and well informed as you know.

"Mr. Yerxa's assays of both the headings and tailings made by Ledoux showed practically no gold! This was naturally a shock to both Howe and Yerxa, especially as so many pannings in the past had showed up well with streaks of pure gold visible to the naked eye! Yerxa stated the first day he was there the ore was run entirely from the dump, and the second day new ore entirely from the mine and that both lots were reddish and seemed mixed with mud! Each day about 14 tons were run through at around mill capacity for six to eight hours. How do you explain the negligible values shown in the assay? Yerxa said that after this running there was no sign of gold on the plates. How do you explain this?

"Have you been able to get any gold since and if not, is this not a very bad showing for our ore? You certainly got very good scrapings of gold when Sutphen and I were last down around the 13th of December 1924 when we took home the nugget valued at around $30.00, which was partially retorted and which I returned to you some weeks ago. I have never, by the way, heard from you concerning its receipt by you!

"I have written a long letter today to Howe. I am giving him an outline of the results to date and he will also receive a letter or report from Yerxa. I shall be guided entirely by his advice as I have great faith in his judgement, fairness, and knowledge!

"I am glad you are pleased with the mill man, but it is of course beyond his power to make gold out of poor ore! I am glad you have had the expert advice of both, Mr. Wright, the Dome geologist and of Mr. DePencier, the General Manager, who from your last letter of the 16th seems to advise you to put some good ore through the mill, showing he had not seen any while there! If all the ore we put on the dump, the 1,500 ton you yourself estimated last summer or fall was poor ore, it was rather a waste of money getting it out at all, was it not?!!

Mr. Yerxa thought the mill was well built and eminently suited to give the best results with free milling ore, such as we have, so there can be no trouble with the mill, but- again- only with the ore! I am of the impression, from talks I have had with him in the past, that Howe will now recommend shutting down the mill and saving all expense, except to keep the pump in the shaft running and to cut the necessary fuel, and to have the ore bodies examined by an outside, unbiased expert on ore, to show conclusively what we have- It is my humble, unexpert opinion that this should have been done long ago the first thing, before any money was put into the mill or machinery which would forestall any possibility of our being really "all dressed up with no place to go!" Mr. Howe even said to me last June, upon the occasion of his first visit to Mineral, that the mill should not have been thought of until we knew all about the ore reserves, and, in this connection, I remember your desire to add shortly another 50- ton unit to the present mill- I am afraid we have put the cart before the horse, but let us hope this is not so, at any rate!

"Now to some business details: Sutphen, whom I telephoned at Morristown last Thursday the 19th to save time, sent you at once a check for $826.66, which you should have received Friday, being payment (final) for the Ford trucks. I am returning notice you sent and suggest you have it receipted and sent back to us, and $500.00 for operating expenses for this week. We will send you $500.00 more the end of this ensuing week but will not send any further funds, POSITIVELY, until the following matters are cleared up satisfactorily. 1) We must have the certified accountants's statement of expenses, disbursements and receipts up to January 1st on their letter head as long ago requested. 2) We must have the long and often promised, but never received, statements for January. 3) we must have your written estimate of any additional betterments or charges for the mill, also a detailed statement of just what your labor requirements are now per week. 4) We must have written, weekly statements of the results of the milling, the amount of ore put through the mill, with the value of gold shown. 5) A written statement from you as to when and how you received the $4,000.00 paid by the bank, (which Bank) in Louisa and why they refuse to give up the other $1,000.00.

"I enclose a letter recently received by me from the insurance people in Richmond which was quite mortifying to me to read- how you can let such matters lapse and not bring same to our attention, I cannot see! Please let Sutphen know at once if this policy payment is correct-also, have you other insurance <u>now in force</u> in sufficient value for our employees and has the <u>premium been paid</u> to date? THIS IS A VITALLY IMPORTANT MATTER! You will also recall the matter of Walton's bill for lumber which you let run so long, without bringing same to payment and found he was correct in the end!

"I had a long conversation with my friend Mr. Richard D. Brixey, yesterday- he is a practical business man, running a large business in railway equipment, wiring etc., being the president of the Kerite Co., of 30 Church St, New York with their plant near Bridgeport,

Conn., and he owns 10,000 shares of our capital stock, which, with my 32,000 constitutes more than "control" of the Twin Vein Co., and we have agreed that things must be run in future in a much more business like manner. For this reason I feel compelled once and for all, to"talk turkey!" I have put over $75,000.00 of my own funds (which was done GRATUITOUSLY!) into this venture, and this has reduced my personal income by over $4,250.00 per annum and I am not a rich man as Mr. Perry probably has led you to suppose! I have gotten some $10,000.00 more from various friends, and I must be held accountable to them as well as the stockholders, as president of the company! I do not propose to let go of this business, until I have gotten to the bottom of it, even if it costs a few thousand more to do so, and even if it is eventually necessary to send down a new General Manager who will keep us better informed and can run things in a more business- like way, and have the directors request your resignation! This I will not do until you have had another month's chance or so, but you are having your last chance now, for our patience is about exhausted! If you will carefully explain the whys and wherefores of our apparent lack of success so far, we will listen carefully, but <u>silence</u> or <u>no attention paid</u> upon your part to our requests for information can only have eventually the above-mentioned result!

"I am well aware that you have now less calls on your time than when the mill was being built, etc. and there is no reason in the world for the uncertain, generalized, unsatisfactory way in which we are kept informed of what is going on, and how the money we supply at great sacrifice is being used- I might even say we are kept in ignorance by lack of any information at important periods!

"In connection with what I have set forth sheet 5, I am well aware you have done very well in many ways, that your salary is over $6,000.00 in arrears, which I would point out has been due largely to the fact we have not made any money nearly as soon

> as you predicted, indeed guaranteed. I am now willing to place before the board of directors the question of giving you some of the 6,000 odd shares still remaining unissued in the treasury, released automatically from my collateral notes, when I was issued the bonds in lieu of my advances of cash to the company for operation and development, but feel sure you do not have the faith in the property you had and would prefer cash of $6,000.00 even to the entire 6,000 shares of stock, even if it were possible in any way for us to issue them to you at $1.00 per share.
>
> "I am keeping a carbon copy of this letter which I consider of the utmost importance to the whole enterprise, and I am sure any stockholder or outside party, such as Mr. Howe, would agree with me as to its necessity and justice!
>
> "I hope we will more thoroughly understand each other in the future, and that you will be able shortly to send us some DEFINATELY favorable report of the result of the operations."[11]

The Colonel had requested Squier suspend his practice of sending embarrassing telegrams to him in Mineral. Squier said he could understand why the Colonel did not want these matters made public knowledge.

> "As we all know, telegrams were read by many local citizens and gossip goes through a small town like fire. I have done this in the past because my letters have so often remained with no reply or attention paid to them. If you want no further telegrams sent about such matters as accounts and the lack of gold, you know how in the future to prevent it."[12]

---

11 February 23, 1925, Letter from Charles B. Squier to Col. Thomas R. Marshall
12 February 23, 1925, Squier

The Colonel is not happy with what Squier said and responded on February 25.

"Your letter of the twenty third was received yesterday afternoon when I came up from the mine. It was long and interesting and I shall try to accept it in the spirit which you say it was written, although you allowed a good deal of acrimony to invade it at the end.

"As you know I have had four men visit the property, one after the other since the twentieth of January, and it required that I be with them constantly. At night they were in my room up to a late hour and that prevented all but a little clerical work being done. Mr. Wright arrived on the twentieth of January and was here for more than a week. Mr. Shoemaker (the new mill man) arrived on February the 8th, Mr. Yerxa arrived on the 9th and was here for two days. Mr. DePencier arrived on the 14th of February and only left here on Sunday the Twenty- Second. All of these men were in the interest of the company and three of them gave considerable assistance in the way of advice and suggestions.

"The statement for the month of January was mailed to Mr. Sutphen on February the 6th at 5:00 PM and if he has not received it I will make a copy and send it to him.

"All of the betterments to the mill have been made by the force regularly employed and with material on hand, with the exception of a few pipe fittings and twenty feet of rubber hose. We are now completing a small assay office, having used the equipment that you saw here which had been bought some time ago at a very small price. The necessary chemicals and a little apparatus required have been bought at a cost of $110.90. This was absolutely necessary to have to enable us to run the mill with any success and certainly as to what we were doing. Mr. Howe advised that we have it at once. All assaying can be done by us here.

"We have succeeded in turning up the mill to such an extent that now we can put through the mill the full capacity of 50 tons per twenty-four hours and with a very small loss in the tails. We are steaming the plates this week and are making a clean up of the mill, we will start with clean plates and I will be in a position to state the amount of ore put through the mill and the recovery with some degree of accuracy.

"In my last letter I suggested adding to the force underground to enable us to feed the mill to capacity. It will require 15 men at $ 2.50 per day and one leader at $3.00 per day. Mr. Shoemaker's salary is two hundred dollars per month that should be paid weekly."[13]

According to the Colonel's daily load tally sheet they hauled 23 loads on February 19, 17 loads on the February 20, and fewer loads each successive day until February 24 when they hauled only 9 loads.[14] Each truck was capable of hauling one ton per load. The Colonel overstated what was put through the mill, because the numbers show they never put anything close to 50 tons per day through it as the Colonel had led Squier to believe.

---

13 February 25, 1925, Letter from Col. Thomas R. Marshal to Charles B. Squier
14 Talley sheet, Col. Thomas R. Marshall

ANOTHER IRON IN THE FIRE

While all of these items were on his plate, the Colonel had a side deal going with Mr. DePencier consisting of an agreement for him to take over an option on the Virginia Lead & Zinc Corporation's mine in Spotsylvania County, Virginia. This deal between the Colonel and DePencier was so secret that the telegrams between them were in code. The Colonel was sent a World War I code book by H. P. DePencier so they could send telegrams back and forth without fear of being exposed by the telegraph operator in Mineral. During the time the Colonel claimed he was busy with company business he had taken a little trip to Richmond for a meeting with the receiver of the ValZinCo Mine, during which he negotiated an option on the mine.

In 1909 the Spotsylvania property, or later Valzinco Mine, was controlled by Mr. Elam and Mr. Jeffries before it was worked by the Continental Development Corporation in 1910. During this period the Colonel was working for the Continental Corporation as a mining engineer. The Corporation was formed on November 8th, 1908 with its headquarters in New York City. An option on the Spotsylvania Pyrites property was obtained by Colonel Marshall for the Continental Development Corporation on December 8, 1909.

A mine report, submitted by Mr. W. G. Eberhardt, a Mining Engineer employed by Ricketts & Banks, a Mining, Metallurgical and Chemical engineering firm, detailed the Pyrites property in Spotsylvania County.

> "This property consisted of about 900 acres of well timbered land and had been reported on most favorably by several engineers, including Mr. Eberhardt, who believed it was a good pyrites property."[1]

---

[1] 1909 Mine Report, W. G. Eberhardt

ANOTHER IRON IN THE FIRE

The ore obtained could be traced by the gossan (hydrated oxide of iron, usually found at the decomposed outcrop of a mineral vein[2]) outcrop, which ran through the entire length of the property and at some places was 50 to 75 feet wide. The problem of its treatment into marketable products was a cause for concern.

Eberhardt continued,

> "Within certain limits we have done this and herewith append a statement based upon prices quoted us by the New Jersey Zinc Company and what can be obtained from the buyers of lead ore. (This type of ore was called a complex ore because it contained lead, zinc, pyrite, iron, copper and some quartz and which made it more difficult to separate into its individual mineral products.)
>
> "The option on the property has been renewed by Colonel Thomas R Marshall until the 8th of January, but we are still awaiting extension papers. The purchase price is $65,000.00.and it will be necessary to make further expenditures if we should determine the property is such as this Company desires to acquire. It will be necessary not only to arrange for the purchase price of the property in the near future, but also for the installation of a plant capable of treating the ore therefrom. The total expenditures for both purposes and working capital will probably be in the neighborhood of $150,000.00 to $175,000.00
>
> "On November the 14th the assay from the 150 foot level arrived. The report showed Lead content at 11.70%, Zinc 26.48%, copper 0.76&, Iron 10.23%, sulfur 22.21% and silica (insoluble matter which can be reduced to 9%) 24%."[3]

Development of the mine continued under the guidance of Colonel Marshall, and the shaft was sunk to a depth of 165 feet. The Continental Development

---

[2] Raymond, R. W., A Glossary of Mining and Metallurgical Terms, from Vol. IX, Transactions of The American Institute of Mining Engineers, Easton, Pa., The Institute pg 44
[3] 1909 Mine Report by W. G. Eberhardt

Company was not financially able to continue and work finally stopped. During his time of employment with the Continental Development Company the Colonel had allowed his salary to lapse for some period of time. The Colonel eventually filed a lawsuit to collect his overdue salary and other money he believed he was owed.

On March 8, 1912 the lawsuit brought by the Colonel was settled which covered all claims, disputes, salary and expenses. Colonel Marshall received $1,100.00 of which he was ordered by the court to pay $543.40 to four other men who had provided services and done work for the company. The court also ordered the Colonel to pay the "costs upon the pending judgments in Virginia of $119.50".[4]

The Colonel was awarded all of the Company's interest and property including the plant, machinery and ore on the premises at the time. On October 4th, 1912 the Continental Development Company was officially dissolved and Colonel Marshall was the proud owner of a lead and zinc mine.[5]

After the settlement the mine was renamed the Marshall Mine. In August of 1914 the Colonel and William Seton Gordon of New York entered into an agreement to work together in an effort to market the mine to whomever would advance the $150,000 cash money needed to operate the mine. The corporation they formed was called the Dominion Zinc and Lead Corporation with an authorized capital stock of $1,000,000. The Corporation's offer was if someone invested $150,000, they would in turn receive $250,000 dollars par value of company stock.. The Colonel would receive for his services, stock in the company of the par value of $250,000.

The mine was later sold to the Virginia Lead and Zinc Corporation and was operated in conjunction with the Valcooper Mine in Louisa County, Virginia. The Virginia Lead and Zinc Corporation operated the mines until they went into receivership after 1918.[6]

The Colonel's attention to business was still not dedicated exclusively to that of the Twin Vein Mine. On February 20, 1925 he had received a telegram from his

---

4   Court papers of Col. Thomas R. Marshall
5   Court papers continued
6   Court papers continued

prospective buyer in code, (fore, excellent, atones, opera, plethoric, presumption, abstains, secured), which read as follows:

"for examination at once please preserve absolute secrecy."[7]

Another encoded telegram from Porcupine, Ontario dated February 26, 1925 read,

"winning, tamely, overhaul, orchestra, openness, testaments, oval, atones, Richmond, year, funded, passes, fourfold, orchestra, fore, excellent, atones, opera, plethoric, presumption, abstains, secured.".

After being decoded it read as follows:

"will take over option on terms outlined at Richmond meeting. Writing full particulars forward option for examination at once."[8]

The Colonel's reply followed on February 27, after being decoded it read,

"will go Richmond Monday for written option forwarding from there."[9]

H. P. DePencier sent the Colonel a letter and option for the Virginia Lead & Zinc Corporation on February 28. DePencier had some reservations regarding the discrepancy between the average assay value reported by the company in their statement to the shareholders and the average set by Ricketts and Banks. In fact, it was so great that he did not make up his mind until he had given the proposition additional consideration.

---

7 February 20, 1925, Telegram from H. P. De Pencier to Col. Thomas R. Marshall
8 February 26, 1925, Telegram from H. P. De Pencier to Col. Thomas R. Marshll
9 February 27, 1925, Telegram from Col. Thomas R. Marshall to H. P. De Pencier

Mr. DePencier was a very cautious man and for good reason, the value of a mine is quite frequently overstated.. He decided, that the only way to settle the question was by doing some exploration work, and with this in view, he wired the Colonel to procure the option, under those conditions. Mr. DePencier had also instructed the Colonel to acquire options on properties to the north and south of the mine property. This was a very common practice and it allowed for the expansion of the mine without having to pay very high prices after the mining operation proved to be a success. The option included a clause, giving Colonel Marshall the exclusive right to purchase the lands described in it.

"The land was to be free from any encumbrance whatsoever, this applied to taxes, mechanics' lien or other indebtedness not specified. It called for a complete inventory of all equipment, machinery.[10]

Meanwhile, Charles Squier still had not received the information and reports he had continuously requested from the Colonel. The mine continued to struggle as production was quite low even though they had a state of the art processing plant. It was still thought that the presence of mud in the ore dump could be causing the very fine gold to wash through the plant and be lost.

Squier fired off another telegram informing the Colonel that they were sending funds for only two weeks operation and he was to run the mill at full capacity with 250 tons of the best ore. The message included another request for a full and detailed report of the results and if they were unfavorable he was to cease operations. Squier demanded the original letter from Dome Mines and their assay of Twin Vein ore, which according to the Colonel, showed a value of sixty dollars per ton. Squier told the Colonel, "It is no use in avoiding this."[11]

Colonel responded on March 4,

> "I have your last letters and telegrams before me and will try to answer them as fully as possible, to make you understand the situation here and comply with your requests.

---

10 February 28, 1925, Letter from H. P. De Pencier to Col. Thomas R. Marshall
11 March 2, 1925, Telegram from Charles B. Squier to Col. Thomas R. Marshall

ANOTHER IRON IN THE FIRE

"I have with me as an assistant to manage the mill a young man who has been well trained by one of the best Mill Men in the whole country. We are both working with all the energy and intelligence that we have to make the property show a profit.

"The Mill as a mechanical unit is working and functioning well and we are able to put through it the full load of <u>Twenty-Five Tons</u> in <u>Ten Hours</u>.

"There is on the dump a large pile of ore taken from the shaft, it is mixed with much fine material that was broken with the Ore, which has made it hard to put through the mill up to now. Mr. Shoemaker and I have examined it and discussed the point of continuing to run it in the mill. As the fines carry some value, Mr. Shoemaker advises and I concur with him that it is best to continue running it and to run with it some fresh ore from the shaft. I have put <u>Ten Men</u> in the shaft and we are breaking some good ore to run with the ore on the dump, and this week we will be able to report the amount put through the mill and the value of the recovery.

"Yesterday we retorted the amount of amalgam on hand and it netted a little more than ten ounces, refined of all but the silver in the amalgam. It is impossible to state exactly the number of tons of ore that produced it because of the adjusting that we were doing, but this week that can be given exactly.

"When you and Sutphen were here I put through the mill the best ore available in order to show you that the plates would catch the gold put over them and you saw a fair amount of recovery, with the same grade of ore we can do as well and better now.

"I do not wish to criticize Mr. Yerxa but to judge by what he did while here, I don't know what he came for. He did not inspect the ore workings under ground, only a casual look at the ore on the dump, he took only two samples of the ore as it came from the rod mill and from the amalgam traps (and at a time when he knew that the fine ore from the dump was going to the mill), I did not expect his samples to show much value.

"Since you were here we have had with us three men from the Dome Mines Ltd. who took the trouble to examine everything here, both the ore and the equipment, each were here for a week giving themselves a sufficient time to digest the situation. They said that we had a lot of fine gold in our ore, that we had a good plant for its size, that they believed that we had the values and that we should do a good business if we stood to it and worked out the problems.

"I am making up a duplicate of the statement for January and will try to get it off tomorrow with the statement for February.

"Enclosed you will find the paid note for the last payment on the trucks, I send it rather than get the notice receipted.

"I did not pay the Compensation Insurance because I did not have the money to pay it with. I had told you that it would have to be paid and gave the approximate amount, but it was long time getting a statement and bill from the Insurance Co.

"If there is any other subject that I have not referred to, please write me and it will have my attention. I do not know what you refer to in your telegram "there is no use avoiding this", I am sure that no one who understands a mining property and who has seen this one would pronounce it a "fake"- It may be a little difficult to save the values and make a profit immediately after assembling the equipment but it can and will be done.

I recommend that you and Sutphen come down and see first hand what is being done."[12]

Colonel Marshall shipped one sealed package of gold bullion valued at $300 to the Superintendent of the Philadelphia Mint on March the 6th.[13]

---

12 March 4, 1925, Letter from Col. Thomas R. Marshall to Charles B. Squier
13 March 6, 1925, Receipt for gold from American Railway Express

It should be noted that this is a very small amount of gold considering the processing rate of 50 tons of ore per twenty-four hours. With a conservative figure of four days or 200 tons of ore being processed, the $300 of bullion is very bad news for the Colonel and the future of the Twin Vein Mine. They shipped only 14.5 ounces to the mint and this amount is in line with the assay which was preformed by Ledoux and Company on February 18, 1925 which showed a mere .01 ounces of gold per ton before being processed.[14]

On March 9 Mr. L. M. Williams, Esquier, Receiver (someone who preserves property during litigation) for the Virginia Lead and Zinc Corporation in Richmond, Virginia received a letter of introduction from Colonel Marshall.

> "My principal, which is one of the largest mining companies in the United States, authorized me to say to you that they will give you two hundred dollars per month for six months for the right of exploring your Virginia Lead and Zinc property, upon the condition that they shall have the right at any time within six months to buy the property from you at two hundred thousand dollars cash.
>
> "My principal will also agree to spend not less than twenty five thousand dollars in diamond drilling and exploring the property within the next six months and will give you full access to all the findings from the drill holes. You shall have access to the log showing the results of the drilling every thirty days."[15]

---

14 February 18, 1925 assay by Ledoux and Co.
15 March 9, 1925, Letter from Col. Thomas R. Marshall to L. M. Williams

DISAGREEMENTS

The Colonel received another tough communication form Charles Squier on March the 10, 1925.

"I have been intending to write you several days ago, but have been prevented from doing so by a slight attack of the grippe (and old word for influenza) from which, I am happy to say, I have now practically recovered. I have before me your last two letters, of Feb. 25th ultimo, and of March 4th, which I have gone over carefully and considerately- they are somewhat longer than you are wont to write, but not very practical or business like and much too general to be convincing- they are not the kind of reports that a company's officers have every right to demand from the general manager in charge of its property!

"Your excuse about having four different men at Mineral, during several weeks time, with whom you had to confer, is not a good one- you could in several short half- hour periods during that time have written a few short letters, "quite to the point", which could have succinctly answered several perfectly simple questions satisfactorily! Mr. Sutphen has not yet received your January statement or your February statement- I will call him again tomorrow morning to get the "latest" news- such dilatoriness upon your part is unpardonable. You say in one letter you sent him the January statement on February 6th Ultimo, and in a subsequent letter mailed by you after February 6th you say you are "going" to send it at once- such statements plainly do not "gee"!

DISAGREEMENTS

"Sutphen sent you last Wednesday, the 4th, $660.00, being $500 for regular labor and operation, $50.00 for your Canadian "Dome" mill-man, and $110.00 for the supplies for the assay plant mentioned in your letter of 25th of Feb. ult. now before me here. Your same letter states you need $40.50 per diem for fifteen additional men with leader for mining of new ore- this meaning about $250.00 per week- $15.00 per diem- 6 men- should run the shaft-house and mill on about $105 per week, allowing for Sunday- and six men for getting fuel, about $90.00 per week- so your labor bill cannot run over $450.00 per week, even with the considerable additional force under-ground. Do you frequently go down in the mine, as otherwise how do ignorant miners know how to follow the trend of the ore veins?

"I have as yet no reply to my IMPORTANT questions as to whether the 1,200 tons you had on the dump long ago, of which you say not over 200 has been used, was not bad stuff and just a waste? Also, where is that report of the stuff refined for us, some months ago at Dome Mines- you surely must have some letter from them for us to see?

"When is the interest due on the loan obtained last summer form the Louisa Bank- I suppose they are duly acquainted with the fact that, in as much as the money was paid to you, without orders from us here, instead of to the company's treasurer, at a time when we had several pressing bills here to pay, such as the insurance bill from Richmond, which you seem to have quite ignored according to letters received from the agent by me recently, that we can technically repudiate such loan, and that their subsequent withholding of $1,000 of the amount they agreed to furnish can be treated as illegal usury! I must comment that the Virginia methods of doing business seem often not only antediluvian, but highly irregular!

"I do not see any point to your remarks about Mr. Yerxa's report, which was satisfactory and quite UNBIASED by any false optimism!

It was just another confirmation in my mind of the undeniable fact that no expense for mill or other equipment should have ever been incurred before the ore bodies had been thoroughly opened up and blocked out by an unbiased expert and a full report made of same; and it looks as though our ore was not very good or in sufficient quantities to make the operation pay!

"When you do not answer our pertinent questions, and you are in a position to do so, if you wanted to, it only make us suspicious! I cannot understand how you can have built your mill and equipment so well and carefully, how you can always have your accounts apparently in good order whenever we are in Mineral (always without any duplicates, however), and how you can run the rest of it in so slipshod a manner, when it comes to furnishing information to the people up north, who are "sweating blood" to supply the continuous drain of funds without any return! However, we are now about at the end, because under such conditions I am not going to "put up" any more money, and the other stockholders have repeatedly demonstrated their inability to do so! If the ore is no good, why don't you admit it, and then we can try to sell the property for what it may be worth You several times told me and others that you had some people in mind who would like to take the property off our hands; well, why not "trot them out"- you have, however, said a great many things, which never turned out, so I am very skeptical now!

"Mr. Howe, whom you know and have faith in, advised, as I let you know several weeks ago, running the mill- full tilt with good ore for two weeks, using at lea-st 250 tons in all- if results were not gratifying then he thought it was no use sending more money after bad! I am mailing him tonight a copy of this letter to you, with your two last letters to me, as he is interested and asked to be kept informed of all developments! My "night- letter" telegram of March 2nd., copy

DISAGREEMENTS

of which I am sending Howe also gives the plan to you, so you know what to expect and plan for accordingly!

"Sutphen, who paid the insurance bill recently, which we never knew anything about, and which they claim they went after you for information about at least 12 times over several months last year(!), will send you $500.00 more tomorrow which will reach you not later than Friday, to run full- tilt this week, as at last- we must then know exact, certified results- if unsatisfactory, we will close down, with the idea of either investigating the ore more throughly, or of trying to sell out the property, in which case there will be nothing left for the stockholders, and your past- due salary will rank pro- rata only with the amount obtained with my bonds!

"You do not seem impressed by the fact that I have personally "sunk" over $80,000.00 in this fool hardy undertaking, and for a long, dreary period of over fifteen months, have entirely financed the thing out of my own pocket, and I am getting pretty sick of it all!

"After this week you must shut down all expense, except for two men to keep the pump at the shaft running and two more for the necessary fuel for that one boiler- also, we must be notified just what this will cost, or I shall presume it will cost $2.50 per man- two shifts at the pump and boiler or 4 men and three for fuel at most, or a total of seven, @$2.50 each for a total of $17.50 per diem, for a total of $100 per week, or less- this is all we will send after this week, until we have before us all questions asked, all accounts demanded and all reports necessary to make me think with expert advice here, there is any use in proceeding further! You must take stock generally after this week, and close down in the interim, as there will be no further funds- THIS IS QUITE FINAL!

"You, perhaps know very few gold mines pay, unless operated on a large scale of tonnage or with bonanza ore running at $1,000.00 per ton as is found in the Yukon!

ANATOMY OF A GOLD MINE

"I regret exceedingly the peremptory tone of this letter, but it is the "last straw that breaks the camel's back!" Your own peculiarly lax methods of keeping us informed have brought about this letter and others of a semi- disagreeable nature, which my own best interests, as well as my responsibility to the other stockholders, have, rendered unavoidable.

You continue to run this property almost with as little concern for others interests, as though it were practically your own! Almost all the money which has gone into it, you never had anything to do with obtaining! You are only a minority stockholder, if not a large one! There are just $60,000 worth of bonds ahead of your stock or any other stock to be paid off first! These are undeniable facts! Furthermore, we are not conducting an experiment into gold- mining in Virginia, but are interested in the purely, cold blooded question of profits!

"When simple questions are asked or easily obtained information is required from our manager, we want it at once, without any unnecessary delays or "stalling", and we are most positively going to have it in the future, or have some other more business- like manager! It is now up to you to explain and make good- this is your <u>last chance</u>!"[1]

The Colonel's reply of March 12 is short and swift for the moment.

"I will answer it tonight in the way that such a letter should be answered. "I will not be so undignified as to follow your example in the use of your verbage (sic) or your veiled innuendos. Since you have in your opinion made such a bad business venture, I shall be glad to have from you a definite proposition to take over your equity interest in the Twin-Vein Mining Co. Inc. I feel sure I can find a business man to join me."[2]

---

1 March 10, 1925, Letter from Charles B. Squier to Col. Thomas R. Marshall
2 March 12, 1925, Letter from Col. Thomas R. Marshall to Charles B. Squier

DISAGREEMENTS

On March 14 the Colonel responds in greater detail to Squier's March 10th letter.

"The letter is unbecoming in you and it is offensive to me and I regret that I am not in New York to answer it personally. When you write to me again please be more careful of your verbage *(sic)* and keep your irritation under control you have no one but yourself to blame for my attitude for you have kept me handicapped from the very first by the failure to supply me with the necessary funds to enable me to do what should have been done and you have held back my salary when I have so often told you that I actually needed it. You have forced me to personally borrow the money to pay the labor on a number of weekends and you have written me letters that were so disagreeable that I have submitted them to members of your board to read in order that they might see what I was contending with.

"Your trouble, Mr. Squier, is that you put too high a value on your money, it makes you so arrogant and insolent, two very disagreeable traits in a man when you have to be associated with him in any way. I dislike to speak so plainly but I would be derelict to myself if under the circumstances I failed to do so.

"Mr. Howe, Mr. DePencier and others who have been down here and looked over the work done here, have said that my work has been done in an intelligent and economical way, but that I had not had money enough to do the work that should have been done. I will submit it to any capable critic.

"I have been doing everything in my power, under the circumstances to push the business ahead, for pride in my profession makes me want to prove the property a good one and that my judgment was not in fault.

"To answer your questions categorically, the ore on the dump is good to go through the mill, in the dump there is rich ore, but as the fines carried some value and I tried to save it, the result being that the large percentage of fines has reduced the percent value per ton of ore as it now stands. I have pointed out to the men who have been here, especially so to Mr. Howe and they have advised using it in the mill to recover the values although it is of a lower percentage than clean ore would be.

"I have commenced work on the east vein in hope of getting some higher grade ore to put "through the mill with the ore now on the dump. The first assay of this vein shows value and I think it will improve and Mr. Shoemaker agrees with me in this opinion.

"Mr. Shoemaker says he can make the mill pay with the ore he has been able to see and he states he is satisfied the property has a large tonnage of good ore. I am glad that some one other than myself has that opinion as to the property.

"My advice to you is that you continue to operate the mill for the next two weeks in order to give us time to get the actual data that you want, the assay of the ore in place which will go into the mill. No shorter time will suffice now that we have a good mill man and the outfit to assay the different samples to show us what we are actually doing. If you decide against this please notify me at once and I will know exactly what to do. If I had my salary I would do it myself.

"Just here allow me to call your attention to the position that my salary account holds relative to the other claims on the property. It is a workman's or mechanics' lien which in this state comes first before any other. I will be pleased if you will make a payment on account of it as it is greatly in arrears.

"The loan made to the company by the First National Bank of Louisa will be due on the 15th of April. I was given written authority by the board of directors to make this loan and the Attorney of the Company prepared the papers and came here personally to see that it was legally done; you have been given all of the particulars often.

DISAGREEMENTS

"I have directed all of the underground work and have personally seen that it was done, if any mistakes were made it is my fault. Mr. Evans, the accountant who wrote up the books will make up the certified statement that you desire on Tuesday, March the 17th and I will forward it to the Treasurer immediately. I trust that I have given you all of the information that you have asked for, and will follow with all data that we obtain. I have no desire to be unfriendly or disagreeable but I think that when you reflect a little you will acknowledge that I have had a good deal to contend with and have been working under great disadvantage."[3]

On March 21, Mr. Williams, Receiver of the defunct Valzinco Mine in Spotsylvania County, Virginia told the Colonel, that they were prepared to accept the option for $250,000, which would be good until October 1, 1925. This was all based on the memorandum that he had given the Colonel the day before, with the stipulation that they were to begin development work on the mine during the month of April 1925. The work was to continue in a serious manner and they were expected to accept the option from Williams as Receiver, which would be subject to approval by the Court. Williams said they would not have to wait until he could give the Colonel a deed of bargain and sale.

Williams advised the Colonel that he represented a majority of stockholders and they proposed to foreclose on the property and give the Colonel title to it. Williams believed they could close the deal in sixty days.[4]

The Colonel had better learn to duck as things really began to heat up when Squier replied to the Colonel's letter of March. Your letters of the 14th and 17th insts were duly received and the contents carefully noted. Your remarks as to verbiage, control of irritation, etc., I would not descend to your level to answer. They are childish and unwarranted in the extreme!

---

3 March 14, 1925, Letter from Col. Thomas R. Marshall to Charles B. Squier
4 March 21, 1925, Letter from Williams to Col. Thomas R. Marshall

"However, whatever remarks I have felt constrained to make in the best interests of the company have been JUSTIFIED by your entirely satisfyingly unpractical and unbusinesslike manner of "sending in no statements of expenditures, making generalized statements of the results of operation and in general, telling us <u>nothing</u>"! Well, we don't swallow this sort of thing for ever- I may not know what is going on at Mineral, but I can get very excellent expert advice here in this great city as to just what should be reported and as to just what should be the results! You have killed the goose that laid the golden eggs!

"Now, to get down to business: don't you think it is about time you made a formal report of the results of the last two weeks turnover before the mill was closed down: How many tons of ore actually went over the plates, whether 250 tons, as Mr. Howe named as a minium, or more, and exactly what was the gold recovery obtained- have you received same from the Philadelphia mint, or am I to understand that the mint check for some odd $70.00 sent Sutphen the last time (very recently) was the result of processing 250 tons of ore, less than 30 cents per ton! Sutphen said you thought the results were very disappointing yourself! Do you think you know good ore when you see it?!!!

"Please state at once the cost of the following two operations: running night and day the pump for the shaft and mine, including fuel; and removing the pump from the mine, thereby flooding the mine, but shutting off all expense! <u>We</u> must make this decision- it is fairer to say: <u>I must</u>, etc.!

"I think the following will be of extreme interest to you; my attorney recently culled the following from the latest book on Virginia statutes and law. In re lien of the general manager of a mine?: "Quoting the Virginia Code of 1924: S6438: "All clerks, Mechanics ...and laborers, who furnish their services and labor to any mining...company...shall have a prior lien in the franchises, gross earnings, and in all real estate and personal property of said company...to the extent of the monies due them by said company for such wages****.

DISAGREEMENTS

"The president is not within this language- nor does designating him as "general manager" bring him within the class of employees sought to be protected... .

Conclusion: manager has no lien for salary!
Opinion rendered by : Dos Passos Brothers, 68, Williams Street, New York City.

"I am not attempting to use the above, except in case of necessity, as I appreciate the value of services you have rendered the company in some respects, but WE WANT COLD FACTS, AND NOT FOOLISHNESS! Make your report of the last two weeks of operation, and have your Richmond certified public accountant make up on his letterhead the reports of outgo and income for last year and for January and February of 1925! If you know what is good for you, you will comply with the above reasonable requests!

"Sutphen gave me the letters from the Dome Mine, Limited and I am not surprised you withheld them so long- the results are unconvincing. Also, why did you come to New York last Friday, and with Mr. DePencier? Why did you not apprise me of your coming and have an interview with me? Obviously, because I should have asked you some questions you could have not answered- you are unfortunately, my dear sir, dealing with practical northern businessmen, and we are going to get to the bottom of this mine, if it means "firing" you, and having a thorough report made by some trustworthy and unbiased party, before we make any move looking toward selling out the property!

"I am sorry if the "verbiage" of this letter offends you, but, again, I must remark, you have only to thank yourself for the reasons producing such an attitude! A sensible, businesslike reply will facilitate matters greatly, and will not be bad for your own, personal best interests!"[5]

---

5   March 26, 1925 Letter, from Charles B. Squier to Col. Thomas R. Marshall

Once again, the Colonel seemed to ignore the last communication from Charles Squier as the mill was still running for a third week after he was told to run for two weeks and shut down. There was still no reply to Charles Squier's letter of March 26 and Squier fired off another letter to the Colonel three days later.

THE CAVE-IN

On March 29 Charles Squier informed the Colonel in another letter.

"I shall endeavor to stick strictly to business even though your continued way of sending us no information of any definite kind is very annoying and unsatisfactory in the extreme.

"First: How much ore in tons did you actually put through the mill in the last two weeks of operation? Second: Just where did the ore come from? State whether from the dump or mine, and, if from the mine- new ore, from which levels? Third: What are the new, net gold recovery results from the above tonnage put through in the above time?

"Mr. Howe thinks there is no reason why you should not be able to answer these questions very simply! Mr. Yerxa states the mill is perfectly able to give full recoveries from our kind of ore now. Thus, it is easy to see what the ore runs!

"Why did H. P. DePencier come to Mineral the second time, and had the Dome Mines people at any past time, before our crowd exercised the option, wanted to consider buying the property? (Charles Squier is not yet aware of the Colonel's other dealings concerning the mine in Spotsylvania County.)

"Sutphen showed me your letter Friday- you had received a telegram well over three weeks ago to run the mill the two weeks provided for and to shut down until the results were known, so, why did you have to run up a bill of $340.00 approximately for labor the third week? This is unnecessary, unless explained to our entire satisfaction! I did not send any money this week, nor can I send much more any week- I have suffered considerable losses in the sudden and sharp fall in the securities markets recently, and am not able to continue pumping money out of my own pockets into a venture which seems to have little chance of ever making any money!

"You estimated that $50,000.00 would be ample to put the property at least on a paying basis- well considerably over $80,00.00.00 have disappeared into it so far, and all we have seen is a paltry $235.00 in returns! I will not consider selling out, until we have had the ore bodies thoroughly examined, however, by some outside, unbiased expert- you have made so many wild statements as to earnings and values that I really believe that you are far too optimistic on the property, and I feel it better to get some more rational party's estimate! Furthermore, we most certainly are, at least out of my pocket, not going to conduct a groping expedition to find "somewhere" some pay dirt, which might just as easily be half- way to Louisa C. H.! If the Dome Mines people are interested in our property to buy, let them make a WRITTEN offer, none other will be considered!"[1]

The Colonel had commissioned the services of William McKendree Evans & Company Certified Public Accountants in order to have the books brought up to date as per Charles Squier's demand. The cost of making up the accounts by the Richmond firm was $331.00.

Squier continues his letter of March 29th.

"In re the bill of Mr. Evans, in the first place, $331.00 seems very high indeed for the three or four days spent at Mineral- you will remember that we had sent down Mr. Barker, a good accountant, who was quite capable of making up your accounts, and would have done them for $25.00, if you had at least assisted him to see

---

1   March 29, 1925, Letter from Charles B,. Squier to Col. Thomas R. Marshall

where and what they were, instead of acting in the way you did, as to his coming! You agreed to pay the Certified Accountants' charges last December in New York out of your personal funds before Sutphen as a witness, also in a letter around that time, if you have no funds to pay the bill with, which I think is unreasonably large (!) we will pay the bill, when adjusted downwards, and debit your salary account that much! Incidently, I can secure the services of a thoroughly competent mine manager here for $350.00 per month, one who will render regular and businesslike reports, so I see no reason why the $500.00 rate should be continued, especially by a company that is pressed for funds! Please remember no personal liability attaches to any officer of the company for debts, but only to the company itself.

"I have written Mr. Evans in Richmond, stating what is set forth above for his information, and advising he settle the matter with you directly as you are the only one who knows what time and expense were used!

"I have also written the First National Bank of Louisa, asking about the loan, why only $4,000.00 was paid, why the money was irregularly paid to you, and not to the treasurer here, and that we will of course only be obligated to pay the interest and principal on the amount furnished- I trust, in this connection, you did not sign any receipt for more than the $4,000 actually received- even if you did, you were not duly authorized to do so, and it would not stand as good, when we show we only received four thousand dollars as you are not one of the company's officers empowered to sign such receipts!

"If you ask any reputable attorney either in Richmond or any other large Virginia town, where people are up to date and acquainted with the Virginia law, you will ascertain your salary, as general manager, does not rank as a mechanics lien, etc and ranks after bonded indebtedness, etc. Also, that you have signed papers which make it quite impossible for you to recover any damages from either Coghill or Perry, either as syndicate members or stockholders- I am setting this information forth merely for your information!

"Please let me know at once the minimum expense possible to keep the shaft-house boiler and pump running PER WEEK, which we will probably do for a month also- the expense of taking the pump out altogether!

"I appreciate all of the difficulties you have had, and am very sorry, but were they not largely your own fault in that in the very beginning you jumped at the conclusion we had a large amount of valuable ore, when we had no proof of same and the mill should not have ever been put up, and all that expense incurred, before we knew just where we were in REAL values?

"The maximum amount I can afford to put up is $1,000.00 more, and some of this must be set aside for expert analysis of the ore bodies- and this sum can be advanced only during the month of April up to May first!

"Sutphen and I had a long talk last Monday at lunch in the Downtown Club with Colonel Tainter, the engineer who made a favorable report about the mine, and who really feels a moral obligation in having gotten the syndicate members into the mine property! He still feels his samples were widely and well taken, although they could have been tampered with by anyone at Mineral after he left, as they were subsequently sent to New York by express and not taken with him, which is always safer."[2]

The mine could have been salted before Colonel Tainter took his samples. This practice has been in use as long as people have been selling mines. One of the ways the mine could have been salted is by the use of a shotgun. This method of salting involves the replacement of lead shot with gold dust, after which the perpetrator fires the weapon at the walls in different locations throughout the mine. The gold

---

2   March 29, 1925, Squier

dust which is soft will adhere to the rock surfaces in the mine and this will cause a geologist to inadvertently collect salted samples of ore.

When the samples are assayed, they will show good value and someone will buy a worthless mine. If the mine was salted, the identity of who salted it is not known at this time, however, generally the suspects are limited to a very few who will profit.

Squier continued.

> "He tells me there is a small gold mine operating on small values near the Great Falls of the Potomac River on the Maryland side very near Washington and I am going down to Washington this coming month to investigate this mine through the Bureau of Mines, if this has been operating for some years on similar ores at some small profit, why should we not be able to do the same?
>
> "There is no use of Sutphen or I coming to Mineral now, as we do not know enough of the practical side to find out anything more than you can answer very simply in letters, if you want to do so. If you have an occasion to come to New York, let me see you for a short interview- I have no intention of getting mad, but of simply asking you questions of a perfectly reasonable character, which I doubt very much you can satisfactorily answer!"[3]

Colonel Marshall replied on March 31.

> "Your letter of the Twenty- Ninth was received, I hope to have the assays completed by tonight that we have made on all of the levels which will complete the assay map promised. It will give you all the data requested in your letter."
>
> "DePencier has at no time been interested in the purchase of the Twin Vein Mine property and he has made no advances to me

---

3   March 29, 1925, Squier

nor have I to him. He, Mr. Dowsett and Mr. Wright of the Dome Mines Limited have been very kind in helping me to solve the problem here and have been of great help to me. Mr. Wright when here saw in my room samples of ore from a mine in an adjacent county that interested him very much, and he requested me to allow him to take them home with him together with my reports on the same. They so interested Mr. DePencier that he has made two trips here to look at the property. Had I wished to interest him in the gold of this district, I have control of five properties that contain a greater acreage and a longer strike of ore than the Twin Vein contains.

"As to Mr. Evans' bill for the work done on the companies accounts, I determined to select the best Accountant in the state, and one widely known, because I knew that only such a one would satisfy your characteristics. I told him that I expected to pay his bill and he replied that I would be very foolish to do so, as it was a perfectly correct charge against the company and he did not think the company would allow me to pay it out of my pocket. I therefore acted on his suggestion and sent it in to see what your attitude would be. If you had paid my salary which is just and equitable, and you know that I have earned it, you would not be bothered with these little matters.

"As to the loan in the Bank in Louisa, as you state that you have written to the bank on the subject, I assume that you will be given all the facts in the case. I have repeatedly done so myself, and besides, the attorney for the company, Mr. Battle prepared all of the legal papers and superintended the transaction and I presume that he made a report to you.

"The mill was closed down as you directed and all of the labor has been laid off except enough to run the shaft boiler and pump. You ask for the exact amount to do this. It will require two men on each shift, day and night, light and lubricating oil amounting to $24.50 to $26.00 per day of 24 hours providing no accident or breakdown occurs. I am also sending you the maps of the under-

THE CAVE-IN

ground workings and the results of the assays of the ore taken from the headings (the gold content of the ore as it enters the mill) and from regular intervals along the drifts.

"During the last two weeks of operation 65 truck loads of ore was put through the mill. Each truck load contained one ton of ore, two thirds of the ore came from the dump and one third from the 75 and 100 foot levels in the mine. (This is a far cry from the fifty tons per day the mill is designed to process.) The recovery from the two clean ups yielded 11.30 Troy ounces of gold and the last retorting appears to carry a good amount of silver so we will not know the fineness (how pure) until we get the mint report.

"The labor has not been paid, although they have been laid-off as per your order, I gave Mr. Sutphen an estimate of what would be needed and I trust that you will have it sent down."[4]

On April 2, the Colonel received a telegram form Charles Squier.

"Sutphen sent you a check yesterday to pay off the men and Mr. Shoemaker as they must not suffer after working so faithfully and all further expenses must be discontinued. Two gentlemen (mining engineers) will arrive in Mineral next Monday morning to inspect the mine and it is quite important you be there. Please wire me if you are available."[5]

On April the 6 Squier sent another letter to the Colonel.

"Replying to your last letter received and duly perused, as per my telegram of Sunday evening last, I am sending you herewith enclosed a check for $125.00 which seems to me ample to keep

---

[4] March 31, 1925, Letter from Col. Thomas R. Marshall to Charles B. Squier
[5] April 2, 1925, Telegram Charles B. Squier to Col. Thomas R. Marshall

the shaft pump and boiler in operation during the closing down of the mill. This is for last week, and we will endeavor to have a like amount in your hands by the end of this week for the same payment. You say you estimate this expense to be $24.50 to $26.00 per day, thus: 4 men in two shifts to run the pump @ $2.50 =$10.00; not over three men to cut and haul wood fuel in twelve hours- 3 cords being necessary for the boiler for 24 hours @$2.50 = $7.50, or $17.50 per day, as you know, the lubricating oil would not amount to 50 cents for some considerable time, and is therefore quite negligible, and I think you have no electric lights at the shafthouse sic yet, although probably in the mine you have- so that hand lanterns alone are quite en-ough sic, as we used them long before the little dynamo was put in, so I think $20.00 per day is quite enough to properly run the property on.

"Please let me have your estimate for having the pump taken out, as these expenses without any income can not go on positively! I have had some affairs go wrong lately and I can simply not finance the mine any further, so we will have to cut off all expenses until the company's affairs can be adjusted. I am not going to inconvenience myself further in a cause which seems to be hopeless and which you promised would be productive long ago!

"I am very sorry if your salary is so long overdue, but it was you who kept urging me to finance the property saying it would soon be on at least a paying basis, and assuring me in several letters you were willing to let your salary drift in arrea-rs, until returns came in to justify your prognostications. The company is without funds and I as an individual, am in no way responsible, and also unwilling to pay for what others should pay for pro rata, as they share alike in the benefits. I shall propose next election that the stock be changed to assessable shares, make each one do his or her part, without all this misunderstanding! There never was, and certainly now isn't any plausible reason why one stockholder should bear the whole

THE CAVE-IN

strain, which hurts the two, but mostly the former! I think you will see the justice in what I say, with due consideration. If your delay in receiving your salary is causing you inconvenience, the loss of return of over $80,000.00 cash advanced is likewise not pleasant for me. I am living at a rate of nearly my present income, less taxes and am quite unwilling to jeopardize what my family has been accustomed to any further.

"A short and quite unsatisfactory letter from the bank at Louisa came this morning- we will pay off that loan, when the particular conditions as to your obtaining it are cleared up, but not before, and we will pay $4,000.00 with interest, and not $5,000.00 unless they can show you received for the company the other $1,000.00.

"Mr Evans of Richmond has not responded to my letter- maybe he is away now, and will soon return- he must also satisfy us as to his ridiculously large charge, before being paid, and he will have to be paid by you, as agreed, on account of your unexplained and unnecessary delays in accounting for funds received- his statement is just a "balance sheet" and not itemized at all or does he state he saw all of the corresponding vouchers? ALL OF THESE MATTERS ARE GOING TO BE CLEARED UP, BEFORE WE BUDGE AN INCH!"[6]

Colonel Marshall received bad news on April 6 from Williams regarding the option on the Valzinco mine property. Williams informed the Colonel that there was no use in submitting any offer that did not obligate the Colonel's associates to spend a minimum of twenty-five thousand dollars on diamond drilling and de-watering the mine. This time period was to begin when they signed the option on October first. Williams also wanted the Colonel to put up a bond to guarantee he would stick to the terms of the agreement. Williams advised the Colonel to work through a good bonding company or an individual of large means. This would guarantee the expenditure of twenty five-thousand dollars, or, the Colonel's

---

6   April 6, 1925,Lettter from Charles B. Squier to Col. Thomas R. Marshall

buyers could put twenty-five thousand dollars in escrow at a bank in Richmond, Virginia which would be held and from which they could draw funds as the work progressed. Williams indicated that if after pumping the mine out they decided that it was not what they expected and believed it did not justify further expenditures, they would be allowed to cancel the option, provided they gave one week's notice. He also required that the Colonel's buyer leave the mine free of water. A lot of conditions and money just to have a look, the diamond drilling could greatly benefit the owners.[7]

Squier sent the Colonel a telegram saying the two engineers may not arrive until Thursday the ninth and he would keep the Colonel informed.[8]

On April 7 the Colonel received another telegram from Squier.

> "The two parties may not arrive until Friday." He has still not heard from Mr. Evans and he wanted to know where the accounts are for January, February and March, Squier told the Colonel he seemed as "dilatory" as usual.[9]

On April 8, Squier told the Colonel,

> "I interviewed Mr. Sutphen today and he tells me the two gentlemen, who were to arrive last Monday A.M. will not arrive until Friday. The engineer, who is acting as the advisor to the other, has been detained on important business in Montreal- we expect them tomorrow morning, and I wired you last night they would be somewhat delayed!"[10]

---

7   April 6, 1925, Letter from Virginia Lead and Zinc Co. to Col. Thomas R. Marshall
8   April 6, 1925, Telegram from Charles B. Squier to Col. Thomas R. Marshall
9   April 7, 1925, Telegram from Charles B. Squier to Col. Thomas R. Marshall
10 April 8, 1925, Letter from Charles B. Squier to Col. Thomas R. Marshall

KNOCK DOWN DRAG OUT

Squier was shocked by the list of large expenses submitted by the Colonel which had not been previously declared.

> "In looking over the statement furnished by Mr. Mc Evans, I note some items which need explanation: first, traveling expense: $1,182.89- how much of this total represents your ten day trip to Canada to the Dome Mines property last autumn? Are there any items in this $1,182.89 not chargeable to your own personal charge account, that is;.did you not incur all of these "traveling expenses"? Secondly fuel, $3,963.33: does this mean <u>all</u> <u>labor</u> and how many cords of wood does this represent; wages: $9,477.53: does this mean all labor charges, etc. exclusive of fuel; salaries: $8,333.34: does this mean all salary due you only to date?
>
> "You have never explained what justified your last visit to New York, and if this were chargeable to the company's account?!"[1]

All of the Colonel's hefty and finally documented charges seem to come out of the blue.

This seemingly inflated list of expenses is reminiscent of Colonel Marshall's previous suit against the Continental Development Corporation.

Squier continued,

> "Did you agree to give the First National Bank of Louisa a $5,000 first mortgage on our property for only $4,000 advanced; if so, you

---

[1] April 8, 1925, Squier

were not empowered to do so, and were thus acting personally with <u>personal liability</u> only. What is meant, in Mr. Evans' statements, of a $1,000.00 Certificate of Deposit in the First National Bank of Louisa under assets? Your estimate of $24.50 to $26.00 per day for running the shaft pump is too high and is not itemized, <u>as usual</u>. Seven men are all needed, for both shifts, two to three men cutting the necessary wood in eight hours for 24 hours of operation, making 7 times $2.50 per day- some men are only paid $2.00! or $17.50- how do you arrive at $25.0 per day when lubricating oil can not be over $2.00 per week, it is not necessary to run the electric light plant when lanterns can easily be used, as for months in the past? I think $20.00 per day is all that is necessary, if you disagree, kindly let me have the details! I instructed Sutphen today to send you a check for $125.00 for this week's Pay-roll!

"It is quite evident to me that you, Mr. Evans and the bank are somewhat in Collusion!

I am writing to my attorneys in Charlottesville for elucidation of all of these peculiar and unexplained details- How can you expect us to settle your salary account when it is so mixed up with other accounts and when your statements for the last three months are noticeable by their absence, I will leave up to any high court <u>without local prejudice</u> to unravel!

"I have already several times asked you for the cost of raising the pump out of the mine, to cut down on expenses so please let me have your figures at once, so as not to let us feel there is some unexplained reason why you do not wish to do so!"[2]

A telegram of April 9 informed the Colonel that the two mining engineers, Mr. de Sabla and Mr. Livingston would arrive the next day. Squier asked the Colonel

---

2   April 8, 1925, Squier

to "kindly extend them all courtesies and they will probably remain over the weekend."[3]

Squier wrote the Colonel on April 12, 1925,

"I have received back from Mr. Howe the letters which passed between you and the Dome Mines people, which seem to show good values on the second level, around $12.00 per ton- would it not mean that, in mining, only half of such value could be counted on in a large amount to tonnage, on account of poorer ore showing? I will hold these letters for the present, in case we have to show them to some expert here for his opinion. I also have received the so-called "sketch" or map- plan of the mine made by Mr. Shoemaker- I had understood that he was only an expert in mill operation, so it is funny he would attempt such other work; but, in any event, it is more curious that his report is so poor, in comparison with the good showing mentioned in the Dome Mines letters. I also understand from a good authority that the particles of gold we saw after washing in pans may be merely pyrite, which is difficult to distinguish from gold, except after pouring a certain powerful acid (nitric) over same- is this true?'

"You have probably by now shown the two gentlemen the property quite fully, and I suppose Sutphen or I will see them soon and get their view of the property's merits, if there are indeed any!

"Please (again) let me know the cost of removing the pump from the shaft, to cut down the expense- this is the third time I have asked for this information, so, unless you reply to this very reasonable question, I must presume you do not want to, as has frequently happened in the past with other entirely reasonable questions, which have been ignored! I shall take up the matter of the strange

---

[3] April 9, 1925, Telegram from Charles B. Squier to Col. Thomas R. Marshall

loan of the bank at Louisa with the Comptroller of the Currency, Washington, D.C."[4]

The anxiously awaited reply from William McKendree Evans arrived on April 14 and Charles Squier had to be shocked by what it said.

"It is our belief that the duties of a Public Accountant cover a larger field than is covered by mere figures. From the careful reading of your letters of March twenty ninth and April 5th, it is very clear to us that there is friction in the operations of the Twin Vein Mining Company which is not to the benefit of this, or any business proposition. For that reason, we are writing you very frankly of our impressions, and observations, during our work for your company. We want to make this communication frank, clear and convincing, as we think it will be to your benefit, as the president of the Twin Vein Mining Company, as well as the Company.

"You appear to take things for granted, and jump at conclusions which are not warranted. We will, therefore, for the benefit of your company, lay before you in reply to your two letters, all the facts that came under our observation, as we found no disposition to hide anything. Taking up your letter of March twenty ninth, we will answer it as written. You state that you were surprised to receive our bill for three hundred and eleven dollars and forty cents, that the account stands against Colonel Marshall and that you had sent down a young public accountant, who was to do the whole job for $25.00.

"At the request of your manager we undertook to provide a system of accounting for the Twin Vein Mining Company, arranging proper records and books, writing into this book the entire transactions for the year 1924. Colonel Marshall stated to the writer that he

---

[4] April 12, 1925, Letter from Charles B. Squier to Col. Thomas R. Marshall

> knew nothing about bookkeeping; that he thought it necessary to show the monies he had received from your office, the amounts expended, the cash on hand and to charge the balance to his personal account, taking into account his salary. You see, like other professionals and many business men, his mind does not run along accounting lines. The writer explained to Colonel Marshall, that would be a very unsatisfactory way of procedure, and advised the making of a proper method of accounting, with books of record, and the proper arrangement of his expenditures. This, we were instructed by him as your manager, to do.

If, as you state, this charge was to be bourn by Colonel Marshall, and he being satisfied with the correctness of our charges, having directed you to pay the bill and charge it to his personal account, your inquiry as to how this charge was arrived at, would be immaterial. We, however, do not take that view of the matter.

> "On taking up this work at Mineral after preparation of a method of accounting for your company, we found that the only books of any character, were a bank pass book and a cheque book; there were vouchers galore, a whole box of them.
>
> "The writer found that it had been necessary for Colonel Marshall to advance from his personal funds, both by cheque and out of his pocket, funds for the operation of your mines.

Your office was written to for a statement, which did not arrive during my stay in Mineral. Having no books or record, things were pretty much mixed. You as a business man, will no doubt understand. There was only one way to work out this proposition- First, to establish the amount of receipts from your office. Your office was written to for a statement, which did not arrive during my stay at Mineral. I understand that when it did arrive, it was a good many hundred dollars short of the amount we had credited to your office, my instructions being to give you credit for all the bank pass book would show as having been deposited. I suggested to

Colonel Marshall to have your office send him all cheques you had sent him, so that they might be traced through the Bank of Louisa.

"It was necessary to examine every item of expenditure to determine how it had been paid, and to arrange it for proper entry into the books. You will therefore see that every item of expenditure of every character was examined by me, and that <u>Colonel Marshall's say-so was not taken for it.</u>

"The expenditures consisted of pay rolls, both for construction, operation, and about every other thing. In the matter of fuel, the wood, of course, was standing- it required cutting and hauling. The pay rolls and expense vouchers make up the charge for fuel.

"You say Colonel Marshall's salary is $6,000.00 per annum. He has only credited himself with $5,000.00 per annum. My recollection is that the remainder is for the salary of the superintendent.

"When the loan of $5,000.00 was made with the Bank of Louisa, they required that 20% of the loan should remain on deposit; therefore, you were paying interest on $5,000.00 and having use of only $4,000.00, Therefore, $4,000.00 plus the one thousand dollar Certificate of Deposit, will retire the $5,000.00 loan.

"You further say the report sent you was only a balance sheet. That is absolutely correct, but will you kindly inform me how it would have been possible to make any other? The statement shows your capital, assets, expenditures, and liabilities, in so far as they appear.

"There had been no income from the operations against which these cost items could be charged. Therefore, no loss or gain. After twenty five years of experience as accountants, we are at a loss to know how the report could have been other than as presented.

"You also say, that we do not state that we have examined the vouchers, but have apparently taken Colonel Marshall's say- so. Please again refer to our report, and you will find as follows:

> "This book when prepared, was sent by your manager to your New York office. If you did not examine it, it was your own fault. Every item was plainly set forth. We told Colonel Marshall that this work was a proper and usual charge to the Company. That is how we did the work, and look to the Company for the payment of our bill.
>
> If you do not mind, there are one or two points on which we would like to be informed. First, what did you expect to get from your Public Accountant for $25.00? Second, how any Public Accountant would for $25.00 travel from New York to Mineral, Va. and undertake to do a piece of work, the extent of which, the conditions obtaining, or the time it would take to do it, were unknown quantities to him, is beyond our experience. The most charitable conclusion we can put to it is, that you may have misunderstood his terms, he meaning $25.00 per diem, the usual charge. It took me, and I think I am a fast and steady worker, 100 hours or 13-1/3 days. For this he would have made a princely sum of 25 cents per diem."[5]

Charles Squier's attitude seemed to change and on April 15 he informed the Colonel,

> "Mr. de Sabla and Mr. Livingston were back here Monday morning, and I have had several long conferences with them since, and would have written sooner, were it not that some very pressing matters detained me until now.
>
> "You will recall that you and I had certain differences upon the occasion of your trip to New York last December (1924), mainly in regard to the continued delay upon your part of furnishing any accounting of funds received and expended! Up to that time I had utter faith in your integrity and judgment! After you promised to set right the accounts at once and admitted in Mr. Sutphen's

---

5   April 14, 1925, Letter from McKendree Evans to Charles B. Squier

presence that you had been very remiss in same, I felt appeased. Since then, as time went on, and none of the promised accountings ever appeared, and the mine seemed to be getting nowheres with earnings, I felt discouraged and somewhat suspicious, and I think, if you will try to place yourself in my position you will see such attitude was rather justifiable!

"I am happy to report that Mr.de Sabla in whom I have the utmost confidence, reports that he believes you have all of your accounts in fine order (in Mineral, which we have never seen!), that you have done your utmost for the company, that you have done all the work in question well and very economically. He says the only fault he can find is that you should not have recommended the installation of an expensive $20,000 mill (as you will recall Tainter in his initial report also advised) before further investigation of the ore bodies, and that you were generally and without proper proof entirely too optimistic as to values. Mr. de Sabla, with whom I have had several conferences due to Mr. Sutphen's advice, thinks I have been unfortunate in some ways in my criticism of you and your work, and I, therefore wish to go on record as begging your pardon and apologizing for and in regard to any unjust criticisms I may have made, if same prove to be so- you will perhaps understand that misunderstanding at either end, without proper information, has been the greatest cause of same! I trust this may pave the way to reestablish the relations we once held!

"Mr. de Sabla suggests that we should work together to liquidate our interests to the best advantage of both, and, with that end in view, has suggested the following plan.

"That the property {but not too much road frontage to kill the rest in the rear} be sold in lots or otherwise, and that you be paid the balance of your salary due as to (which we have no definite figures yet), from the proceeds of said sales, as I personally have no further funds available, and you know the company has none. All of the stock would probably be wiped out, but the value of the mine seems quite negligible (unless you can prevail upon someone else to buy it as a <u>gold mine</u>, and not as mere real estate or farm land), and so it can't be helped, and your salary and my considerable, gratuitous advances against bonds must rank ahead of the stock!

"Mr. de Sabla has many mining connections and says he has just seen some people who are interested in the purchase of the plant and equipment, if a price can be agreed upon. There is little doubt that a sale can be effected; but the price must be F.O.B.{freight on board, freight paid by buyer of equipment} rail cars at Mineral and so I would thank you to let me know what it would cost to take the mill and the shaft equipment down and transport them to the local railway station- this should be about the same as erection, less cost of buildings and the foundations?

"The loan of the First National Bank at Louisa was paid in cash ($4,000) today by my attorneys from Charlottesville, Virginia, Mssrs. Perkins and Battle- I can assure you that to me this, with my present large outstanding losses in Wall Street "cramped" my style quite as much as your over due salary must be proving inconvenient to you. However, I made a special effort, which I hope you will appreciate, as the bank could have foreclosed on the property, and forced a sale might have even meant you would not have gotten your full salary due, which can now be liquidated in due time!

"You must remember that this is an incorporated company, that there is no obligation upon my part to finance same, except as I may elect to do so, and that the company has no funds worth mentioning except perhaps $250.00 at this time!

"A special meeting of the directors called for next week will request your resignation as general manager as of May 1st, simply to arrest further expense, pending non- operation of the property. I shall see that your salary up to that point is recognized as full and justifiable, and ranking pro rata with the bonds I hold, even though same is not legally so, because I deem same your just due, and I will see that same is liquidated first of all from the sale of assets! In view of the fact that your over optimistic advice at to the value of the mine has caused me to "sink" far more into the property than I would otherwise ever considered, I think you will see the fairness of my attitude!"[6]

The Colonel had written a letter to Squier on April 13 which was not received until two days later. Unfortunately, it did not provide the information Squier had previously requested.

Apparently the Colonel did not follow instructions given relative to the lay off of all of the men, as Mr. Shoemaker was still working and Squier scolded the Colonel,

"Your letter of the 13th has just come to hand, and you do not explain the detail of the cost of raising the pump- also we did not authorize you to keep Mr. Shoemaker so long but only as to such time as he was needed, his discharge is quite in order!"[7]

It appears that Shoemaker and the Colonel were desperately searching for some gold value which will save the mine.

Squier continued.

"You say Gold dust found in the pans after washing. I will say that no intelligent mining man or metallurgist would be deceived by the residue found in our pans'- true, but INEXPERIENCED people like myself and Sutphen could easily be so mistaken!

"Mr. de Sabla thinks it should only cost $25.00 or two men several days to remove the shaft pump from the mine- please explain how you arrive at the figure of $100.00!"[8]

---

6   April 15, 1925, Letter from Charles B. Squier to Col. Thomas R. Marshall
7   April 15, 1925, Squier
8   April 15, 1925, Squier

On April 17 the Colonel's last chance for a good profit on the Valzinco faded in a letter from Douglas Wright and H. P. DePencier.

> "After the annual meeting of the Dome Mines company in Toronto Canada, H.P. says he could not find the time to give the Valzinco property full consideration and he regrets the unavoidable delay in advising you of his decision.
>
> "I have decided that we cannot go forward with this proposition for the assay plan shows it to be altogether too small a proposition for me to interest the Company in. We might have been prepared to proceed under the terms of William's earlier letter but the conditions outlined in his letter of June 4th 1925, obligating us to spend a minimum of twenty five thousand dollars, makes the entire project impossible.
>
> "Mr. Wright (Geologist and Mining Engineer) told me that in the event of the Dome Mine not being interested, he thought he could turn it over for you to another mining concern, so I had him present it to them on Wednesday last Their reply was that they were not interested under the conditions of Williams letter, but would make an examination provided they were given sufficient time and you were able to get it under the original terms, without any riders as to work required or monies to be expended.
>
> "I would therefore suggest that you let the matter rest for the present, for Mr. Allen is trying to interest parties of English "capital" and Mr Williams probably feels he can make a deal with them, and that may account for his impossible "rider" conditions in the letter of April the sixth"[9]

This has to be devastating news for Colonel Marshall who was so close to collecting the big payoff when everything seems to go wrong at once.

---

9   April 17, 1925, Letter from H. P. De Pencier to Col. Thomas R. Marshall

ANATOMY OF A GOLD MINE

The Colonel receives some helpful information on April 22 from Mr. Wright.

> "I placed it. {the Valzinco property} before another concern who are reputable mining people and who are satisfied with somewhat smaller properties than this Company is prepared to handle. I saw their representative, Mr. M. B. Huston of The Tonopah Mining Company last week and showed him the plans, reports, etc., relative to the property. He, I might state, like Mr. DePencier, felt that the assay map condemned the property and was not willing to proceed under the option as amended by Mr. Williams letter of April the sixth.
>
> "Mr. Huston might be interested in the property as originally arranged under Mr. Williams letter of March the 21st. Personally, I am of the opinion that Allen's "English Crowd" will not be as game as he thinks when all the data is placed before them. I think you will have an opportunity of dealing on this property on even more favorable terms. When you do, and have it properly tied up, I would suggest you write Mr. M. B. Huston, Chief Engineer of the Engineering Division, Tonopah Mining Company of Nevada, Bullitt Building, Philadelphia, Pennsylvania, open the subject with him again and see if he is interested in further information."[10]

The Tonopah Mining Company was one of the largest mining companies in the American West.

On April 19th Squier informed the Colonel of his plans for the future of the mine.

> "At the board of directors meeting called for the 22nd., next Wednesday, the directors will, in the usual formal way, request your resignation as of May1st, to stop all unnecessary expenses, as set

---

[10] April 22, 1925, Letter from H. P. De Pencier to Col. Thomas R. Marshall

forth in my last long letter. Also, we will probably authorize and empower you to sell off some of the company land fronting on the main road, but in this case only 50 feet of road frontage with 300 in depth, in lots, or elsewhere, in which case you must submit to us first what you propose to sell, but, ALWAYS RESERVING THE MINING AND MINERALOGICAL RIGHTS, to us on all land sold! Out of such sales your salary to May 1st can be gradually liquidated in cash payments, which is now largely in arrears and do you know the exact amount of your salary due still to May1st?"[11]

On April 20, the Colonel replied to Squier's letter.

"I accept the letter in the spirit that you indicate and will cooperate with you to the best of my ability to liquidate company so as to bring you out nearly whole as possible. At no time have I had any desire to do otherwise than cooperate with you for the best interest and success of the company.

"I think I am in a position to liquidate the company sooner than by the suggestions of Mr. De Sabler *(sic)*, to sell the land next to the highway (which will take some time) and scrap the equipment. I saw how you were feeling about the property and have been looking about to see if I could interest others in the venture. You know I wrote you that I thought I could find one to take your place and relieve you of your bad bargain. I believe that I am in position to accomplish it, and think it can be done in 30 days if you will cooperate with me. I will not be able to get my party here before the end of the month, and I will have to be able to show them the conditions in the shaft. If you will keep the shaft dry until I can get them here I feel sure that I can get us both out with but little loss to you. I have the Walnut Grove property on one side and the Luce on the other

---

11   April 19, 1925 Letter from Charles B. Squier to Col. Thomas R. Marshall

side of our property, and by combining them into a larger property and adding territory that is considered more valuable makes it attractive to the new people."[12]

The Colonel's idea of combining properties is very interesting considering that he never signed the contract transferring the options to Charles Squier in December of 1923. Could the Colonel have been intentionally holding out on Charles Squier for just such an occasion or was he planning to sell the property to the company at a later date when the mine was producing gold for a big payoff?

The Colonel Marshall continued.

> "The expense to you would be only running the pump for ten days or two weeks at the greatest. Please consider this proposition and write me as soon as possible, in order that I will lose no time in communicating with the other people. <u>Please act quickly.</u>
>
> "To take down and lift the pump, pipes rails and anything of value under ground will require, two men on top (Hoist Man and Boiler Man) and three or four men in the shaft, for the pump and pipe is large and heavy, the time consumed would be not less than three days. If it can be done in less time it surely will be done. The fuel will be two cords of wood each day.
>
> "I am preparing a complete statement of the indebtedness of the company to date and hope to have it in the mail tomorrow."[13]

Colonel Marshall is attempting a reorganization, hoping to find new investors who will keep the mine operating. He updated Charles Squier on April 22,

> "Your night message of last night was received this morning. I have at once taken the subject up with some friends of mine by

---

[12] April 20, 1925, Letter from Col. Thomas R. Marshall to Charles B. Squier
[13] April 20, 1925, Marshall

letter, but would have gone to see them in person but for the fact that I am short of funds as my salary has not been paid for so long a time. You ask me to tell you the amount now due me.

"Mr. Evans' statement showed that on January 1st the company owed me $5,909.36--- four months of this year have passed amounting to $1,666.66 – On January of this year I was paid $500.00 which leaves a total balance of $7,076.00 — if you can manage it I will appreciate your making a partial payment on the account for it will enable me to more actively push the reorganization and the sooner relieve you of the burden."[14]

On April 26 Colonel Marshall received a telegram from Charles Squier.

"Are you coming up within the next two days or are you going to meet with Mr. Sutphen on May 2nd after the stockholders meeting at Mineral? In any event bring all the records and accounts you have to date. Sutphen, you and I can then discuss the best means of settling everything."[15]

On May 1 the stockholders' meeting was held and the Colonel was no longer the General Manager of the Twin Vein Mine. The Colonel was fired by Charles Squier. In spite of all of the reconciliations offered by Squier, the Colonel claimed he had not received any part of the overdue salary. The Colonel had been in communication with Sutphen concerning some arrangements relative to the reorganization of the company, and Squier was not very happy to hear about the backdoor approach.

May was a very tough month for Squier; the mine was a bust, problems on Wall Street continued and then his wife filed for divorce. Squier claimed the divorce was caused by Mr. Horace R. Paige, in France, and that he was happily married to Olive beginning in 1913.[16]

---

14 April 22, 1925, Letter from Col. Thomas R. Marshall to Charles B. Squier
15 April 26, 1925, Letter from Charles B. Squier to Col. Thomas R. Marshall
16 Squier Asks Million in Alienation Suit, New York Times, November 23, 1926

ANATOMY OF A GOLD MINE

On May 16 Charles Squier let the Colonel know,

"Your various communications to our Mr. Sutphen have been duly forwarded to me, and, in this connection, I would say letters directed to me directly are subject to less delay and are shown to Sutphen later, if of any importance.

"In regard to the question of Mr. Evans' bill, and of the other bills you ran up to May 1st as General Manager, I am getting some information as to the status of various debts under the Virginia Statutes, which are not so easy to access here; also Barker has not finished making up the books, but when he does, then we can check up on the extremely large charges for labor, especially since August 1st (1924) to date: It being plain that since that date, the showing of expenses must have been mainly for labor, as everything else was settled long before! When this work has been finished I will write you about the results! I cannot help but agree with Mr. De Sabla's view that, while you built our mill and shaft house well and economically, you were over extravagant in keeping on experimenting with a nearly and now proven hopeless situation, which you should have apprised us of long ago.

"You perhaps do not know that I have recently ascertained that the Ricswan Company, owners of the Slate Hill Mine property, under Mr. McSween's guidance, had an option on the Twin Vein Mine property, under which they expended around $6.000.00 some years ago, and that it was they who explored the shaft long before you came to Mineral, and that their resulting investigation of the property made them, with McSween's advice, abandon any idea of value.

"The gold ore values, if any exist in paying quantities in the entire region, are in the lower sulfide ores, exposed at the Slate Hill Mine, and this knowledge caused me to suspect the Dome Mines people were interested in the idea of a large combination of local properties to mill a large daily tonnage of low grade ore, as in their Ontario mine, which is probably the only hope of the entire region.

Mr. McSween, whatever his other faults, seems to have been quite honest in advising his clients early in the game to abandon the hope of values in paying quantities in the oxidized (The upper most part of a mineral deposit) ores on top, and seems also not to have wanted to continue to spend other people's money on foolish expectations!

"I am sorry for you that the whole thing has turned out as it has, but I can only call your attention to the undeniable fact that you are careless with other people's money, characteristically careless of details of each step which would soon have proven the failure of an optimistically unfounded and persisted-in idea, and quite loathe to ever admit in the face of failure that you were in any way wrong or at fault!

"We went to the expense of bringing you up to New York the last time, not so much as to go over books and accounts, as to talk over the prospective purchasers you mysteriously mentioned as having for the property, but upon due questioning, you seemed quite hazy as to anything of any definite reliance in that direction!

"In regard to the various bills now outstanding, your long overdue accounts for the period of January1st to May1st 1925 seemed to show all moneys sent down expended for labor, with about $1,000.00 in unpaid bills for supplies, etc. to boot! Your letter written from the Pennsylvania Hotel, this city the night you were here last, as per my request, however, contained no statement that to the best of your knowledge there were no other subsequent bills to meet than those listed in your said letter- in view of these facts, the question of accounts outstanding is too muddled at present to make me believe anything is to be gained by paying a few of said bills, when others constantly appear-None of the charges vs. the company are, vs me personally nor am I in any way personally liable- A VERY DEFINITE STATEMENT from you as to the entire amount of these accounts would be quite acceptable at this time!"[17]

---

17   May 16, 1925, Letter from Charles B. Squier to Col. Thomas R. Marshall

Colonel Marshall wasted no time firing back at Charles Squier on May 17.

"Your letter of the 16th was received this morning. I left in the hands of Mr. Sutphen a list of all unpaid accounts as well as a list of the paid vouchers and a statement of Mr. Shoemaker's salary. There can be no controversy over these for there is such a thing as morality even in the keenest commercial transactions.

"The bill of Ledoux and Company, amounting to twenty dollars, I understand from .Mr. Sutphen was paid. The claim of Allis-Chalmers for the man sent here to inspect the installation of the machinery was considered by me to be an improper charge, I so wrote them and went in person to their New York Office and stated same. That is the only item to my knowledge that has not been brought to the attention of the company in my last statement.

"An early settlement of the companies' indebtedness to me will be much appreciated."[18]

With the demise of the mining deal in Spotsylvania County things wind down in connection with the Dome Mines. On May 19 the Colonel received a letter from his friend Douglas Wright.

"None of us have heard from you recently and we have just presumed that you are, for the time being, too busy to write.

"If it is not too much trouble, would you be kind enough to mail the code book loaned you, to me at your early convenience, as we procured these books in England and being short the one loaned you causes considerable inconvenience.

---

18 May 17, 1925, Letter from Col. Thomas R. Marshall to Charles B. Squier

> "Did you write Mr. Huston of the Tonapah Mines in regard to the Virginia Lead and Zinc Company property in Spotsylvania County, Virginia and if so with what results?"[19]

The Colonel had asked Sutphen if he could be appointed Receiver for the Company. This position would allow him to control the assets of the Company and disburse funds to creditors such as himself.

The Colonel received an answer on May 22, 1925 to his question of being designated Receiver from Van Tassel Sutphen.

> "It isn't quite clear to me why you wish my consent as to your appointment as Receiver inasmuch as my interest in the property is negligible. Personally I should be very glad to have you take charge and am quite willing to have you do so, but you understand that I cannot take any step which would be prejudicial to Mr. Squier's interests as I owe him loyal support so long as I am an officer of the Company.
>
> "I spoke to him this morning of what you wrote me regarding Mr. Graves and the hardware company and gathered that he did not intend to do anything about it."[20]

On Sunday May 24 Charles Squier informed the Colonel,

> "With considerable difficulty, I have finally placed today in Mr. Sutphen's hands sufficient funds to pay off the several bills outstanding, which you totaled up to over $255.00 with various local firms, also to pay McEvans accounting bill of $331.00. The checks should go out tonight, thus leaving no bills to pay or accounts overdue, except the charge for some of Shoemaker's time, which you say

---

19 May 19, 1925, Letter from Douglas Wright to Col. Thomas R. Marshall
20 May 22, 1925, Letter from Van Tassel Sutphen to Col. Thomas R. Marshall

you have paid out of your own funds and your overdue salary account, regarding which I have this to say: on the strength of your supposedly expert opinion I have advanced, as much for the good of the other stockholders as myself proportionately, in which you enter to the extent of 15,000 shares, a very large sum of money, some of which toward the end seems to have been expended by you needlessly in not manfully admitting the failure of the enterprise-therefore, why should <u>I personally</u> pay such salary more than any other large holder, when I am at present making no attempt to foreclose the bonds I hold against the property, and when I have not agreed to do so, unless the property produced at least in a small way what you promised or set forth positively it would do!

"I have already indicated that you may submit to us any offers you can get on selling certain blocks of the company's land, out of which your salary can be gradually paid off, but, for some mysterious reason you do not desire to do so, although such parcels would have to be sold 'ex-mining rights!' We will also be pleased to hear from you of any prospective purchaser of the entire property, with the terms offered fully set forth in writing, although I presume, from your conversation upon the occasion of your last visit here, you have none such!

"You will remember you wrote us to the effect you would have to be advanced certain funds to be able to leave Mineral and go some distance away to confer with certain prospective purchasers, but when advanced funds to come to New York and talk it over, you had nothing to say of any account in this direction; such actions are automatically unconvincing! I shall be in touch with powerful interests here who will ascertain just what possible interest the Dome Mines, Ltd. management may have had in gold properties in and around Mineral, Va. and why such negotiations, if any, should not have been carried out here with our officers, rather than with our <u>former</u> General Manager in Mineral.

> "You already know we are quite well aware of the fact that the only plausible or possible gold values in the whole district lie in the development of the possible large bodies of the low-grade sulphite ores underlying the oxidized and now leached areas! Upon no other ground would any prospective purchaser, who is posted about mining, which we were <u>not</u> (!) be interested!"[21]

Gold is known to run with pyrite, not bound chemically but physically attached to the mineral itself.

> "I am writing to Mr. W.F. Proffitt of Pendleton to henceforth assume the guardianship or watchmanship of the Twin Vein property, for which position he and his brother are well fitted as to trustworthiness and proximity of residence, and for which services they have submitted a reasonable offer.
>
> "Also, at any time that he may elect to do so, Mr. McSween of the Slate Hill Mine property is to be permitted to examine our mill, with the idea of finding out if it will mill their ore satisfactorily and he will have written authorization from me to do so."[22]

Apparently Squier was unaware of the closure of the Slate Hill mine on January 1st.

Colonel Marshall lectures Squier on May 26.

> "Your letter of the Twenty-Fourth is before me and I am glad to learn that you have ordered the outstanding bills paid by the Treasurer.
>
> "You are making a mistake in employing the two Pofitt men to be watchmen of the property. If you were here and investigated

---

21 May 24, 1925, Letter from Charles B. Squier to Col. Thomas R. Marshall
22 May 24, 1925, Squier

the matter you would yourself decide that it will not do, I have a good interest in what is here and I would not be willing to place the two buildings in their charge. I hope you will not carry that plan out. If you want corroboration of my opinion it can be furnished you.

"Anyone that you wish to inspect the Mill will have my consent but the allowing of McSween to do so will accomplish nothing, for he knows nothing about them and would not know the difference between a concentration plant from an amalgamation mill. (A concentration plant employs water and or air in conjunction with gravity to separate the lighter or less valuable material from the heavier and more valuable minerals). The man is ignorant and knows nothing about mining or milling.

"I have nothing in common with the man nor does any respectable one here care to have anything to do with him. His credit is not good here. You can ascertain that by inquiry if you wish.

"I must again refer to the obligations that the company are due to me, you could not have supposed that I paid Mr. Shoemaker or the paid vouchers that I sent, or gave, to Mr. Sutphen out of my salary for my salary has not been paid. I am not willing to believe that you will decline to settle the obligation <u>even</u> if my salary is not paid."[23]

On May 26 Squier updated the Colonel,

"Since writing you yesterday, I have duly ascertained from sources close to the New Jersey Zinc Company that the Dome Mines people are not at all interested in the possibilities of gold in Virginia. This leaves it clear that there will be no bid there!"[24]

---

23 May 26, 1925, Letter from Col. Thomas R. Marshall to Charles B. Squier
24 May 26, 1925, Letter from Charles B. Squier to Col. Thomas R. Marshall

It is not surprising that Charles B. Squier could secure reliable information as to the intentions of the Dome Mines. He would have had connections within the New Jersey Zinc Company which his father helped establish.[25]

Squier paid no attention to the Colonel concerning the watchmen.

> "I am instructing Mr. Proffitt to take charge of the property as of June 1st. If you have anyone acting as watchman during this month he is hereafter discharged, and please let me know to whom to send the check for $75.00, which is all the job is worth for a month!
>
> "Let me know if it will be necessary to oil the machinery of the mill from time to time to avoid rust or deterioration, and what that should cost per month, and also if it is possible to <u>bond</u> the caretaker of the property! Mr. McSween will shortly inspect the property with a letter authorized by my signature to show him every courtesy!"[26]

Squier, to the chagrin of the Colonel had given his nemesis, McSween, authorization to inspect the mill and then had the audacity to ask the Colonel "to show him every courtesy".

On May 29 the Colonel received a communication from his friend Van Tassel Sutphen,

> "I have repeatedly assured Mr. Squier that the Dome Mines people were not interested in the Twin Vein, but he would not believe me.
>
> "I can't tell you exactly what the books show about your overdue salary, as Charles Squier has all of the accounts in his possession. To the best of my recollection, it is around $7,000 and Mr. Squier quoted that amount in round figures when I was talking to him on the telephone this morning.

---

25   The First Hundred Years of the New Jersey Zinc Company. New York: The New Jersey Zinc Company, 1949, pg 21
26   May 26, 1925, Letter from Charles B. Squier to Col. Thomas R. Marshall

> "Of course, I don't know anything about Proffitt, and Mr. Squier has handled all that part of the business himself.
>
> "The present Board of Directors is as follows: Colonel Thomas R. Marshall, Mineral Virginia, Charles B. Squier, 521 Park Avenue, New York, Van Tassel Sutphen, Morristown, New Jersey and Harry A Ushe, 730 5th Avenue, New York. I shall be very glad to submit any offer that you may be able to make to the Company, and to assist in any other way possible"[27]

Sutphen was well aware as to why the information was requested, the Colonel was going to sue.

This was the last communication between the Twin Vein Mining Company Offices in New York City and Colonel Marshall until July 2, 1925 when he filed a lawsuit in the Louisa County Circuit Court against Charles B Squier, Eugene A. Perry, Junior; James H. Coghill and his friend Van Tassel Sutphen. The Colonel was represented by Gordon and Gordon in Louisa.

With the demise of the Twin Vein Mine the Colonel found himself in a very bad situation, no job and no further funds from the New York people. The only chance he had for collecting any cash was to use the lawsuit to take over the Twin Vein Property and collect his $5,000.00 from the Dolans. Unfortunately, the Colonel was nearly broke and he had to finance the legal wars out of his own pocket.

In the suit Colonel Marshall contended that

> "he was the owner of an option upon the mining property of Gertrude L Dolan lying near Pendleton in the County of Louisa, Virginia. It consisted of upwards of 700 acres of land deemed very valuable for gold; that this option gave complainant the right to purchase the said property for the sum of $25,000 and your complainant, during the lifetime of the option had negotiations with Jason Coghill and Eugene Perry for the promotion of the Corpora-

---

[27] May 29, 1925, Letter from Van Tassel Sutphen to Col. Thomas R. Marshall

tion to mine and operate the property as a gold mine and for other metals; that Coghill and Perry assured complainant that they were amply able to finance the proposition, and your complainant had, and still has, the utmost faith in the value of the property for mining purposes that it was agreed between your complainant and the said Coghill and Perry that they would put up the sum of $50,000 to pay the option price for the property and the estimated cost of the necessary machinery and fixtures to properly equip the property for mining purposes of $25,000.00 and it was further agreed that your complainant should have 49% of the capital stock of the Corporation and that the said Coghill and Perry should have the remaining 51% of the stock in consideration of the sum of $50,000.00 with the further understanding that they would furnish the money necessary to properly finance and pay the cost of operating the mine."[28]

Eugene Perry and James Coghill disagreed,

"in the year 1923 they were approached by Colonel Marshall, who advised them that he was the owner of an option on a certain tract of land in Louisa County, Virginia upon which there were very valuable gold deposits. The Colonel said that he was a mining engineer of experience, and he was satisfied that the deposits on the tract of land were exceedingly valuable and that the land could be purchased for $25,000.00, and a mine with all necessary equipment for the recovery of gold could be installed on the property for a maximum of $15,000.00 making a total investment of $40,000.00."[29]

---

28 Colonel Marshall vs Charles B. Squier & Twin Vein Mining, July 2, 1925, Gordon & Gordon
29 Answers to Suit, May 22, 1926, Perkins, McNutt, Battle & Rinehart

Perry and Coghill advised Colonel Marshall that they did not have the necessary funds to purchase the property and install the mining equipment, but they were in close touch with men of means whom they believed could be interested in the proposition; as a result, Colonel Marshall, Mr. Perry and Mr. Coghill agreed that they would jointly promote the proposition and attempt to interest certain parties who will be able to develop the property.[30]

> "They attempted by every proper means in their power to interest men of sufficient financial standing in the proposition to take over and develop the property, and in order to secure the necessary backing, Perry and Mr. Coghill at their own expense, employed and paid for the services of a distinguished gold-mining expert from New York, Colonel Tainter, who went to Louisa County, investigated the situation and made a report which did not, in any way, verify the statements which the Colonel had made to them; the report was in fact so discouraging that Perry and Coghill found it even more difficult to secure financial assistance."
>
> "About this time however, Perry and Coghill got in touch with Mr. Charles B Squier, a gentleman of large means and a close personal friend of Eugene A. Perry. Mr. Squier offered to put up the sum of $10,000.00, which was the cash payment demanded by the Dolans for the property, provided the control of the corporation, represented by a majority of the shares of stock outstanding were given him. Perry and Coghill thereupon got in touch with Colonel Marshall, and suggested to him a re-allotment of the stock of the contemplated Corporation, to which he at first objected.. Colonel Marshall, however, agreed to go to New York, and thereupon a new agreement was entered into between them and said Charles B. Squier, by which Colonel Marshall agreed to accept 15,000 shares of stock in said Corporation."

---

30 Answers to Suit, May 22, 1926, Perkins, Mcnutt. Battle & Rinehart

> "The Corporation having been organized the stock was issued in accordance with this final understanding, and although the stock holders of the Corporation will show issues of stock to numerous parties this stock was issued at the direction of the owners thereof as provided in the aforesaid agreement. Upon the organization of the Corporation, Mr. Squier advised your Respondents and said Marshall that he would advance to said Corporation the amount which had been indicated by said Marshall as sufficient to install and put in operation the necessary mining financial equipment, etc., to the maximum amount of $25,000.00.

Colonel Marshall assured Perry, Coghill and Squier that the amount indicated would be amply sufficient for the purpose. At that time the company was indebted to Mrs. Dolan in the sum of $15,000 for deferred purchase money (mortgage), on the property payable nine months from the date of the purchase. Colonel Marshall assured Perry, Coghill and Squier that the mine would be in operation long before the expiration of said nine months, and he was confident that the earnings therefrom would be ample to take care of the Dolan bonds.

The Colonel asserted that Perry and Coghill had agreed to fund the costs related to developing the mine. Their answer was,

> "They emphatically deny that they, at any time, had obligated themselves in any way to furnish the necessary funds to purchase and operate the property, or to furnish any sums in connection therewith, nor so far as they are advised and believe did said Squier at any time, in any way, bind himself to furnish any money to the Company other than hereinbefore set out."[31]
>
> "Colonel Marshall further represented that the Perry and Coghill, after the organization of the Company as herein stated below, without his knowledge or consent sold in one Chas. B Squier for the

---

31 Answers to Suit, May 22, 1926, Perkins, McNutt, Battle & Rinehart

sum of $10,000 thirty-four thousand five hundred shares of capital stock of the Company and that this $10,000 was used, as Colonel Marshall afterwards ascertained, to pay the cash payment on the property. The said option having been closed by the purchase of the property from Mrs. Dolan for the sum of $25,000, $10,000 paid in cash and the residue of $15,000 upon a credit of nine months with a deed of trust securing the same to Mrs. Dolan."[32]

According to the Colonel,

"Originally the Twin Vein Mining Company was chartered by the State Corporation Commission of Virginia on May 10, 1923. It was lodged with the Secretary the Commonwealth on July 3, 1923 and it was then recorded in the Clerks Office of The Louisa Circuit Court on July 12, 1923. The maximum stock authorized was $375,000 with a minimum amount of stock issued to be $100,000 divided into shares of five dollars each which were to be full paid and non-assessable."[33]

"Colonel Marshall felt cheated because shortly before the company was organized Perry came to Mineral with his Attorney John S. Battle of Charlottesville, Virginia and presented to the Colonel a paper providing for a change in the distribution of the stock. The Colonel's original 49% was reduced to 12% which the Colonel refused to sign. He claimed that Mr. Perry induced him to go with him to New York to see Charles Squier who he said was putting up the money. When they arrived and had a conference between Colonel Marshall, Perry, Coghill and Mr. Squier, they all concurred, that the company could not be organized unless the Colonel would accept less than 49% the capital stock. Colonel Marshall at first refused, stating that $10,000.00 had been paid upon the property, and Mrs. Dolan would

---

32 Answers to Suit, May 22, 1926, Perkins, McNutt, Battle & Rinehart
33 Col. Marshall vs Charles B. Squire & Twin Vein Mining, July 2, 1925, Gordon & Gordon

hold this as damages if they did not want to carry the deal through. After some discussion the Colonel agreed, in order to make the Corporation possible and he surrendered all of his stock except 20% of the capital stock and upon this basis the Company was organized

"Squier agreed to advance the remaining $40,000 to pay the balance due upon the property and the cost of its equipment of $25,000; that said $40,000 was to be advanced upon notes of the Corporation; and secured by the Treasury or unsold stock of the Corporation, that the stock issued to your Complainant was to be fully paid and non-assessable representing your Complainant's option aforesaid, and your complainant insisted that no stock be issued until the necessary funds were provided for financing the operation of the Corporation, but his protest was disregarded and the stock was issued."[34]

Court records show that approximately 75,000 shares of stock were issued at a face value of five dollars each. The Board Members and several friends held the larger number of shares, Charles B. Squier, 32,019 shares, Colonel T. R. Marshall 15,000 shares, J. H. Coghill 7,110, shares, John S. Battle 500, Van Tassel Sutphen 1,135 shares and Richard D. Brixey 10,000 shares, these shareholders accounted for 65,745 shares of the 75,000 shares available, removing the 15,000 shares the Colonel held from the total reveals a controlling interest of 50,747 shares.[35]

Colonel Marshall claimed,

"that after the organization of the Twin Vein Mining Corporation he was elected by the Board of Directors of the Corporation the General Manager at a salary of $5,000 a year. In the capacity of General Manager he was in active control and management of the mining and milling operations of the Twin Vein Mine until the execution of the mortgage upon the property of the company

---

[34] Col. Marshall vs Charles B. Squier & Twin Vein Mining, July 2, 1925, Gordon & Gordon
[35] Col. Marshall vs Charles B. Squier & Twin Vein Mining, July 2, 1925, Gordon & Gordon

when he resigned his position as General Manager and a member of the Board of Directors of the company."[36] That is not exactly what Charles Squier's letters to the Colonel stated, the Colonel had been given a very clear exit date.

The Colonel swore that Mr. Squier being the controlling influence furnished certain funds to finance the company until the execution of the mortgage, but not a sufficient amount to pay off all the labor and the Colonel paid the balance of the labor and supplies for the company out of his own pocket which amounted to $1,250.42. The Colonel also swore that Charles Squier and the office of the Twin Vein Mining Company owed him as of May 1, 1925, $7,076.00 in salaries, for a total of $8,386.42.[37] The Colonel had made very similar claims in connection with the lead and zinc mine owned by the Continental Development Corporation.

The officers of the Twin Vein Mining Company indicated that they were not sure as to what amount if any was due the Colonel in regard his salary or advancements made by him for labor and supplies. They also asserted that Colonel Marshall had never rendered an accounting to the company for the operation of the mine during the time he was in charge and they asked the Colonel to render a full accounting for all gold which was recovered and for all the money received by him as General Manager of the Company's works including at least two shipments of gold sent to the Philadelphia Mint and the $750 paid to the Colonel for the small hand powered stamp mill from the Dolan Mine.[38]

The Colonel continued his efforts to take over the mine by outlining the details concerning the purchase of the Dolan property.

"Gertrude L. Dolan and R.E. Dolan, her husband, conveyed to the Twin Vein Mining Company the tract of 776 acres of land by a deed dated July 23, 1923 which was recorded on November 17, 1923 and on that same day the property was conveyed to the

---

36 Col. Marshall vs Charles B. Squier & Twin Vein Mining, July 2, 1925, Gordon & Gordon
37 Col. Marshall vs Charles B. Squier & Twin Vein Mining, July 2, 1925, Gordon & Gordon
38 Answers to Suit, May 22, 1926, Perkins, McNutt, Battle & Rinehart

company in trust to secure the remaining $15,000 for the purchase money of the purchase which deed of trust had been paid off and properly released on the first day of December 1924. On December1st, 1924 the Twin Vein Mining Company executed a deed of trust conveying All its property, real and personal including the mining equipment to W. Allen Perkins, trustee, in trust to secure an issue of $80,000 of bonds."[39]

Court records show there were five bonds issued all payable to Charles B Squier, bond number one was for $20,000, due and payable on June 1, 1925, bond number two was also $20,000 due and payable to Charles Squier on December 1, 1925, bond number three was for $20,000 due and payable on June 1, 1926, bond number four was in the amount of $16,500 and was due and payable to Charles Squier on December the first 1926, bond number five was in the amount of $3,500 and was to be paid to the bearer and was due and payable on December 1, 1926.[40]

The Colonel stated, The deed contains a statement that was submitted to the State Corporation Commission along with other papers to make the bonds legal and binding obligations of the company and further states that the vote of the stockholders meeting directing the issuance of these bonds in the securing of them by a mortgage trust deed upon the property, was unanimous, which is not true. I was present at the stockholders meeting in protest against the execution of this trust deed upon the ground that the corporation had no right to put a lien upon this property which affected and would probably destroy the value of my stock in the company without my consent and when the vote was taken I declined to vote upon the proposition as soon as it had been carried I decided to resign my position with the company effective May 1, 1925.[41]

Charles Squier asserted that he had no personal knowledge of any early negotiations between James Coghill, Eugene Perry and the Colonel pertaining to the purchase of the Dolan property. He had agreed to advance $10,000 and additional

---

39 Col. Marshall vs Charles B. Squier & Twin Vein Mining, July 2, 1925, Gordon & Gordon
40 File Box 192, 109- 1928 file 013, Louisa County Court House
41 Col. Marshall vs Charles B. Squier & Twin Vein Mining, July 2, 1925, Gordon & Gordon

funds for the purchase and installation of the machinery which was not to exceed $25,000, provided stock was issued to him which would insure the control of the corporation. Squier reiterated that the Colonel attended a conference in New York when the arrangement were made.[42]

Squier challenged the Colonel's claims beginning with his desire to briefly detail the history of the company since his connection with it.

> "The company was originally organized with capital stock in the amount set out in the bill, which stock was allocated to Colonel Marshall, Mr. Coghill and Mr. Perry. This allotment was made with the full knowledge and consent of Colonel Thomas R Marshall, who was one of the organizers and directors of the corporation.
>
> "Colonel Marshall stated that he was a Mining Engineer of large experience and had accurate and detailed knowledge of the company's property, and if the proper machinery could be installed on the company's property it would yield very large returns in gold, and if the necessary funds were forthcoming the machinery could be installed and in proper running order in a short time.
>
> "The Colonel said that as soon as the mill was put in operation it would yield sufficient returns to pay the cost of operation and meet the amount due the Dolans on account of the purchase price of the property and quickly pay the cost of the investments. I then agreed to advance to a sufficient sum to install the mill and put it in operation, not however, to exceed the sum of $25,000. I advanced the $25,000 upon the company's notes executed to me as the various accounts were turned over.
>
> "Colonel Marshall was given absolute control of the construction of the company's plant, superintending, directing its erection and the installation of the equipment. Numerous delays occurred

---

42 Answer to Suit by Charles B. Squier, May 22, 1926, Perkins, McNutt, Battle & Rinehart

before the completion of the plant and it was sometime later than the time set before it was actually put the operation.

"The $15,000 due Ms. Dolan, fell due and I, although under no obligation to do so, when a foreclosure of the lien was threatened, advanced the amount necessary to pay this lien with interest, taking the company's notes for the advancement.

"When the mill was put in operation no gold was recovered. To operate the mine and the mill were both expensive. Excuse after excuse was given by Colonel Marshall for the failure of the mill to recover the gold which he maintained was in the ore, and I for some months continued to advance large sums of money to meet the company's payroll and other expenses.

"My patience had become about exhausted, and seeing that the mill was yielding no income, I requested the directors carry out their agreement to give me security for the large sum of money I had advanced at that time, amounting to some $61,200.00. This proposition was approved by the directors of the company, and Colonel Marshall gave his consent to it. The Directors of the company then called a meeting of its stockholders to be held in Mineral, Virginia and I was advised and believed that the proxies for the meeting were drawn and executed in the joint names of John S. Battle and Thomas R Marshall.

"At this meeting, Colonel Marshall for the first time indicated his unwillingness to the bond issue for the purpose of securing your complainant the large sum advanced by him and refused to vote the proxies in favor of the proposition, the meeting thereupon adjourned.

"Upon learning of the refusal of Colonel Marshall I declined and refused to advance any further sums of money to meet its pay roll the result of which was that the company was very seriously embarrassed for funds, and when I, who was then in Europe, learned of the situation cabled my approval of the bond issue of $5,000 to secure funds from one of the banks in Louisa to meet the company's pay roll. After this issue of bond was approved by the directors and stockholders a deed of trust was executed in the amount advanced by the Louisa Bank. Upon returning from abroad I was advised by Colonel Marshall that he had reconsidered his decision with reference to the issue of bonds to secure the amount secured by me and that he would approve the bond issue. In the meantime the $5,000.00, borrowed from the bank in Louisa came due and I, rather than have the lien foreclose, again advanced the necessary funds to pay this loan.

"Feeling that I was entitled to such security as it might give the company's directors, I again called a meeting of the stockholders of the company to consider the creation of a bond issue of $80,000.00, the bonds to be delivered to me upon the surrender by Colonel Marshall of the company's notes which he had received for money advanced by him to the company for the amount of bonds to be transferred to him.

"At the meeting of stockholders, Colonel Marshall stated that he agreed not to oppose the issue of bonds, but that he was not satisfied with the stock distribution which had been made a year or more ago and feeling that his rights, if any he had, in connection herewith might be affected he would like to be excused from voting on the bond issue. Upon being assured that it was his right to refrain from voting Colonel Marshall did not vote upon the issue of bonds, the bond issue being approved by all stockholders represented at the meeting except Colonel Marshall.

According to Charles Squier,

"Colonel Marshall's statements with reference to the inaccurate statement in the deed of trust, that the bond issue was unanimously approved by the stockholders, is probably inaccurate, as a matter of fact the deed of trust was drawn before the stockholders meeting in order that it might be presented at that meeting and the word unanimous was inadvertently left in the deed when it was executed."[43]

The Colonel swore that Coghill and Perry had agreed to properly finance the corporation and claimed fraud upon his rights and that Charles Squier had knowledge thereof and participated in the fraud; and that he had the right after the organization of the company to have it properly financed and give to the property a fair opportunity to demonstrate its value.[44]

Perry and Coghill claimed that,

> "They never at any time agreed to properly finance the corporation as stated by Colonel Marshall. They did agree to attempt to interest men of means in the proposition, and they succeed in doing so, which is evidenced by the fact that Mr. Squier has expended some $80,000 in an effort to develop the property."[45]

Squier noted,

> "He had not at any time proposed or obligated himself in any way to finance the project but, he has advanced sufficient money to bring the mill into operation and to run it for some six or eight months, and so far the property has not only failed to pay the operating cost but has yielded practically no return.
>
> "A sale at public auction of the property should be avoided if possible, and I can see no reason for the appointment of a receiver. The property is at present under the care of a competent caretaker and will be preserved for such disposition as a company may see fit to make in the future."[46]

---

43 Answer to Suit by Charles B. Squier, May 22, 1926, Perkins, McNutt, Battle & Rinehart
44 Col. Marshall vs Charles B. Squier & Twin Vein Mining, July 2, 1925, Gordon & Gordon
45 Answer to Suit by Coghill & Perry, May 22, 1926, Perkins, McNutt, Battle & Rinehart
46 Answer to Suit by Charles B. Squier, May 22, 1926, Perkins, McNutt, Battle & Rinehart

The Colonel still contended that, "The property is very valuable and can be made very remunerative if it's properly managed and financed. He further stated that since his resignation there was no one legally responsible for the care and preservation of the property consisting of a lot of costly and valuable machinery, which may be greatly damaged or even stolen by depredators unless someone is appointed by the court to preserve and protect the same.[47]

Perry and Coghill slam the Colonel's claim that the property is very valuable.

> "They hope that Colonel Marshall is correct in his allegation that the property is very valuable. They would suggest, however, that the Colonel was furnished with ample funds and installed on the property the most up-to-date machinery and equipment obtainable and operated both the mine and machinery for 6 to 8 months at large expense, and so far as they are advised has never to this day shown any gross profit to say nothing of a net profit from the operation."[48]

The Colonel claimed he would never have reduced his percentage in the property from 49% to 20% except upon the assurance of Coghill and Perry that they had already put up the money for the operating expenses of the mine, of which Charles Squier was fully advised. The Colonel continues,

> "it was at the insistence of Charles Squier that the deed of trust upon the property was given and that while Squier was in Europe he sent his attorney John S. Battle to Mineral to hold a stockholders meeting for the purpose of putting a lien on the property, but upon the objection and protest of Colonel Marshall he adjourned the meeting without action. The Colonel said, that upon a former occasion, attorney Perkins said to him that he had told Mr. Squier

---

47 Col. Marshall vs Charles B. Squier & Twin Vein Mining, July 2, 1925, Gordon & Gordon
48 Answer to Suit by Coghill & Perry, May 22, 1926, Perkins, McNutt, Battle & Rinehart

that the court would upset this deed of trust, and it was after the return of Charles Squier from Europe that the lien was placed upon the property."[49]

The Colonel believes that,

> "Both Coghill and Perry are bankrupt and an execution against them would be useless and that they have disposed of their stock, or the greater portion of it."

The Colonel calls Charles Squier a cheat and contends that

> "Squier for a mere nominal consideration acquired the stock for the purpose of speculation and exploitation rather than for mining and placing the deed of trust upon the property, and the issuance of the bonds thereby secured was a part and parcel of a scheme on his part to acquire the entire possession of the property."[50]

The Colonel again makes his play for total control of the $80,000 property, contending that

> "the mine property is exceedingly valuable for gold and if permitted to do so at any time during the progress of the suit, he can make a sale of the property privately, subject to the approval of the court, for a price greatly in excess of what it could be sold for at auction. He asks that a Receiver be appointed to take control of the mine property to preserve and protect it until he can get a judgment from a court against Squier and all of the stockholders to require them to further finance the proper operation of the

---

[49] Col. Marshall vs Charles B. Squier & Twin Vein Mining, July 2, 1925, Gordon & Gordon
[50] Col. Marshall vs Charles B. Squier & Twin Vein Mining, July 2, 1925, Gordon & Gordon

mining property for a sufficient time to fully develop it and place it upon a paying basis. He also requested that an injunction should be granted enjoining and restraining the Twin Vein Mining Corporation and Charles B. Squier personally or as President of the Company or any of their agents from selling, transferring or otherwise disposing of the bonds secured by the trust deed. The Colonel also wanted the deed of trust securing the bonds to be declared fraudulent and invalid as to Complainant and all other stockholders of the company and finally that he may have all such other further and general relief as the nature of his case requires."[51]

In other words he wants everything.

The Colonel has a lot of legal irons in the fire and on September 9, 1925, the Colonel's attorney R. L. Gordon, Jr. writes Ernest B. Upton, the attorney who has been handling the hunt for the Dolans in Cripple Creek,.Colorado, inquiring as to the status of that case.

Mr. Upton replied on September the 24, 1925,

"I have neglected answering your letter of the 9th in the matter of Marshall verses the Dolans. I have not yet obtained judgement and you may assure Mr. Marshall that undoubtedly it will run along for a year before we get to trial time. We only have two terms of District Court in this county a year and as the judges are here for only a few days at a time it is a slow process to get matters at issue; that is, to get motions and demurrers disposed of, and as you know one cannot devote time exclusively to one matter so that in our profession we have to do the best we can to move all things along as fast as convenient, and I am personally in rather a peculiar position here.

---

51 Col. Marshall vs Charles B. Squier & Twin Vein Mining, July 2, 1925, Gordon & Gordon

"I have just a little more work than I can keep right up to date and there is not field enough here to justify my getting a man with whom I would wish to associate. There are three other attorneys here but they are all past seventy two and I cannot make use of any of them for assistance now.

"I have not taken up the motion of the defendant's attorneys to make the complaint more specific. I wish you would give this matter some attention. You have a copy of the complaint and a copy of the motion and you are able to reach the facts a little better in consultation with Mr. Marshall and I would like your opinion as to whether or not you consider the contract for employment a written contract and if so what constitutes that contract, or whether you consider it an oral contract and if so what constitutes the same; also give me your opinion as to the date of the promise to pay the $5,000. I want to be prepared on these things before the argument of the motion and prepared to amend the complaint in accordance with your opinion if the Court grants the motion. I want you to advise me fully on these matters and then I will take up the motion outside of this county by agreement with Court and counsel. In order to get any speed in these matters I have to go to Colorado Springs because outside of three days of court here, the early part of September we have not had any court since the motion was filed and will not have any further attendance of the Judges before next February."[52]

It appears that the Colonel has a long wait ahead while he and his attorneys chase the Dolans across the country from town to town.

Meanwhile, the Colonel has a new idea to put some money in his pocket. The mine sits idle and the standing timber is a very tempting and ready source of income. On October 14, 1925 he entered into an agreement with Walter Harley, a local timberman. Harley agreed to cut and deliver at the railroad, the railroad ties

---

[52] September 9, 1925, Letter from R. L. Gordon to Ernest Upton

that can be cut off the land of the Louisa Mine Tract also known as the Twin Vein Mining Company Property, not to exceed 5,000 ties. This arrangement could be a product of the talks with Charles Squier which would allow the Colonel to sell some of the ready assets of the property to provide funds to pay the Colonel and other obligations. Colonel Marshall and Walter Harley agree to split the proceeds 50-50.[53]

On January 4, 1926, Colonel Marshall again contacted H.P. DePencier of the Dome Mines in an effort to reignite the deal on the Spotsylvania mine property.[54] On January 12 he received a reply from Douglas Wright.

> "I took the opportunity of discussing the matter with Mr. DePencier and he was pleased to hear from you again as you had more or less just fallen out of the picture.
>
> "I discussed both of these things with Mr. DePencier and he does not feel that we can reopen the negotiations at the present time. We were both pleased to learn that you anticipate winning your contention in connection with the lawsuit with which you have been tied up during the past year."[55]

This was the last iron the Colonel had in the fire, all of the larger gold mines in the area have closed, the pyrite mines have been closed for years and there is no interest in the lead and zinc mine he hoped to sell for a good profit. The mining industry around Mineral is no more.

Unfortunately, the Slate Hill Mine which had been closed was now in the hands of the Master Commissioner in Chancery. McSween, the miners and the creditors had filed suit against the Ricswan Mining Co. in an effort to recover the money they were owed.

The property was evaluated and it was decided that an auction was the most expedient method for the liquidation of the property. The Commissioner set the

---

53 September 24 1925, Letter from Ernest Upton to R. L. Gordon
54 October 14, 1925, Agreement between Col. Marshall and Walter Harley
55 January 4, 1926, Letter from Col. Thomas R. Marshall to H. P. DePencier

auction for Saturday, January 9 at 11:00 A. M. The property and mine were sold to Carl H. Nolting for $3,800. The proceeds were distributed to the miners and creditors, however, McSween as Manager did not recover anything for his past due salary.[56]

A search of the Chancery records of the Louisa County Circuit Court found no record that the Colonel's suit against Charles Squier and the others was ever litigated. One possibility for the absence of any resolution either way could be due to the Colonel's lack of funds, which made it impossible for him to prosecute the suit because he could not pay the legal fee.

The ending of the Slate Hill Manager's claims against the Ricswan Mining Company may have convinced the Colonel that he would not prevail in the suit against Charles Squier and he may have dropped it. In the Book of Record at the Louisa County Courthouse there is a reference to the file, Thomas R. Marshall vs Twin Vein Mining Co. listed as "out" and could not be located. This file may hold the answer. However, Charles Squier was paying the Colonel something on the salary owed each month as he said he would. Van Tassel Sutphen wrote the Colonel a short note on January 29, 1926,

> "Herewith is the February cheque. What is new? I have not seen C. B. S. and hear nothing from him. I saw Colonel Tainter the other day. He was much surprised and indeed cut up when I told him of all that had happened, and the apparent failure of the mine to produce anything."[57]

---

56 January 12, 1926, Letter from Douglas Wright to Col. Thomas R. Marshall
57 January 29, 1926, Note from Van Tassel Sutphen to Col Thomas R. Marshall

THE WHYS AND WHEREFORES

What caused the failure of the Twin Vein Mine? According to the Engineering and Mining Journal,

> "One of the favorite ways for an inexperienced mining man to show his faith in a property is to build a reduction plant popularly called a mill, before the requisite ore is developed. Sometimes, people want to make an impression on investors, promising good returns on their money. But more often premature mill construction is the result of unwarranted optimism, of a desire to have someplace to treat the ore as it is mined from the grass- roots down. This is especially true when there are no facilities nearby to treat the ore, so sure is the promoter that an ore body will be found that he takes a chance. If the ore is there, he is considered long- headed and his reputation is considerably augmented; if not, he had better move at least 5,000 miles away and start, afresh."[1]

It appears that there are multiple human components which contributed to the failure of the mine, beginning with an early indication of some dishonesty on the Colonel's part. First, he did not inform his employer that the ore had run out on two levels in the mine, instead he told only Dolan. This crucial information, by itself, would have caused Squier to close the mine on the spot. Then there is the un-

---

[1] Engineering and Mining Journal, September 9, 1922, Vol. 114, No. 11, New York, McGraw Hill pg 442

favorable assay the Colonel apparently withheld, which also would have caused Charles Squier to rethink the wisdom of his involvement in the mine.

Additionally, there are the Colonel's constant, overly optimistic and sometimes, misleading statements concerning the property's value. The Colonel's statements regarding the extreme value of the Twin Vein Mine were diametrically opposed to those of McSween, who had abandoned it earlier. Most probably the use of the diamond drill would have prevented the loss of Charles Squier's money. On the other hand, the Colonel would not have had a job during tough economic times. There are similarities in regard to the ending for this mine, and the one in Spotsylvania County, such as the Colonel's salary in arrears, money supposedly not paid by Charles Squier and other charges out of the blue.

There is the question, was the mine salted, and if so, by whom? Usually all one has to do is follow the money and the Dolans are the only people who gained monetarily. There was the sample which was sent in by Dolan which assayed at $100.10 per ton. Certainly the subsequent assays taken never approached the $100 value and that sample should have been discarded because there was only Dolan's word that it actually came from the Twin Vein Mine. It could just as easily have come from some mine in Cripple Creek, Colorado. Charles Squier, Coghill, Perry, and the stockholders all lost money. As for the Colonel, it is impossible to be sure, but he may have in the end, gotten most of his money.

Geologic and equipment issues existed from the very beginning, starting with the inability of the small 3 ton stamp mill to recover any gold, if there was any, in fact to be recovered. Sometimes gold can have an irony coating which will prevent it from being caught by the mercury. Gold-bearing quartz veins in Mineral are made up of alternating layers of quartz and thin layers of iron oxide. The gold-bearing veins are also accompanied by varying amounts of clay. Clay is sometimes referred to as "gold robber" because the fine gold will float off with the clay into the tailings pile. The presence of red mud in the ore would have a similar effect. The absence of a large and reliable supply of clean water could have interfered with the plant's ability to operate at its normal rate.

The Twin Vein mine was employing Pierce Amalgamators as the final stage of processing in an effort to solve this problem, but were they preforming as well as expected? Some miners did not like them. Gold could have been lost onto the tailings pile if any of the machines were leaking oil which can cause the gold to float on top of the water instead of moving along the bottom and over the amalgamating plates where it would normally be trapped.

So many individual things or a combination of several could have been responsible for the failure to recover the millions in gold that Charles Squier and the others hoped would be theirs, but it looks as though there never was any significant gold in the old mine after all.

THE RETURN

The equipment bought from Allis-Chalmers is believed to have been sold by Charles Squier and anything remaining could have been sold to one of the numerous scrap iron dealers traveling across the country prior to World War II.

As far as can be determined from the court records, the Twin Vein was abandoned. The property sat idle until the early part of July in 1935 when Charles Squier returned from Paris, France. He asked that the Twin Vein Mine and its 776 acres of land be advertized for sale under the terms of the deed to satisfy the lien he held. W. Allen Perkins was the trustee of the property and it was advertized for sale on the of July 7, 1935. It was then offered for sale at public auction at the front door of the Louisa Courthouse on Saturday August 31, 1935 at 12:00 noon.[1] "At which time and place the property was CRIED for sale at public auction and was purchased by C. B. Squier for the sum of $12,500.00."[2]

The $80,060.00 which Charles Squier invested in the mine is gone. With the $12,500.00 added for the buy back, he had a total of $92,560.00 invested in the property. In 1935 the value of gold was $20.67 per ounce. Charles Squier's total investment in the property would equal 4,475.085 ounces of gold. By comparison at today's rate of $1,200 per ounce his total investment would be worth $5,370,102.00

Charles B. Squier went back to Paris and apparently never returned to the United States. R. L. Gordon was elected to the Virginia House of Delegates. The Colonel's pursuit of the Dolans continued for some time. The Colonel eventually went to work as an Engineer for the Virginia Department of Highways and he passed away on February 13, 1939 at the age of 79.[3]

---

1   Deed Book 45, pg. 198, Louisa County Court House
2   Deed Book 45, pg. 476, Louisa County Court House
3   Colonel T. R. Marshall Long an Engineer, New York Times, February 14, 1939

The mill building, head frame and shaft house were eventually torn down and the materials were probably reused.

Today the acreage remains nearly intact, several small parcels of varying size and some lots were sold off.

THE END

www.ingramcontent.com/pod-product-compliance
Lightning Source LLC
Chambersburg PA
CBHW080529170426
43195CB00016B/2516